War Pigeons

War Pigeons
*Winged Couriers in the
U.S. Military, 1878–1957*

Elizabeth G. Macalaster

McFarland & Company, Inc., Publishers
Jefferson, North Carolina

Frontispiece: Engraving of homing pigeons with messages tied to a foot on one pigeon and to the tail feathers of another.

LIBRARY OF CONGRESS CATALOGUING-IN-PUBLICATION DATA

Names: Macalaster, Elizabeth G., author.
Title: War pigeons : winged couriers in the U.S. military, 1878–1957 / Elizabeth G. Macalaster.
Description: Jefferson, NC : McFarland & Company, Inc., Publishers, 2020 Includes bibliographical references and index.
Identifiers: LCCN 2020037799 | ISBN 9781476680804 (paperback : acid free paper) ∞
ISBN 9781476640563 (ebook)
Subjects: LCSH: Homing pigeons—War use—United States—History—20th century. | Homing pigeons—War use—United States—History—19th century.
Classification: LCC UH90 .M28 2020 | DDC 355.4/24—dc23
LC record available at https://lccn.loc.gov/2020037799

BRITISH LIBRARY CATALOGUING DATA ARE AVAILABLE

ISBN (print) 978-1-4766-8080-4
ISBN (ebook) 978-1-4766-4056-3

© 2020 Elizabeth G. Macalaster. All rights reserved

No part of this book may be reproduced or transmitted in any form or by any means, electronic or mechanical, including photocopying or recording, or by any information storage and retrieval system, without permission in writing from the publisher.

Front cover photograph: Celebrated Navy pigeon Peerless Pilot being released off of France in World War I. Neither the altitude nor the cold bothered Peerless Pilot or any other pigeon messenger (courtesy Naval History and Heritage Command)

Printed in the United States of America

*McFarland & Company, Inc., Publishers
Box 611, Jefferson, North Carolina 28640
www.mcfarlandpub.com*

To the pigeons
and their pigeoneers
who served America
with courage and distinction

Acknowledgments

I would like to thank my friends and family for their interest and support over the years during which I explored this somewhat unusual topic of homing pigeons. I know they will never look at a pigeon in the same way again. I especially thank my writers' group; Stephanie Greene, Chrysler Szarlan, and Amie Swift; Tom DeRosa, who was a pigeoneer at Fort Monmouth; his good friend Bob Carney, who introduced us; Frank Quatrochi, a pigeoneer during the Korean War; Jennifer Spangler, a journalist and pigeon aficionado with an excellent blog; Deone Roberts at the American Racing Pigeon Union; John Baldwin, pilot; Joe Gluckert, Portsmouth Naval Shipyard historian; military historian Frank Blazich, Jr., for his review of the manuscript; and Ronald Hart, who improved many of the photographs.

Table of Contents

Acknowledgments — vi
Prologue: John Silver — 1
Preface — 3

1. The First Feathered Recruits — 7
2. Pigeons for Sea Duty — 22
3. Put to the Test — 49
4. Into the Breach — 65
5. More, Farther, Faster — 95
6. A Call for Champions — 110
7. Staying Power — 152

Afterword — 162
Appendix A. Instructions on Reception, Care and Training of Homing Pigeons in Newly Installed Lofts at U.S. Navy Air Bases — 167
Appendix B. Henri Marion's Patent for a Message Holder — 176
Chapter Notes — 179
Bibliography — 187
Index — 195

A bird of the air shall carry the voice and that which hath wings shall tell the matter.—Ecclesiastes 10:20

Prologue: John Silver

In the fall of 1918, more than a million American servicemen took part in the 47-day Meuse-Argonne Offensive of World War I, and more than 400 pigeons served beside them. Tangles of barbed wire, machine gun nests and enemy-filled trenches carved the French countryside. Nothing lived above the ground, and the trenches filled with dead and wounded. Gas attacks occurred on the hour. Machine gun fire and bursting shells shattered the air.

The U.S. Army Signal Corps used mainly field telegraph and telephone to communicate to headquarters and other divisions, but the wires connecting them didn't last long. They were shredded to bits by artillery fire, and wheels and tracks of vehicles. Countless linesmen were killed as they stepped out of the trenches to repair lines. Additional messages were sent with human and dog couriers, but the terrain was heavily forested and cut by deep ravines, making movement treacherous. Under fire and gas attacks, these means of communication proved utterly useless. Only homing pigeons, flying high above the ruin, could reach headquarters with important messages that relayed the status of the allies' positions, their needs, their plans.

Earlier that year, in January, a pigeon had hatched in a cold, damp loft not far from the trenches in the Argonne Forest. The gangly and nearly featherless squab grew quickly, and in a few weeks, he was turned over to an experienced handler, a member of the Signal Corps. Rigorous training that included flying home from miles away over rough terrain and through all kinds of weather turned the youngster into a swift soldier pigeon. Fast and assured, the handsome blue-barred cock stood out among the other young birds and became one of the Signal Corps' best.

In August, the pigeon was seven months old and left for the front, where the Allies were holding against the Germans. He gained a reputation for acrobatic and fast flying skills that were tested time and time

Prologue

again, as the bird conveyed information from the embattled trenches 25 miles back to headquarters in Rampont.

On September 26, nine American divisions began an assault against the Germans along a 24-mile front from the Argonne Forest to the Meuse River. The goal was to capture a German rail hub at Verdun, thus breaking the rail network that supported the German Army in France and Flanders. Intense fighting caused heavy losses on both sides, but by early October, the U.S. First Army, headed by General John J. Pershing, penetrated the formidable Hindenburg Line, the main line of defense set by the Germans. After this punishing campaign, Pershing's men badly needed rest, reorganization, and replacements.

On October 21, the swift, bullet-dodging pigeon was released from the trenches at 2:35 p.m. with a message for headquarters. Just then, the enemy laid down a fierce bombardment. With sinking hearts, the men watched from the trenches as shells burst all around the pigeon. Concussions tossed the bird up and hammered him down toward the ground. It didn't seem possible he would survive, let alone fly. But then, as the soldiers stared in disbelief, the pigeon, struggling to stay aloft in the aftermath of the shells, somehow regained altitude and found his course to Rampont.

The bird made the 25 miles in 25 minutes, despite the flak that surely had hit him. He arrived at his loft in terrible condition. He had been hit in the chest by shrapnel, and a leg was missing, the message capsule hanging by the ligaments of what was left of it. Still, he had gotten the message through.

The blue barred cock was among 442 pigeons at the Meuse-Argonne Offensive. The feathered soldiers delivered 402 messages, over distances from 12 to 30 miles. Not a single message was lost.

Weeks of care repaired all but the bird's leg. He was named John Silver, after the one-legged pirate in Robert Louis Stevenson's *Treasure Island*. John Silver retired from service in 1921, and took on mascot duty with the U.S. Army Signal Corps, Honolulu, Hawaii. The hero pigeon died December 6, 1935, at the age of 17 years, 11 months.

John Silver was mounted and given to the National Museum of the U.S. Air Force in Dayton, Ohio. He stands in the Early Years Gallery, looking out from among famous airplanes and other war artifacts.

Preface

The extraordinary abilities of homing pigeons like John Silver caught my attention while I was researching stories about women spies for another, earlier book. I came across an article about homing pigeons operating as spies in World War I. A pigeon was outfitted with an aluminum breast harness to which a tiny, time-delayed camera was attached, and then released to fly over landscapes of interest. Spying was done on the wing, the camera snapping photos of the ground below at regular intervals. When the pigeon returned to its loft, the film was developed, and photos reviewed. The Germans used pigeon spies in World War I, and there are claims that the birds lugged cameras for both Allied forces and Axis powers throughout World War II. I was intrigued. How could a pigeon that weighs barely a pound fly straight home through storms, gas, exploding shells, smoke, and gunfire, with a capsule on its leg and sometimes a camera hanging from its body?

Is this the same bird that is maligned for gathering in congenial flocks, cooing and cleaning up city streets of discarded food? Yes, it is. Homing pigeons are the same species as a common street pigeon, *Columba livia.* However, homers are a combination of several different breeds of *Columba livia* including the Antwerp Smerle, French Cumulet, and the English Carrier, Dragoon, and Horseman, developed in Belgium in the early 1800s. What resulted from years of meticulous breeding is a super-bird with an aerodynamic and muscular body and a heightened ability to find home—an athlete of incomparable skills.

As a sport, pigeon racing began in Belgium in 1818, when the first long-distance race of 100 miles was held. The sport grew in popularity, and by the end of that century, spread to Holland, France, Great Britain, Canada and the United States. Now, well-trained homing pigeons routinely fly 600-mile races without stopping, averaging nearly 60 miles per hour, and most astonishing, starting from a place they've never been before. They win purses up to a million dollars. These are not your average street birds.

Preface

Homing pigeons come in a variety of colors, the most common being blue gray, with dark bars or checks on the wings. They can be a reddish color as well, and also grizzled, with white on the head, back and wings. But owners of homing pigeons aren't concerned much about color; they breed birds for speed, endurance and an ability to find home.

Although the exact details remain a mystery, the homer relies on a number of built-in directional aids to navigate. All sorts of theories are tossed around: pigeons use the sun's position to orient themselves, and they have a kind of internal "compass" that senses the earth's magnetic field, allowing them to discriminate between going toward the pole or the equator; superb hearing, vision and smell are important guides; pigeons learn about their home area, perhaps using visual, sound and smell cues to form a kind of map, and they get better with practice. Researchers continue to experiment, speculate and propose new theories, but the precise mechanism used by pigeons to find their way remains their secret.

Beyond the nearly mythic navigational abilities of homing pigeons is their motivation to reach home as quickly as possible, at all costs. They have been seen walking back to their lofts, dragging broken wings. Home is a familiar place where there is food, shelter and safety—and, most important, where their mates and nests await. Pigeons mate only once and form a strong and enduring bond with that chosen partner. There is no better place to be. This bond with home is aptly illustrated by an example cited by Major General Donald R. Cameron in his 1890 article, "An Aid to National Defense." Scamp was born in a Utica, New York, loft, and when just a young squeaker no more than three weeks old, moved to a loft in Northampton, Massachusetts. Here, he began training flights from a direction southwest of Northampton. All was well until he was released from White Plains, New York, 105 miles away. Instead of returning to Northampton, Scamp made his way directly to the place where he was born—Utica, 153 miles away. He was returned to Northampton and kept a prisoner in the Massachusetts loft until his keeper believed him to be completely settled at home again. However, accompanied by a mate, Scamp deserted at the first opportunity, and the pair was found that same day in the loft in Utica, in the nesting spot where Scamp had hatched.

Since ancient times, militaries all over the world have taken advantage of this intractable urge. The swift and loyal pigeon became a life-saving alternative for sending messages when telegraph and telephone lines were down, radio was out, where the terrain was impossible

Preface

for horses or dogs, or when conditions were so horrible, human couriers couldn't get through.

Given their stellar military service and extraordinary physiology, the public's general dislike of pigeons is puzzling. Despite prodigious feats during several wars, pigeons have lost their heroic luster, unlike other war animals—dogs and horses—who remain beloved. The flocks that gather in city parks and on buildings are either lost or AWOL racing pigeons, or their progeny; or, they are descendants of war birds. These are intelligent birds that have adapted easily to city living. Buildings offer exactly the nooks and crannies they like for nesting, and humans leave consistent food sources. Bits of donuts, bagels, pizza—perfect.

Overcrowding of pigeons in some cities has produced acidic dung that destroys buildings and statues. But pigeons are not filthy, and they do not spread disease any more than any other animal. Studies are trying to find humane ways to regulate city pigeon populations, but meanwhile, public perception of pigeons as "flying rats" remains in sharp contrast to the true nature of these descendants of racers and honorable veterans. We have forgotten all too quickly.

I knew the Army had used pigeons in both world wars, but I was surprised to learn that the Navy was the first branch of the U.S. military to officially include them in their ranks. I couldn't imagine birds being released far out to sea with no place to rest, no landmarks or map to follow. I investigated further and uncovered the little-known, but pivotal role pigeons played in naval communications from the late 1800s through World War II.

In fact, as I mined deeper and deeper into the role of pigeons in military communications, I discovered that they served in all branches of the military as well as with other government entities. Homing pigeons served with the Office of Strategic Services and the Central Intelligence Agency, the Civil Air Patrol, the U.S. Forest Service, Civilian Defense Councils and the National Guard. They even accompanied small naval and Coast Guard boats doing reconnaissance off the East Coast during World War II.

From 1878 through the Korean War—75 years—homing pigeons served America, here and on three other continents. Their widespread value as a vital means of communication is even more compelling because in many instances their role remained unsung.

To achieve the most complete chronicle of pigeon messengers in the U.S. military, I turned to both primary and secondary sources. Where I could, I used military and government records, such as the U.S.

Preface

National Archives and Records Administration's (NARA's) records of the Navy's use of homing pigeons. This material included orders, memos and letters that set up the initial Navy lofts in 1896. Some primary sources, such as original Army manuals for pigeoneers, were available online. So was Army pigeoneer Frank Hauck's diary from World War II. Secondary sources—books, newspapers, journal and magazine articles—broadened the narrative of the pigeons' service. The most powerful sources were personal communications, real conversations with former military pigeoneers or their relatives. Their voices returned the stories to life.

After months of trips to museums, libraries and archives around the country, after many exchanges with pigeoneers, pigeon fanciers, historians and military personnel, here is the unforgettable story of military pigeons, an accounting of a remarkable service to our country.

Author Note: Homing pigeons have often been called carrier pigeons, but that's a misnomer. They are two different breeds, the Carrier having been developed originally in England for its looks, not to carry messages.

Chapter 1

The First Feathered Recruits

> *I believe that by securing the best clans of birds, and with proper care and training, they [pigeons] can be made quite useful.*—General Nelson A. Miles (Report of the Secretary of War, 1875)

Homing pigeons got their start as messengers in the United States not with the military, but with newspapers. Since the 1830s, newspapers and stockbrokers, particularly in England and France, had used homing pigeons to carry news and the latest stock quotes. Information was sometimes flown from Boulogne France, across the English Channel directly to London, a distance of 135 miles. In the summertime, messages would arrive in London by mid-day, whereas the Paris mail could not be expected before midnight.[1] With feathered couriers in service, fortunes, like that of the Rothchild family, were made in the stock exchange. Aware of the successful pigeon couriers used by stockbrokers and news services in Britain and Europe, some American papers set up their own pigeon messenger services, eager to try out any method that might increase the speed of information flow. In the 1840s, both the *New York Sun* and the *Baltimore Sun* newspapers profited from swift pigeon posts. Arunah S. Abell, the *Baltimore Sun's* owner, was particularly impressed with the work of homing pigeons and organized a pigeon express of 400 to 500 birds to convey news between Washington, D.C., New York, Philadelphia, and Baltimore.[2] Farther north, Daniel H. Craig, editor and proprietor of the *Boston Daily Mail* in the early 1840s, would leave Boston harbor in a fast schooner to meet incoming Cunard-line mail steamships, carrying with him a crate of homing pigeons. On the ship, Craig gathered news from London and Liverpool journals and wrote summaries of them on tissue paper. He then fastened the papers to the legs of his pigeons and released the birds out a porthole. In a matter of minutes, the feathered couriers arrived at their loft near Craig's Boston office. Craig and his pigeons served newspapers in Boston, New York,

War Pigeons

Philadelphia, Baltimore and Washington, and Craig gained a reputation for scooping the news.[3]

By the Civil War, pigeons had been carrying information in North America credibly for a couple of decades, but records do not show any official use of them during that war, although they might have flown casually between families or towns. Homing pigeons had been imported from England and Europe at this point for racing, but an organization of clubs and fanciers hadn't yet formed. Perhaps the Army lacked the expertise needed for training or had too few birds available to cover the enormous territory involved in the war. Instead, the Army relied on flags, torches and the telegraph for signaling. To coordinate communications, the Army created the Signal Corps, the world's first organization of its kind. Under Chief Signal Officer Albert J. Myer, over 15,000 miles of telegraph cable were laid with mobile units developed to keep up with moving troops.[4]

Following the Civil War, a tide of migration flooded the western two thirds of the nation. White Americans thirsted for adventure, land and gold, and arteries of settlers and miners snaked across the Plains. The Union Pacific and Central Pacific railroads joined in Utah on May 10, 1869, accelerating the westward flow of people. Many of these settlers were hard-edged trappers, miners and traders with little respect for law or treaty. Native Americans, particularly the Plains Indians, stood squarely in the path of progress and put them on a collision course with the unrestrained intruders.

The Army was sent to defend the settlement of the frontier and quell those Indians who opposed non–Indian occupation of any lands. However, a post–Civil War force of fewer than 10,000 enlisted soldiers faced a patrol range of two million square miles of inhospitable land and more than 200,000 Indians, among them, skilled and unorthodox warriors. Except during major campaigns, troops remained scattered across the frontier at more than 100 outposts, forts and cantonments, sometimes hundreds of miles apart. Their campaigns against the Indians were characterized by widespread skirmishes, pursuits, massacres, raids and battles.[5]

Beyond the frontier's impossible expanse was its weather—as much a challenge to the soldiers as the enemy. Primarily a high plateau of semiarid grassland, the Plains cover a quarter of the interior of the North American continent. In the U.S., the Plains encompass about 500 miles East-West, and 2000 miles North-South, and include Montana, North and South Dakota, eastern Wyoming, Nebraska, eastern

Chapter 1. The First Feathered Recruits

Colorado, Kansas, eastern New Mexico, western Texas and western Oklahoma. In contrast to the confined, relatively tame landscape of the East, frontier soldiers faced a mostly flat and treeless expanse, with a few tree-covered mountains, low hills and stream valleys. They were struck by the harsh climate, with below-freezing temperatures and wind in winter, and hot humid summers, marked in some places by heavy rainfall, hail, wind and tornadoes that slashed across the open land.

The far-reaching network of Army posts across a formidable land forced commanders to establish a dependable communications system in order to fight campaigns and administer daily duties. They turned to the Signal Corps, which built and maintained thousands of miles of telegraph lines. In addition to the Army's needs, further demand for telegraph lines came from the nonstop flow of explorers, miners and settlers.

From the outset, the frontier telegraph system fell prey to problems. The construction, alone, of telegraph lines was daunting. For starters, the Great Plains and Southwest lacked good timber to build poles. The Signal Corps specified that the ideal wood was red cedar or black locust, and failing that, white cedar, sassafras, yellow pine and white oak. But often, the easiest to procure were willow and cottonwood, which lasted only a year.[6] Hauling the poles, digging holes and clearing land was laborious for both men and animals. In addition, sandstorms, snowstorms, prairie fires, thunderstorms and floods that battered the land throughout the year, threatened the whole operation. Indians, and sometimes cowboys and other outlaws, burned down signal stations and cut the lines. Poor equipment constantly hampered transmission of messages.

Still, demand for the telegraph escalated in 1873 when the Signal Corps took on weather reporting. Weather had been studied since colonial times. Benjamin Franklin theorized about the origin and movement of storms, and Thomas Jefferson had kept a daily journal of weather observations. In 1849, under its first Secretary Joseph Henry, the Smithsonian Institution organized the country's first telegraph system of weather reporting. Volunteer observers sent reports to the Smithsonian via commercial telegraph, and from those, the first weather maps were produced.[7] But after the Civil War, commerce and agriculture spread so rapidly, that the need for a national weather service became clear. Lacking the funds to operate one, Joseph Henry urged Congress to take it on. The duties of such a service were assigned to the military because it was thought that military discipline would secure promptness, regularity and accuracy in the required observations.

War Pigeons

In 1870, after receiving a Congressional mandate, the War Department made the Signal Corps responsible for weather forecasting. Telegraph lines were extended first along the eastern seaboard, to help warn of storms in conjunction with the Life-Saving Service. Then, weather stations were built throughout the country in eight districts, with forecasts sent three times a day to Washington, all via telegraph. Signal Service traffic became the biggest daily use of military telegraph lines. (The Signal Corps was sometimes referred to as the Signal Service.)

In the early 1870s, the Signal Corps began to experiment with two new modes of communication to augment the telegraph—homing pigeons and heliographs. The Siege of Paris, August 1870–January 1871, had thrust homing pigeons into the international spotlight and opened the world's eyes to their value as reliable and vital couriers. For five months, the Prussians, a strong German state, had besieged Paris, cutting off supplies and all contact with the outside world. Balloons could leave the city, but prevailing winds kept them from returning. Homing pigeons provided the solution. Pigeons donated by Paris clubs left with aeronauts in balloons heading to Tours, the provisional government set up about 150 miles away from Paris. There, the birds were outfitted with messages and released to fly home to their Paris lofts. At first, the messages were handwritten on very thin paper, rolled up tightly, inserted into a small goose quill pierced at both ends, and tied to a tail feather. In December, thanks to M. René Dagron's expertise in microphotography, messages were photographed and reduced to tiny bits of text. Hundreds of these messages could be inserted into a single quill. The Parisians, the large majority of whom had never heard of the capability of homing pigeons, were astounded at the unexpected success of their flights.

Of the 302 birds sent from Paris during the siege, only 57 returned, but those few that did became heroes to all of France. One hundred fifty thousand official dispatches and one million private notes were carried by the pigeons to Paris.[8]

When the siege ended, stories of the pigeons' heroic flights were publicized around the world. Commemorative souvenirs, such as medals, stamps and postcards, were sold, and a statue honoring the pigeons and aeronauts of the balloons was built at Porte des Ternes, Paris. It was designed by Frédéric Auguste Bartoldi, the same artist who designed the Statue of Liberty. (During the German occupation of Paris in World War II, the statue at Porte des Ternes was destroyed.)

The unexpected triumph of pigeon messengers at the Siege of Paris convinced European governments that pigeons were valuable military

Chapter 1. The First Feathered Recruits

tools and resulted in a flurry of pigeon stations. France, Germany, Italy, Spain, Turkey, Russia, Denmark and Belgium all established intricate pigeon messenger networks, and their militaries devoted time and money to keep the pigeons in training and to improve the stock. In some countries, the War Ministries fixed the direction of races, even offering prizes. In return, the military could rely on the services of many thousand privately trained birds to supplement the work required during a war or in an emergency.

Beyond newspaper articles and reports, Americans may have learned about the heroic pigeons from American diplomat Elihu Washburne and the colony of Americans staying in Paris throughout the siege. Washburne aided American and other foreign nationals with food and fuel, and helped many of them leave Paris safely. In his diary and letters written during the ordeal, Washburne referred to information being received via homing pigeon from Léon Gambetta, the French war minister who was raising troops in the provinces outside Paris.

> Nobody can tell how long we are in for it and to what extremes we might be pushed. I first put the siege at sixty days and here we are at sixty-six and no light ahead. The French seem to be getting more and more "uppish" every day. Gambetta sends his proclamations pinned to a pigeon's tail, and tells of a great many things in the provinces, and then all at once, here in Paris, "pop goes the weasel."[9]

Military personnel undoubtedly heard about the Paris pigeons from three U.S. Army officers—Major General Philip H. Sheridan, Brigadier General James W. Forsyth, and Colonel William B. Hazen, who had gone to Prussia to observe the conflict. After the Civil War, the Army had made an effort to increase the professionalism of its ranks. Professional journals were created and postgraduate schools founded. Army officers traveled to Asia and Europe to study how other armies functioned. As invited guests of the King of Prussia, Major General Sheridan and his aide, Brigadier General Forsyth, and later, Colonel Hazen, observed the German tactics during its siege of Paris. Colonel Hazen kept a diary during the siege and wrote about his experiences as an observer. The focus of his observations was the organization and education of the French and German armies, and some of those aspects he compared with the U.S. Army. Hazen mentioned the use of balloons by besieged civilians to communicate in one direction, out of Paris, but he did not add that pigeons brought messages back. Nonetheless, he, Sheridan and Forsyth would have known about their use, as the Prussian Army sought to shoot down the pigeons and sent falcons to kill them.

War Pigeons

While impressed with how the German military operated, the officers must have been further inspired by the skills of the pigeons, and likely brought those accounts home.

One officer, General Nelson A. Miles, was particularly interested. An ambitious, imposing soldier, General Miles had made a name for himself first in the Civil War, and then, in the campaigns against the Indians. In 1875, commanding the 5th Infantry, he had been victorious at Red River, Texas, against the Southern Cheyenne, Comanche and Kiowa, and again, a year later in the wintry Northern Plains against the Sioux and Northern Cheyenne. Leading the 5th Infantry through Montana, he had forced the surrender of Chief Joseph's band of Nez Perce in 1877. If there was one thing he'd learned from years of fighting Indians, it was to leave nothing to chance—including the challenge of maintaining supply lines and communications in the difficult terrain and extreme weather of the Plains.

After the surrender of the Indians at Red River, Miles prepared a wide-ranging report on the campaign. As well as military operations, he described the nature of the territory, the problem of supplies, and need for good communications. Interested in weaponry and technology, he was always on the lookout for ways to strengthen movement and coordination of troops. At this point, he must have heard about homing pigeons, perhaps from Colonel Hazen, for in his report, he stated that flares and

Always interested in improving communications, General Nelson A. Miles advocated the use of pigeons as messengers during the Indian Wars in the late 1880s.

Chapter 1. The First Feathered Recruits

homing pigeons would improve the Army's ability to communicate.[10] That same year he reiterated his belief in the potential of pigeons in an 1875 Annual Report to the Secretary of War. "I believe that genuine carrier pigeons could be raised at frontier posts and to great advantage; they should carry a message across the staked plains in a few hours that would take weeks to send round by the usual route. I would recommend their trial."[11]

The Army followed up on the idea of using homing pigeons in the West. By now, pigeon clubs had sprung up across the country, particularly in the East, among them, the Red Star Pigeon Club of Philadelphia, the Albany County Homing Club of New York, the New York Homing Pigeon Club, and the Old Dominion Homing Pigeon Club of Alexandria, Virginia. These clubs began to organize races, and it wasn't long before American birds were racing over longer and longer distances, often over 200 miles. In June of 1878, for example, pigeons from a club in New York were flown from Steubenville, Ohio, 341 miles to New York. The winner reached its home in an impressive 8 hours, 18 minutes, or at a rate of 1205 yards per minute (41 miles per hour).[12] With such distances routinely covered, birds could surely carry messages across the large expanses of the west, especially if they were trained according to proven methods.

What the Army hadn't counted on was the effort involved to train homing pigeons. In 1882, First Lieutenant William E. Birkhimer prepared a report for the Secretary of War on the feasibility of homing pigeons in the military. He referred to veteran pigeon expert Louis Oflerman's training regime to prepare military birds. It was a precise and time-consuming process used in European garrisons. Young birds, those in their first season, were loosed at three months old from a distance of three miles from home, and then that distance increased, with rest in between, until they learned to fly from 200 miles away. In the second season, the distances over which the birds flew were lengthened until they could fly home from 500 miles away. This took many months to accomplish, but what resulted were strong and reliable messengers. In Germany, for example, birds that followed this regime, "are considered trustworthy from fifty to one hundred miles, if the breed of birds is good; if the birds are reared at the locality to which they are to fly; and if they are acquainted with the country over which they are to travel."[13]

Would such a detailed training strategy work out West? The idea of messages traveling through the air at 40 miles per hour must have appealed to Nelson Miles, who had already encouraged the idea of experimenting with pigeons. He was game to try.

Lieutenant Birkimer reported that in 1878, Chief Signal Officer Albert Myer sent two dozen pigeons from a fancier in Philadelphia to then–Colonel Miles, who was stationed in Montana in the Northern Plains. These twenty-four sleek homing pigeons were the first United States military messenger birds. Able to carry a message at least 100 miles, immune to all but the worst weather, and safe from hostile Indians, they seemed to be the answer to long distance communication on the frontier.

Colonel Miles tried to train and use the pigeons, but, initially, without success. The birds, reported Birkhimer, may not have been the best breed, nor the trainer experienced in his duties. Birkimer did not specify what, if any, training the birds received. But it's clear that whatever was done, was not enough. The birds could not have had time to learn the landscape well, or to construct that crucial map of smells, sounds, and visual cues to help steer them home. Plus, Colonel Miles hadn't anticipated the swift plains hawks and falcons that hunted the pigeons relentlessly. Pigeons are able to out-fly some hawks and other raptors, but not all of them, especially in wide open country that afforded little shelter. Along with the constant threat of winged predators, Lieutenant Birkhimer doubted the ability of soldiers to give the pigeons the careful and elaborate training necessary, and did not recommend that the Army spend time or money on extensive experiments with pigeons.

Birkimer cited later trials by Miles out of Fort Keogh in Montana that produced better results.

> I received, through the Chief Signal Officer of the Army, twelve pigeons—strong, hardy birds, very tractable, and, as far as experimented with, their action was very satisfactory. They bred rapidly, and, when I left Fort Keogh, numbered about fifty. At times, when flying them, we were troubled by a small hawk, which greatly disturbed the birds in their flight, occasionally destroying them. My experiments were successful, and demonstrated the fact that they can be made useful for military service. The longest distance made was about one hundred miles, from the mouth of the Big Horn River, to Fort Keogh, Montana; but they only had a few trials, and were not fully trained. When in Montana, I was unable, through want of time, to make as thorough an investigation as I should have desired. I believe that by securing the best clans of birds, and with proper care and training, they can be made quite useful.[14]

Birkhimer's report included an addendum from the Military Division of the Pacific that discussed the potential use of pigeons at larger

Chapter 1. The First Feathered Recruits

forts, particularly those near railroads. This addition agreed with Miles summation, asserting the pigeons' abilities and their benefit to the Army.

> All of this [training the birds] requires strict attention and gives trouble. But their cost, trouble and expense will be insignificant compared to the benefit they will confer by conveying important information at critical times. The posts in Arizona where pigeons could probably be used to most advantage are Grant and Huachuca. As these posts will have large garrisons they will be the first from which expeditions start; at these large posts someone will probably always be found with a special aptitude and fondness for breeding and training pigeons, and being near the railroad, the birds can readily be sent to increased distance while in training.

As compelling, the addendum recognized the pigeon as more than a means to convey information. This was the flicker of the start of a seven-decade soldier-pigeon bond.

> Anyone with the least fondness for natural history, or of games in which competitive effort enters, cannot but become deeply interested in the breeding and training of pigeons, and in their wonderful voyages, and the voyager so strong of wing and enduring as to be the first to bring from a long distance, across a trackless, hostile country, in a few hours, the news of a victory or a call for help from those in whose fate many interests, attach, cannot but be accorded military recognition and a place in military annals.[15]

Despite the clear potential of pigeons as messengers, as well as some actual successes, the Army did not develop a comprehensive plan for the use of homing pigeons in the West. In 1886, General Miles was sent to Arizona to find and subdue the Apache, who had for a long time terrorized residents of southern Arizona and New Mexico, eluding the Army's attempts to locate them. He arrived at Fort Huachua without a clan of homing pigeons.

But while stationed in Montana, he had also investigated another Signal Corps communications tool, the heliograph, a mirrored instrument that flashed messages across large distances. It was easy to set up and required only the sun, and Miles had already established a line of them that connected Fort Keogh to Fort Custer, 140 miles apart.[16]

By the time he got to Arizona, Miles, now a general, was an expert on the technology. The endless sun that burned through his hat was just what he needed. From his headquarters at Fort Huachua, he organized a campaign against the Apache around a network of heliograph stations supplied by the Signal Corps. Twenty seven of them, set atop mountain peaks, each with its component of guards, telescope, water supply and field glasses, spanned nearly 800 miles.[17]

War Pigeons

The signal officers could identify movements at a distance of 25 miles, and flashed reports back to Miles' advance headquarters at Fort Huachua. The heliographs kept Miles' commanders continuously informed of the Apache's progress over the barren, rugged land. The glinting messages disheartened the Apache, assuring them that troops were in hot pursuit. No matter how Geronimo twisted or dodged, he could not hide, and he surrendered in early September 1886.

Even though the heliograph trumped a pigeon express in the West, the Army left the door open a crack regarding the possibility of a pigeon post in the eastern part of the country where homing pigeons were becoming *de rigueur*. Country physicians carried pigeons to remote patients, leaving instructions on how to release the birds with messages to carry to the doctors back in their town offices. Businessmen in cities communicated with their families in the suburbs via pigeon post, and vacationing stockbrokers had pigeons bring numbers from Wall Street to their summer residences.

More and more racing clubs had formed with birds making record distance journeys, routinely 400–500 miles. Two pigeons exceeded more than 1000 miles. By the 1880s, the Federation of American Homing Pigeon Fanciers had formed and included clubs scattered all over the country. In the New York and New Jersey areas, fanciers trained their birds to fly from boats on the water as well as from points on land. According to an 1886 article in *Century Magazine*, by well-known fancier E.S. Starr, the passenger steamships SS *Waesland* and SS *Circassia*, both used homing pigeons to alert the port of New York of their arrival, liberating birds 300 and 250 miles, respectively, off New Jersey.[18]

Starr reported that pigeons flew readily from yachts. "The use of pigeons by Mr. C.T. Arnoux as message-bearers, in the yacht races of last September," Starr stated, "proves conclusively the value the birds might have as messengers from off the water." Starr related how one newspaper editor responded to receiving news from offshore. "It gives me a peculiar sensation to receive a copy from the hand of one I know to be out of reach upon the water, and to feel that he may talk to me but I cannot answer back. It is a wonder to me after this experience that the officers of any vessel, excursion steamer, yacht, sail or tug boat should be willing to leave the shore without this means of communicating with it."[19] In his article, Starr included charts showing long distance records achieved by American birds as well as a map of mostly east coast routes flown by the pigeons. It looks eerily like the route map at the back of a modern in-flight magazine.

Chapter 1. The First Feathered Recruits

The use of pigeons by Mr. Arnoux was just the beginning of their role on yachts. The rivalry between Boston and New York to produce the winning boat in the America's Cup trials became a passion among fans up and down the eastern seaboard, and they craved news of the racing results. In 1887, Charles Taylor, the *Boston Globe*'s publisher, bought a steamer yacht, the *Ocean Gem*, and equipped it with a pigeon loft. (Perhaps he remembered the successful exploits of Daniel Craig's birds.) The *Globe* racing reporters observed the action from on board the *Ocean Gem*, and at key points, released a few birds carrying reports of the race's progress, such as leader's speed, time at which buoys were passed, changes in weather. Once the birds reached their loft on shore, the news was telegraphed to the *Globe*.[20]

In his 1882 report, Birkimer concluded, "In most cities of the sea-board, there are many birds that could be procured for training for military purposes, and the rail-roads and steamboats afford facilities for training. No branch of the army is so well equipped for this kind of work as the Signal Service."[21] The Signal Service did, in fact, maintain an interest in homing pigeons. The Annual Report of the Chief Signal Officer (W.B. Hazen) to the Secretary of War for 1886 requested appropriations for the next year to include money for pigeons. The money would cover costs for cages, bracelets, feed, etc., of the pigeons that belonged to the Signal Service and pay for continued experiments with them.

The following year's Annual Report of the Chief Signal Officer, now Adolphus W. Greely, remarked that homing pigeons had not recently received much attention from the Service, but that a stock of birds from private fanciers was at his disposal, and that he intended to experiment with pigeons in the coming year, at little cost to the Corps.

> The necessity for such dispatch-bearers is not pronounced in this country; but with a view to familiarizing the Service with these pigeons, as is possible at nominal cost, the Chief Signal Officer has directed that experiments be made from Key West toward Cuba, with the expectation based upon the opinion of experts, that by training these birds in flights from the seaward, would enable a United States squadron in the vicinity of Havana to communicate rapidly and certainly with the naval station at Key West. If such flight is possible from Cuba, it could be eventually extended to the Windward Island, even to Nassau.[22]

With money appropriated, the Signal Corps opened an experimental pigeon station at the Army's barracks in Key West, Florida, in 1888. The barracks had been established in 1831 and were garrisoned in support of Fort Taylor, built between 1845 and 1861. After the Civil War, the barracks were sporadically occupied. But Key West had grown into

War Pigeons

an economically important area, with a deep port, shipping lanes that connected to the rest of the world, and an underwater cable line that linked the U.S. to Cuba. The military found it prudent to maintain bases there.

Greely's annual report for 1888 explained the advantageous position of the Key West pigeon loft with respect to other powers, and that communications from a squadron of ships cruising in nearby waters might, at times, be desired. The Signal Service was given an empty storehouse at the barracks, which was converted into a cote and fully equipped with the latest in recommended food items: Canada peas, small corn, vetches, hemp seed, flax seed, oatmeal, grits, cracked wheat, and rock and common salt. And plenty of fresh water. (This would cost the Army extra, as rain provided the only fresh source.) That a pigeon messenger service would best serve the Navy at that location, didn't appear to hinder the Army's efforts, and training birds to fly over water became a focus of the loft.

Even though the Key West cote was experimental, it came with rigorous regulations on the care of the birds. These were probably the first guidelines written by the Army and would become the prototype for future manuals on the care and training of military homing pigeons. Because the Key West station kept meteorological records, such as haze, fog, clouds, wind, pressure, temperature and humidity, these factors were used to determine to what extent weather affected flight. Registering atmospheric conditions on flight days was probably a first.

Extracts from the regulations were included in Greely's report:

> The register will contain a list of the birds by number, their age, sex, color, distinguishing marks and parentage, and set forth in detail the history of each, with stone as to achievements and capabilities.
>
> In the care of the birds due regard will be paid to cleanliness and ventilation; they will be fed at stated hours, in deference to their regular habits, and the fountains and bath-tubs will be frequently cleaned and supplied with wholesome water, a measure of vital importance to the health of the pigeons.
>
> It is not designed that great speed be developed or exceptional flights be undertaken at the expense of hardiness and reliability, and it must always be kept in view that the chief merit of the birds for military purposes lies in the direction of its service as a messenger. Breeding and training will therefore be mainly directed to the production and development of the most resolute homing qualities.
>
> As it does not appear that the homing pigeon has well recognized points of color that wil assist in breeding for special traits, that much importance attaches to the form and size of the bird, provided there be sufficient length and strength of wing, or that the shape of the head is material, provided there be ample development for brain room, these features may, at first, be safely disregarded in mating for results;

Chapter 1. The First Feathered Recruits

but as experience is gained, advantage should be taken of all points believed from observation to go hand in had with valuable characteristics.

The eye, however, seems worthy of special attention as indicating the degree of intelligence and of persistence in face of difficulties.

The crossing of different stocks becomes a necessity that lack of constitution, strength, and intelligence may not result, as also that by judicious mating the qualities most desired may be combined and reproduced, possibly improved. In this connection, however, it is the opinion of those well qualified to judge that birds bearing kinship nearer than that of second cousin cannot be paired to advantage.

The gradual training of the birds will begin as soon as practicable after they attain sufficient strength for the first short flights. (Old birds from other lofts, and which are provided solely for breeding purposes, will be kept in restraint, as their liberation implies their loss.) They will be made familiar with the appearance of the island from different directions, but the further training and ultimate result will contemplate the invariable employment of the same birds over practically the same course, and special care will therefore be exercised to identify birds trained to different directions. Thus the mark "N" will indicate that the bird bearing it is trained to return from the north (embracing the full quadrant from northwest to northeast), and similarly for east, south, and west. The number of birds composing each group will depend on the necessities of the service in the several directions.

In sending out birds for training flights, sufficient food (small corn, Canada peas, or wheat, etc.) will be fastened to the basket by sack or otherwise to insure a supply for the utmost limit of time till their liberation, and each basket will be tagged with instructions as to feeding and bear a notice conspicuously placed that the birds should at all times have access to a plentiful supply of fresh drinking water. Also that unless their retention aboard ship is apt to carry them beyond reasonable limits, they be not liberated before sunrise or during very stormy weather.

In regard to these latter points it may be remarked that successful flights have been made during storms of wind and rain, and even during the night; but experiments to test the hardiness of the birds under these unfavorable conditions will be made only after the satisfactory demonstration of their reliability and usefulness by daylight in ordinarily favorable weather.

Entrance to an ante-room of the loft by a trap-door is contemplated, that the birds may be kept imprisoned till the message is detached. Until such is provided a substitute may be improvised by requiring the birds to raise a pair of wires hung from a staple at the top, which swing in freely, but falling back against a ledge prevent egress.

Whether the tenacity with which the pigeon seeks its loft after liberation is due to affection for mate and young, or whether it is due to attachment to its home, perch, and nest, it is certain the bird has strong proprietary instincts and dislike of change. All possible deference should be paid to this trait in its character. No bird therefore be forced to vacate the nest and perch originally assigned it, except for the most urgent reasons.

A number corresponding to that of the bird in the register will be so placed with reference to the nest and perch as to indicate the proprietorship.

The birds will be identified by the leg-band, but should bear the service-stamp on the under side of a suitable wing-feather.

War Pigeons

The young birds in their first season may be trained to return home from a distance of 100 miles; in the second season this distance should be somewhat increased; but for the third and subsequent years a return from 400 miles can be accomplished with much certainty unless the weather is so bad as to make flying impossible. It is believed that the question of seasons will not affect the flights materially at Key West, but that throughout the year the birds may be kept in training and be available at any moment for messenger service.

That the birds may become accustomed to the carriage of the message-roll and the chance of loss from picking at the parcel be reduced to the minimum, it will be established as a general rule that the quill intended as the envelope for the protection of the message shall form the habitual equipment of the bird in all its flights, and the methods of attaching the quill and securing the safe transmission of the message will be made the subject of inquiry and practice till the most suitable is definitely determined.

An approved practice abroad is to roll and insert the message slip in the quill, closing the ends of the latter with sealing wax, and piercing near the ends with a red hot steel point, so as not to split, threading the pierced holes with waxed silk thread or fine copper wire, and attaching to the principal tail feather. This feather should be tested by a slight pull to see that it is solid.

Advantage will be taken of the opportunity offered by ready access to the meteorological records of the station to determine as definitely as possible to what extent the speed and reliability of the birds are affected by various atmospheric conditions, such as haze, fog, clouds, wind (direction and velocity), pressure, temperature, and humidity; in fact, careful note will be made of all causes that operate to prevent or delay the return of the birds to the loft, including the ravages of the hawks; and that no less may inadvertently occur through actions of gunners, the residents of the island will be informed that their co-operation to prevent such loss is invited in behalf of the public service, and generally, it is made a duty in connection with the maintenance of the station that the most approved methods be employed of handling and caring for homing pigeons, and adapting them to the carriage of messages under all conditions likely to arise where benefit in a military point might result.[23]

With experienced keepers and specific guidelines on care and training, the 56 birds donated from private sources demonstrated their reliability for carrying messages over land as well as over long stretches of water. They flew without incident from ships in the region to shore, and from Havana, Cuba, to their Key West loft 90 miles away. Greely reported that of their current flock, nine pigeons were reliable for distances of 100 miles over water, five more for distances of 60 miles, while the remaining birds were trained at distances not exceeding 60 miles. This was excellent work, he claimed, for birds ranging in age from one to four months.

However, the pigeon couriers, sure to be a valuable component of the Signal Service, were suddenly grounded. In 1891, the Signal Service

Chapter 1. The First Feathered Recruits

was transferred to a civilian status at the Department of Agriculture and established as the U.S. Weather Bureau. The Army found no further official use for the birds. In fact, the Army didn't officially enlist the help of pigeons again, until World War I.

What of the birds at the Key West cote? They were shipped to the U.S. Naval Academy, in Annapolis, Maryland, where a French professor, convinced of their value to the U.S. Navy in sea communications, couldn't wait to get his hands on them.

Chapter 2

Pigeons for Sea Duty

> *We have got the pigeons, we have got the stations, we have got the ships, and we have got the sea.*—Henri Marion (*Proceedings of the U.S. Naval Institute*, 1896, quoting Manoubia experiment promoters)

    Henri Marion was appointed to the Naval Academy in 1887, as Assistant Professor of French, but almost from the time he arrived, he appeared to have something more important on his mind than explaining French verbs to cadets. He intended to convince the U.S. Navy Department to enlist homing pigeons for sea duty as messengers for ship-to-shore, and possibly shore-to-ship, and ship-to-ship communication.

    At the time, telegraph facilities were available in nearly every port and provided fast connections between the Navy Department in Washington and commanders of squadrons. Out at sea it was a different story. There, the Navy still relied on flag, whistle, horn, and gun signaling during the day, with lights for visual transmission of Morse code at night. Two types of flag signaling were used. The one-flag wig-wag system, originally developed by Albert J. Myer of the Army's Signal Corps, used one flag attached to the end of a 16-foot-long pole that was waved to different positions. Each position was coded. At night, a torch was used in a similar fashion. The International Code of Signals was a system of flags with assigned codes. Flags (and pennants) were hoisted up a ship's halliard and in a group, or singly, conveyed a message. Hundreds of signals were standardized and could be sent quickly by the signalers of one ship and received by all other ships nearby.

    Therein lay the problem. Ships had to be nearby. If ships weren't at anchor, or sailing close enough to each other, signaling was useless. In addition, flags went limp in no wind, or blew the wrong way for good visibility. Pigeons, Professor Marion believed, could vastly improve long-distance communications at sea. With feathered couriers, messages could be sent beyond the reach of sight.

Chapter 2. Pigeons for Sea Duty

Marion's fervent belief in the birds' potential to enhance communications in the U.S. Navy was likely fostered as a boy. Given the depth of knowledge about homing pigeons expressed in his adult correspondence, it's probable that he, or his family, had raised pigeons. At the very least, he had to have worked closely with someone who did raise and race them. Marion's boyhood home, the Loire Valley, France, would have also stoked his passion for the birds. For the medieval city of Tours, situated 130 miles southwest of Paris between the Loire and Cher Rivers, had served as France's provisional government and also as the headquarters of the famed pigeon post during the Franco-Prussian War of 1870–1871.

Henri Marion, a teenager at the time, would have known about the desperate situation inside Paris—a city without fuel or food, reduced to eating rats, consuming even the two beloved zoo elephants, Castor and Pollux—and this last-ditch effort to establish two-way communication. It was impossible not to be deeply impressed.

In 1881, at age 24, Marion married a Parisian, Jeanne Marie Hael, and they arrived in the United States several years later. Why he immigrated or what route he took to his appointment at Annapolis is unknown. He lived briefly in Charleston, South Carolina, perhaps with relatives or other French nationals, and he taught at the Norwood Institute for Girls and Young Ladies on Massachusetts Avenue in Washington, D.C. An ad for the college of modern languages at Norwood listed Marion as a graduate of the Sorbonne in Paris. He may have heard about opportunities at the Academy through those connections. He and Jeanne Marie had two children, Paul and Jeanne. Marion began in the modern languages department at the Naval Academy, teaching first French, and later, Spanish.

While settling into his new life at the Academy, Marion must have kept track of the surge in ranks of pigeons in European armies and navies after the Siege of Paris, and the resulting high-speed winged network of information across the continent. And now England was on the cusp of building her own feathered branch of the military. Just a year before Marion arrived at the Academy, Captain H.T.W. Allatt of the Duke of Cornwall's Light Infantry wrote a lengthy article in the *Journal of the Royal United Services Institution* and presented it at an Institution lecture. Attending that day, was a diverse and influential audience, from high ranking military and naval officers to pigeon experts.

In his lecture, Allatt extolled the value of homing pigeons as part of a military communications plan and the need for England to organize a pigeon messenger system such as those in Europe. Allatt detailed the European military pigeon systems, listing the pigeon posts of France, Germany, Austria, Russia, Italy, Spain, Portugal, Denmark and Belgium. He included a map which resembled an intricate spider web, each piece of web representing a direct flying route between a frontier fortress and inland town. A principal point, usually the capital, served as a central station with which all other stations communicated.

Furthermore, explained Allatt, most of the countries with coastline utilized the system at sea as well. Trials were taking place off the north coast of Germany with birds being trained to fly from ships, and also from shore to ship where young birds had been born and raised in shipboard lofts. The birds did not have any problems recognizing their own ship, among others. Allatt added that Spain had established successful pigeon lofts on its coast.[1]

Captain Allatt concluded that given England's insular position, an organized pigeon messenger system would afford a means of communicating beyond Britain's shores, if the occasion arose. Unlike continental countries, Great Britain's telegraph lines could be severed without any sort of invasion. And submarine cables might be cut by an enemy who never caught sight of the island. It would be a difficult task for the Royal fleet to watch and protect all of the cables that ran from British shores to parts of the globe. In an emergency, he stressed, pigeons offered a means of maintaining direct, cheap and speedy communication with the Continent.

Pleas for a government-funded pigeon messenger service had just begun to stir in this country, mainly with regards to a coast defense system. The design and construction of heavy ordnance in Europe had advanced rapidly, including the development of superior cannon, making the current harbor defense systems in America obsolete. A strong national defense was a topic in much discussion since the Board of Fortification, formed under President Grover Cleveland in 1885, had declared the need to improve the defense of America's coastlines. In its 1886 report, the Board's findings indicated the necessity for a new system to safeguard America's seacoast cities from naval bombardment. A massive construction program of breech-loading cannons, mortars, floating batteries, and submarine mines for some 29 locations along the U.S. coastline had been recommended.

Lieutenant Richard Wainwright, a young naval officer (He later survived the USS *Maine* explosion and continued to fight in the Spanish-American War) and frequent contributor to the *Proceedings of the U.S. Naval Institute*, the go-to journal for naval professionals and

Chapter 2. Pigeons for Sea Duty

civilian experts, wrote an article in a 1889 issue pitching the need for signal stations equipped with pigeon messengers as integral parts of a coast defense system. In referring to the current prominent topic of coast defense, he stated "...the conveying of intelligence from one point of the coast to another will be of utmost importance. With fortifications, we shall always need stations from which the movements of the enemy and the number and character of the vessels can be reported. And when we have a defending fleet, we shall need, in addition to be able to convey such information to our fleet as will enable them to meet the enemy and frustrate his designs."[2] Lieutenant Wainwright emphasized the importance of properly placed and manned pigeon stations along the coast as part of a communications network in an improved defense system. Telegraph alone was not sufficient, and what he described was a network of flag to feather to telegraph wires, with an emphasis on the value of the birds if telegraph or phones lines were cut.

> An ideal system of transmitting intelligence coast wise and to seaward during a coast war would be one in which observation stations, connected by telegraph lines, were established at certain intervals along the coast: at each station, trained men with the necessary equipment for receiving and sending visual signals; at certain of these stations, pigeon lofts for furnishing pigeons to lookout vessels and receiving from them reports, and also for dispatching birds with information to outside stations of the fleet; also lofts at such stations as, from the position of the telegraph lines, are liable to have their connections interrupted, the birds being used to maintain communication when the lines are cut.[3]

With such a system, Wainwright further stated that direction of an enemy would be known, its progress along the coast tracked by observers, and a defending fleet able to engage or follow it. This, he emphasized, would greatly increase the strength of a fleet and effectiveness of national defense.

Wainwright stressed the cost-effectiveness of his plan. He explained that some 300 lighthouses and light ships were well-positioned for signal stations, manned by about 2700 personnel. Two hundred and three life-saving stations on the Atlantic, Gulf and Great Lake coasts were already connected by cable or telegraph, and many used telephones.[4] With a complete set of stations already in place, the country, concluded Wainwright, could put into operation a system of signal stations, including pigeons, at very little cost.

Another proponent for a pigeon post on Marion's side of the Atlantic was Major General Donald R. Cameron, commandant of the Royal Military College in Kingston, Ontario. In 1890, he published *An Aid to*

War Pigeons

National Defense, a slim book detailing the role of homing pigeons as part of Canada's national defense.

Cameron began with an overview of the numerous pigeon societies and success of pigeon messengers in Europe and then asked, "But in Canada, where is the organization? Where are the birds? How many of its people have even heard of them?"[5]

What followed was a detailed description, with specific examples, of why homing pigeons make nearly perfect messengers: their extraordinary homing faculty, power and endurance; their ease of care; their aptitude for long-distance flights, including those over water at the Army's Key West barracks; and their ability to fly in all but the most severe weather.

He stated that several European countries employed pigeons in connection with the defense of their coasts and included the U.S. Key West cote as being a successful coastal station in North America. Cameron dismissed any notion that communications technology had made pigeons dispensable.

> It is now time to submit to those who argue that railways and telegraphs make it unreasonable to promote the establishment of an organized system of pigeon lofts throughout the country—and to others who take no interest in the matter because it has no detachable coupons—it is time to submit to such that they should reconsider their opinion, for it has been shown that during the last fifty years, over the continent of Europe, not the least intelligent and not the least experienced quarter of the world, there has spread an amazing system of railways and telegraph lines, and with those has developed the most wonderful use of messenger pigeon services.[6]

He further emphasized the danger to national security of telegraph wires being cut. "All the details of mobilization, concentration and tactical movements in the country at this moment are dependent upon our telegraph wires. What a slender thread to carry our national safety!"[7]

Cameron listed possibilities for the birds' use outside the military. With a well-organized pigeon post, newspaper men might receive news from Europe days in advance of mail vessels; Eastern Canadian presses could exchange news with western newspapers, and official dispatches might even fly between the British embassy at Washington, D.C., and Ottawa.

And a final entreaty:

> It is earnestly hoped that not a few of those who read this article will consider it a citizen's duty to encourage the breeding and training of messenger pigeons as a means of furnishing abundance of innocent amusement to young and old alike, as

Chapter 2. Pigeons for Sea Duty

useful helps in domestic and personal affairs, as servants of the press, as aids in the transaction of business, as assistants in commerce, as invaluable friends of the mercantile marine, and as indispensable auxiliaries to the navy and army in the time of our country's need.[8]

(Canada did establish an official government pigeon post, which ran between look-out stations at lighthouses on islands off the east coast of Nova Scotia and the citadel in Halifax. It later stretched to Windsor, Ontario. The coastal messenger service began in 1891, but was plagued with a heavy mortality rate among the pigeons, and was discontinued in 1895.)

Although seeds of interest might have germinated, there was no immediate response from either the United States government to heed these sensible requests for the addition of pigeons to national security plans.

With other issues at hand, the United States continued to balk at considering a pigeon messenger service. Post–Civil War reconstruction was only partly working. The south remained economically devastated, while the north experienced rapid economic development.

Isolationism, begun in the colonial period, remained a part of the country's mindset. This would all change with the Spanish-American War in 1898, but America fought the War of 1812, and the Mexican War, 1846–1848, without joining alliances or fighting in Europe. Along with other pressing post–Civil War issues, this isolationist attitude may have contributed to the lack of enthusiasm over a pigeon messenger service, even as part of a coast defense. After all, pigeon posts were a European and British phenomenon. Another consideration might have been insufficient experience with the birds and thus, a lack of confidence in the whole notion.

If Professor Marion was aware of the pronounced disinterest in a government-funded pigeon post, he was certainly not discouraged by it. He clearly believed his new country's navy would prosper with feathered seamen on board its vessels. Living within a naval community at Annapolis, he was well placed to push the notion of a navy pigeon messenger service. Plus, he was more than willing to launch the service right on the Academy grounds and had even scoped out a good spot for a loft.

When Marion began teaching at the Academy, the approximately 174 cadets adhered to a full schedule of academics and athletics. They studied mathematics, engineering, English, history, law, modern languages, as well as practical courses such as seamanship, tactics and navigation. Athletics were mostly intramural and included fencing, boxing, baseball, football and crew. By 1890, the Academy experienced a revival in sports. The Navy "N" was introduced, the same year in which the first Army-Navy game was played. The revival of athletics wasn't limited to football. Baseball, fencing and crew all entered intercollegiate competition.

The crew team kept its shells in a boathouse along with other small boats. The tower of the boathouse, where masts were stepped, became vital to Marion's plans when the first flock of pigeons arrived from Key West. It was in this aerie that he built the Navy's first pigeon loft and established, in 1891, an experimental pigeon station to demonstrate the birds' usefulness.

It took money to care for the birds at the Academy and begin their training, and for that, Marion turned to pigeon fanciers. Anxious to promote their sport and the value of homing pigeons, fanciers along the eastern seaboard indicated that they would support a government initiative to establish a pigeon messenger service and help in any experiments. In keeping with this offer, Professor Marion's endeavor at the Naval Academy was privately funded, but he quickly began his campaign for Federal funding, writing in the influential *Proceedings*. It was to be an uphill battle, but fortunately, Marion had both the rapt attention of the *Proceedings* and the force of the Academy's summer cruises and their young officers behind him.

Professor Marion didn't waste any time beginning his campaign to convince the Navy to fund a pigeon messenger service, writing unremittingly in the *Proceedings of the U.S. Naval Institute* about the success of pigeons as sailors. Less than 20 years old, the *Proceedings* was already a highly influential journal, read widely and relied upon for informative, policy-shaping articles. It was in the fleet where the value of the Naval Institute's forum was truly felt. And it was in the fleet where Marion wanted his pigeons. So the new French professor wrote about the worth of pigeons as sailors abroad, and he wrote about their success as messengers at home, on board Naval Academy ships and other American vessels.

Marion built a careful and compelling argument for a pigeon messenger service, not only as part of the country's coastal defense plan as presented by Lieutenant Wainwright a year earlier, but also as an invaluable component of squadrons at sea where the birds would carry messages from ship to shore, and eventually, he believed, shore to ship. The articles and professional notes Marion wrote in the early 1890s emphasized highly successful experiments with pigeons at sea in

Chapter 2. Pigeons for Sea Duty

European countries, experiments that had resulted in complete systems of government-controlled pigeon stations along their coasts. European navies now possessed clear lines of communication between ships at sea and their home ports with pigeons often arriving at their port lofts many days before dispatch vessels sent at the same time.

In one note, he pointed to the use of pigeons on board French men-of-war vessels. The objective was to establish permanent pigeon cotes on outgoing ships, with pigeons released from shore to fly to their shipboard homes. A pigeon loft was built on the artillery practice ship, *St. Louis*, at Toulon, high on the bridge, about 20 feet forward of the mizzen mast. The loft was painted in bright red and green paint, colors easily seen by pigeons at long distances. In future trials, pigeons were to be released both from the ship to fly to lofts on land, and vice-versa, released from shore to fly to the brightly painted homes on ships. The pigeons so far, reported Marion, had done well.

> A cote has been established on board the artillery practice vessel, *St. Louis*, and the pigeons have become thoroughly accustomed to the report and smoke of the guns, and follow the vessel on her cruise, never mistaking her for another. Their usefulness has been especially appreciated whenever the vessels of the squadron were beyond the range of the heliograph, as they enabled the commander of the fleet to communicate with the shore at long distances when no other means of communication were available.[9]

One especially significant *Proceedings* note summarized pigeon trials made at the United States Training Station at Newport, Rhode Island, on board the USS *New Hampshire*, flagship for the enlisted seamen training program. These trials took place two or three years before Marion began his own test runs from the Naval Academy and must have used a different source of pigeons, perhaps from civilian lofts in nearby Fall River, Massachusetts, where pigeon clubs had been established.

Commander of the *New Hampshire*, Frances J. Higginson, was questioned regarding the viability of a pigeon messenger system along the Atlantic Coast, and Marion included the commander's answer:

> We have at this station erected a pigeon-house and have some choice messenger stock. Although our cote is still in its infancy, we have made some very interesting trials with our birds, and have been much pleased with some of the results. One of the pigeons flew from the Hen and Chicken's Light-ship to our cote, a distance of twelve miles in 16 minutes and 35 seconds.
> Several of our birds were taken to New York on the *Juniata* last year, with intention of liberating them along the coast. The weather, however, was thick and they were not flown. While at Brooklyn, one of the pigeons escaped from the *Juniata* and it was considered lost, as it had never flown a greater distance from Point

War Pigeons

Judith (14 miles from Newport Harbor) but great was our surprise when in a few days the bird arrived at his home here safely and in good condition.

Higginson added,

> I think it would be a good plan for all naval vessels leaving Newport to be supplied with carrier pigeons for the purpose of sending communications ashore and to train them for long distance flights. The use of carrier pigeons as bearers of dispatches would prove of great use to the naval service, and I am heartily in favor of establishing carrier pigeon lofts along the Atlantic Coast. I have no doubt of the success of the undertaking if it were organized and thoroughly executed.[10]

Marion ran with this strong endorsement and in the same *Proceedings* note, fashioned, for the first time, the notion of building a system of lofts at principal navy yards along the Atlantic Coast, initially at: Portsmouth; Boston; Newport (already established); New London; New York; Philadelphia (receiving ship *St. Louis*); Washington, D.C.; Annapolis; Norfolk; Port Royal; Key West; and Pensacola, Florida.

Any commercial or naval ship, he asserted, could be supplied with pigeons from these lofts. During peace time, leaving and approaching vessels with birds on board could report the position of disabled ships and local wrecks, and signal their own needs. In war, ships defending a coast could send transmissions ashore over a distance of several hundred miles, via pigeon express, to signal the approach of the enemy's fleet and report its every movement.

Marion summarized his vision to *Scientific American* in an 1890 interview. "The United States," he explained,

> have no organized service yet, but it is to be hoped that it will soon be established, as numerous experiments have proved that homing pigeons can fly several hundred miles at sea—if liberated in the morning, of course; that birds can be bred and trained on board ship, that they can be accustomed to the noise of the ships, that they can recognize their own ship among others, that they can be relied upon to carry news from the fleet to the shore and under favorable circumstances from the shore to the fleet and from one vessel to another.[11]

Marion then turned to reporting on trials made with pigeon releases during summer cruises out of the Naval Academy, using the Key West stock pigeons he bred in the loft above the boathouse. By now, Marion's boathouse loft would have been filled with a thriving, cooing population of homing pigeons, adults preening, eating, and feeding newborns, youngsters flapping around, absorbing the happenings in the loft. At about six weeks, the youngsters would be allowed outside to exercise. They would have their first view of the Academy grounds,

Chapter 2. Pigeons for Sea Duty

Pigeon cote at the U.S. Naval Training Station, Newport, RI, ca. 1890. This was one of the earliest U.S. military pigeon lofts and probably the one Commander Higginson referred to (Library of Congress, LOT 9756 (F)).

the city of Annapolis with its narrow streets and brick buildings, and the ragged arm of Chesapeake Bay reaching to the ocean. Marion's birds would have begun training at around four months of age, traveling in a crate a short distance from their boathouse loft and released to fly home. With flights from ships on his mind, perhaps Marion took the youngsters in a skiff on the Severn River where they could feel the boat's movement and smell the water. As the birds progressed in their training, Marion would have continually increased the distance from where he released his young fliers until they found their way home from 100 miles away. In no wind, Marion's strongest pigeons would cover the 100 miles in as many minutes.

Summer cruises at the Naval Academy began in 1851, and by 1856, they had become a regular feature of the Academy's program. Cadets learned how a ship ran, from navigation and steering to gunnery and rope climbing, skills that would be necessary for them to run their own ships in the future. The USS *Preble*, a sailing sloop-of-war, was the first practice ship assigned to the Academy. She was followed by a string of other distinguished ships. In 1873, the mighty *Constellation* arrived and for 20 years served as a floating classroom for cadets to learn seamanship. She was also the first practice ship to host Academy homing pigeons.

On one of their training runs, Marion's pigeons likely spotted the masts of the USS *Constellation* moored at the Academy docks. The *Constellation* was a fast sloop-of-war, 176 feet long with a displacement of 1400 tons. She had patrolled around the world, chasing slave ships off West Africa and protecting American shipping from Confederate raids in the Mediterranean during the Civil War. For cadet training, she had been modified for gunnery instruction with a potent battery of one eleven-inch, and eight nine-inch Dahlgren guns, plus one 100-pound Parrott rifle.

For a few summers, room was also made on the spar deck for a small pigeon cote which held a dozen or so homing pigeons. The cote sat atop the ship's capstan where the birds had a view of the ocean, felt its wind, and smelled its saltiness. (When the capstan was in use to lift heavy objects or weigh anchor, the cote was likely set down on the deck.) The pitch and sway of the ship, the creaking and banging, shouts of officers and scurrying of cadets, and the boom of the gun batteries just one deck below would grow as familiar to them as the sights and sounds outside their boathouse loft.

Under the command of Colby M. Chester, those first sea trials in 1892 were reported by Professor Marion in a *Proceedings* article extracted from a report made by Lieutenant W.S. Benson who was on board that cruise and took part in the experiments.

> On June 6, the day the *Constellation* sailed from Annapolis, ten pigeons from the Naval Academy loft were taken on board and released at different distances down the Chesapeake Bay, the last at a distance of 35 miles, and two requesting that certain stores that had been omitted from the outfit be sent down to the ship by the *Phlox*.[12]

All of the birds, said Benson, returned in good time and all messages were safely delivered. Before the *Constellation* left Newport, Rhode Island, on her return trip to Annapolis, Benson reported that birds from lofts other than the Naval Academy were released from the ship.

> ... through the exertions of E.S. Starr, of Philadelphia, at the request of Professor Marion, pigeons were sent to the ship from lofts in Philadelphia, Woodbury, NJ,

Chapter 2. Pigeons for Sea Duty

Atlantic City, Providence and Fall River. During the six days the vessel was at sea, several birds were liberated at 9 a.m. each day (except one when the weather was threatening, with a strong breeze from northward), bearing duplicate messages giving the ship's position, condition of weather for the past twenty-four hours, and other items of interest. In nearly every case these messages were delivered at the respective lofts the same day and the messages repeated to the Superintendent of the Naval Academy by telegraph. The greatest distance from land any birds were liberated was about 90 miles; and those liberated to the northward of their lofts had previously only been flown from the southward, and the owners were under the impression that they could be used successfully from the southward. Their success showed that pigeons could be flown from any direction. These results show that the pigeons service from ship to shore was entirely successful.[13]

Benson stated conclusively that because pigeons fly from any direction to their lofts, from as far out to sea as 100 miles or more, their usefulness to the Navy was inestimable and unlimited. He, as many enthusiasts before him, stressed that an effective service needed to be well organized and the birds well trained by keepers who had a strong attachment to the birds, a sentiment echoed again and again.

Marion reported less satisfactory results from a shore to ship experiment in which birds that had lived briefly on cotes on board the *Constellation*, were taken and left ashore. When released, they did not always fly directly to their "home" loft on the ship, but sometimes landed on other nearby vessels. These birds, emphasized Marion, had not been raised on the *Constellation*, and despite only a brief acclimation period, many still flew to the ship even when she was several miles out under sail. Even with its mixed results, explained Marion, this limited experiment opened a new field for the usefulness of homing pigeons for naval purposes. They could, for example, carry news from a landing party to a vessel stationed near the shore, or serve as couriers between different vessels of a squadron. These semi-satisfactory experiments showed the importance of home to the pigeons, the place where they were born and raised.

At this point, Marion explained the proposed pigeon stations in greater detail, and included a chart showing the stations on the Atlantic Coast with circles of 240 mile-radius around each station, indicating the zone in which trained pigeons could be relied upon to return to their home lofts with a sufficient degree of certainty. "The distance," said Marion, "is equal to one day's run of a vessel making ten knots an hour, and it could be covered by a pigeon in about eight hours, at an average speed of 30 miles per hour, thus gaining 16 hours on the vessel. From these lofts a vessel leaving any of the stations could be supplied with trained pigeons to be liberated at intervals within the prescribed zone of the station to which they belong."[14] For example, the Portsmouth, New Hampshire, loft might send a basket of trained pigeons on an outgoing cruiser that could release them from anywhere within the prescribed 240-mile radius. That could include locations from Portland, Maine, to New London, Connecticut. Any locations farther south than New London, would use birds from overlapping stations.

The message, added Marion, would be written on fine tissue paper, rolled up and inserted into a piece of goose quill, then sealed at both ends and fastened to one of the middle tail feathers of the birds with a copper wire. Each message would be duplicated, in cipher if necessary, and forwarded by two or more birds.

A tightly knit coastal communications system. Marion had laid it out in perfect sense, and it was very convincing.

Commander Chester strongly endorsed Marion's pigeon messenger service and recommended that an appropriation be asked of Congress to carry out the proposed plans of such a service. Yet, no appropriation was made, and Marion was told that while in the past, expenses had been met by private subscriptions, likely from pigeon racing clubs, they would not continue for very long. After all, there was only so much money available.

In 1893, very important pigeon messenger trials took place during the 1893 International Naval Rendezvous at Hampton Roads, Virginia. The event marked the 400th anniversary of Christopher Columbus' arrival in the New World. Beginning April 17, squadrons of U.S. Navy cruisers and gunboats, along with ships from Great Britain, Italy, Germany, Brazil, Holland, Russia and Spain assembled. Since many of the nations were fierce rivals at the time, the gathering of ships was declared a diplomatic triumph. The week's festivities included floats, boats and bicycle races, excursions, fireworks and a grand ball. After a week in Hampton Roads, the fleet traveled as a group to New York City for a parade on the Hudson River.

Reporters covering the rendezvous were intrigued by how the ships communicated. They wrote of the assorted means of signaling—semaphore with red flags, long strings of pennants, and a cacophony of signal guns and whistles.

Most interesting to the reporters was the use of homing pigeons. The event was a noteworthy milestone for the pigeon messenger service, because, a real pigeon network, not an experimental stratagem, delivered official messages. From the dispatch ship, USS *Dolphin*, at

Chapter 2. Pigeons for Sea Duty

Hampton Roads, pigeons flew to Richmond, Virginia, by Richmond birds, to Annapolis via Academy birds, and to the office of the Secretary of Navy by Washington birds. Also, birds were released during the parade from New York harbor to New York, Brooklyn and Newark lofts, and from off Cape May to Woodbury, New Jersey, and from the New Jersey coast to Atlantic City and Philadelphia, with messages forwarded to Washington by wire. Here was solid proof that a pigeon-telegraph network was viable.[15]

April 22 of the rendezvous saw more significant results. Birds from lofts in Richmond, Washington, and Philadelphia were liberated from the USS *Dolphin* in Hampton Roads April 22 under the direction of the Secretary of the Navy. The first message was carried by a naval loft bird to Mr. George Childs, publisher of the *Philadelphia Public Ledger* and pigeon fancier, in Philadelphia by Miss Lila Herbert, the Secretary of Navy's daughter, who released the bird at 6 a.m. The message was transferred at Annapolis to another bird which arrived in Philadelphia at 1:30 p.m. The President and Mrs. Cleveland also received messages from the dispatch boat, *Dolphin*, at Fort Monroe, where two pigeons were released from shortly after 7 a.m. and reached Washington at 12:20 p.m., covering the distance of 135 miles in a little more than five hours in bad weather. Each of the two messages was headed:

U.S. Messenger Pigeon Service. U.S.S. *Dolphin*, off Old Point comfort Light, 7 A.M. and read:

> *To the President and Mrs. Cleveland:*
> We are off in good shape and send greetings to you both.
> M. Margaret Manning,
> widow of Secretary Daniel Manning.

> *My Dear Mrs. Cleveland:*
> We all send you greetings from over the sea.
> Lila Herbert,
> Secretary Herbert's daughter.[16]

President Grover Cleveland expressed surprise at the speed of the service. What better endorsement did the Navy need?

The next month, pigeons berthed on the cruiser *New York*. Mr. Childs provided a cote of pigeons for experiments on board the new ship. Sending birds from deployed ships would prove a two-fold experiment. First, experts believed that only pigeons born in a cote onboard a ship would return there; also, the ship cotes would be mobile, and it remained to be seen if pigeons would home to a moving loft. Initial results from the *New York* on her trial trip from Cramps Shipyard in Philadelphia to Boston, were positive, as reported in the *Internal Revenue Record and Customs Journal*:

> Messages brought by pigeons on May 17 to Philadelphia from the cruiser were from Rear Admiral Belknap to the Secretary of the Navy, and besides information of an official character, gave the start from off Lewes, Del. at 10:30 a.m. and from, "out at sea" to George W. Childs, conveying the compliments of Rear Admiral Belknap, Edgar S. Cramp and Capt. Sargent, with the information that the capes were cleared at 10:30 A.M. The vessel then headed for Boston Light.[17]

That same year, Marion gave an account of a real-time situation on the *Constellation*, which had returned from another successful summer cruise. The report on this subject was made by Commander Chester and stated:

> Twenty-seven pigeons of various ages, and trained up to corresponding lengths of flight, from 20 to 150 miles, were furnished the *Constellation* from the Naval Academy loft when she left Annapolis, the 5th June 1893. The first necessity for sending pigeons occurred about 12 miles from Annapolis, when Thomas Gilkie, seaman, was killed and it was necessary to send the body ashore. As speedy delivery was desired, duplicate messages were sent by two 150-mile birds, telling of the accident, and that the body would be sent ashore in the ship's steam launch. Later, the weather proving unfavorable, two more 150-mile birds were sent with a message, asking that the *Standish* be sent for the body. The message was sent at 9:30 a.m., June 7. The *Standish* was alongside a little after noon of the same day, and brought back the four birds which had carried the messages.[18]

This was no experiment. It was a real emergency during which pigeons transported an important message. Their flight foretold of countless emergencies in which military pigeons would play a vital role. Professor Marion must have been proud of the four birds and keenly aware of the significance of their success.

Flush with the success of the homing pigeons at the Hampton Roads Rendezvous and out at sea as couriers of vital information, Marion began the next year, 1894, newly inspired to continue his campaign for a naval pigeon messenger service.

In 1894, Lieutenant Austin Knight summarized in the *Proceedings* flights made from that summer's cruise on board the *Monongahela*, which had replaced the *Constellation* as a summer practice ship. Knight, another adamant believer in homing pigeons for sea duty, said that the results confirmed the conclusions of reports from preceding years, namely that the shipboard pigeon messenger service worked. The

Chapter 2. Pigeons for Sea Duty

total number of flights was 100, across distances varying from 10 to 100 miles.

Knight included an endorsement from Captain R.L. Phythian, superintendent of the Naval Academy at the time. Not only did the superintendent support the project, he also commended Professor Marion's effort.

> 1. Experiments made with the homing pigeons at the Naval Academy here, in my opinion, demonstrated that their use can be made valuable in receiving communications from vessels operating near the coast, and that the pigeon service should be established on some recognized base.
> 2. Professor Marion's voluntary aid in developing the usefulness of pigeons has been valuable because of his zeal in the cause, and his familiarity with the subject, and I think it merits commendation.[19]

Knight admitted that weather and darkness limited successful flights. Birds need to see, he explained, so in thick fog or darkness they cannot be released if they cannot reach shore by nightfall. He referred to Marion's earlier suggestion to distribute cotes in such a way that a bird reaching the coast at nightfall would recognize and seek refuge at one of these, rather than trying to continue to its own loft. This would not only prove safer for the bird, but a message might be delivered even earlier than if the bird had time to reach its own home. So, the cotes, explained Knight, needed to be established in conspicuous places, near all lighthouses and lightships, built and painted exactly alike. Messages could then be forwarded via telegraph.

The young officer continued the article with a compelling scenario he developed, whereby an enemy fleet is spotted and Washington is alerted via a pigeon network.

> ... let us consider the case of a fleet entrusted with the defense of that part of our coast from Block Island to the capes of the Delaware. Whatever position might be taken up by such a fleet, there would be thrown out many miles beyond it a line of light swift vessels as scouts, and upon the rapidity with which these vessels could communicate with the inner line and with the shore would depend, in large measure the success of the defense. Suppose a vessel of the outer line to discover an enemy's fleet standing to the westward; she could hasten toward the squadron of defense or toward the nearest point of the coast from which it might be possible to communicate with that squadron, with Washington and with the cities threatened, and if not overtaken by an enemy's cruiser or by a shell from a battle-

ship, and if she did not break down, she would ultimately communicate the fact that at a certain time—already long past—an enemy's fleet, of unknown strength, was standing in for some unknown point on the coast. Let us suppose, now, that instead of hastening off herself she could despatch a number of pigeons with the certainty that they would carry the news quite as surely as she could carry it, and far more quickly; and that then holding the enemy in view, she should follow his movements, and from time to time send off new messengers with particulars of his strength, his course and his apparent intentions. It is not difficult to see the immense value of a system which promises the possibility of such service as this.[20]

This was the first time a war plan had been envisioned to convince the Navy Department to enlist pigeons. Yet, no money for building pigeon lofts was included in the Navy appropriations bill for 1894.

Interest in pigeon messenger services continued to surge in other government agencies and private companies, as reported in the *San Francisco Call*. In a June 1895 issue, the *Call* stated that the U.S. Weather Bureau office in San Francisco was considering using homing pigeons to bring weather forecasts from the Farallon Islands to the city, a distance of about 30 miles. According to fancier Edward Koenig, if pigeons were raised in a loft on top of a city building, and trained from that point, they'd be reliable messengers from the Farallons in a few months.[21] A year later, the *Call* published another article about interest in using pigeons to aid in shipping and commerce. Referring to the experiments proposed by the Weather Bureau, the article stated that advantages to taking pigeons on commercial ships to a point within flying range, beyond the Farallon Islands, would include being able to receive reports about wrecks, accidents, fires and bouts of calm weather, which prevented the timely arrival of ships to port.[22]

Despite consistently good results from naval trials as well as increased interest from other organizations, the year 1895 saw the naval homing pigeon messenger service fighting for its life. While the summer practice ships out of the Academy continued to have successful trials, Washington continued to drag its feet on appropriating funds. The pigeon lofts at the Academy were in danger of shutting down.

That year, the famous *Manoubia* experiment off of France toppled any disbelief in the seaworthiness and value of pigeons. The French newspaper, *Figaro*, had claimed that pigeons could not fly 100 miles at sea and would grow seasick if left on board a period of time, and, thus, unable to leave.

The *Le Petit Journal* of Paris gleefully took up the challenge and hired the steamer, *Manoubia*, to prove *Figaro* wrong. About 4500

Chapter 2. Pigeons for Sea Duty

pigeons belonging to various pigeon societies in France, Belgium, Holland and England were placed on the *Manoubia* June 30, 1895, at St. Nazaire. Arrangements for their care and comfort had been made with cabins retrofitted into lofts. The trip lasted 10 days, during which the birds ate, drank, cooed and showed no sign of sea sickness. Of the 4500 birds most were land-lubbers, with few ever having flown over water.

Four tosses took place:

> 800 pigeons were liberated at about 91 miles from the nearest shore, Pointe du Croisic;
> 1600 pigeons were liberated at about 125 miles from Pointe du Croisic;
> 600 pigeons were liberated at about 187.5 miles from Pointe du Croisic;
> 1500 pigeons were liberated at about 312.5 miles from Pointe du Croisic.

Only 16 pigeons out of 4500 refused to seek land and their home lofts.[23] That's a greater than 99.6 percent success rate.

The results surpassed the most optimistic expectations of the promoters and completely dispelled any notions made by *Figaro*.

But even *Manoubia* failed to move the Navy Department that year. Marion received a sympathetic letter from Major A.D. Greely, Chief Signals Officer of the Army, who spoke of the original Key West Army, who spoke of the original Key West pigeons:

> These pigeons were originally received as donations from owners of the lofts in the United States whose birds had made the best flights. They were sent to Key West barracks, where a loft was established. From this stock young birds were bred which, at first, were trained for short distances and gradually extended until flights had been made from Havana to Key West. It seems, however, that you have been more successful, from the fact that birds under your training and liberated at sea at a distance of 102 miles off Cape Henry returned to Annapolis. It is therefore to be regretted that for lack of funds the maintenance of the station at the Naval Academy has been discontinued as well as the future establishment of lofts at the most suitable naval stations on the Atlantic, Gulf, and Pacific coasts.[24]

The following year, a *Proceedings* article by Professor Marion was one of a very different tone. In July of 1896, he delivered a stirring lecture to the Naval War College at Newport, Rhode Island, reprinted in the *Proceedings*. Marion first related the success of pigeon messenger services in Europe, and then summarized results of experiments in the United States. He ended his talk with stunning news:

War Pigeons

Since then, through personal efforts aided by articles periodically published in the *Proceedings of the U.S. Naval Institute*, to which belongs the credit of having kept this work before the Navy, this service has been officially recognized this year by the Honorable Secretary of the Navy and lofts are to be established at several of the principal navy-yards by the Bureau of Equipment, viz. at Boston, Newport, New York, Norfolk, Key West and Mare Island. No breeding and experimental station has yet been designated, but it is to be hoped that one will be established, as this service would be incomplete without it, its main object being the creation and breeding of a strain or type of "naval" pigeon capable of performing fast and continuous long-distance flights over water. With that addition and a suitable appropriation by Congress for its support, this new service, under competent and intelligent supervision, is destined to render at a trifling cost valuable assistance to the systems of naval signals and coast defense as advocated respectively by Lieutenant-Commander R. Wainwright and Lieutenant Niblack in their admirable articles in the *Proceedings of the Naval Institute*, and to become one of the best of its kind in the world.[25]

Perhaps it was the indisputable results of *Manoubia* that finally swayed the Navy Department, or perhaps politics, or public opinion, or some combination of pressures. Whatever proved the final push, pigeons were finally accepted for sea duty.

A memo from the Secretary of Navy, Hilary A. Herbert, on January 11, 1896, to Commodore William T. Chadwick, Chief of the Bureau of Equipment, set things in motion, not just for the Navy, but for the entire American military:

Sir:

You are authorized to establish, in accordance with the Bureau's request of the 23rd, ultimo, Pigeon Cotes for homing pigeons at the following points, viz: Boston, Newport, New York, Norfolk, Key West and Mare island. The receiving ships at the several points mentioned may be utilized in the establishment of these Cotes.

Very respectfully,
Signed, Hilary A. Herbert
Secretary[26]

The Bureau of Equipment (BOE) sent blueprints to the six Navy yards, setting precise standards for loft construction. All lofts were to be patterned after the one in the tower of the boat house at the Naval Academy—two stories, twelve feet square, and painted red and white vertical stripes. Portable lofts were also designed, so cotes could be moved around a particular station or placed on board a ship. Birds would be purchased. Experienced and devoted keepers were to be hired, from the Navy, if possible, or from private lofts if not. Training the birds was to begin immediately, with a focus on flying them from over water.

Chapter 2. Pigeons for Sea Duty

Pigeon Cote at the Mare Island Navy Base, 1902. It later was converted to the base's first radio station (official U.S. Navy photograph).

Size, historical relationship with pigeons, strategic locations, and likely, politics, influenced which yards were chosen. Mare Island Navy base in California, the nation's first Pacific naval installation, boasted one of the most successful pigeon cotes and messenger systems. Joseph N. Richards, proprietor of the Vallejo Homing Pigeon Lofts, worked in the base Steam Engineering department and applied for position of pigeon keeper. He was a 20-year veteran pigeon flier and had already been flying his pigeons for the Navy, explaining in a letter to Commander Bowman McCalla, equipment officer at the base, "My birds have at all times been at the disposal of the officers in command of the naval vessels on this station. At the request of Professor Marion of the Naval Academy at Annapolis, I have sent my data of the flights of my birds from the various naval vessels of this station."[27] Richards understood the importance of consistent care and rigorous training. He gave his birds systematic practice flights from the sea by sending them out on regular steamers from San Francisco, as well on departing naval vessels, which liberated the birds with messages at different distances from port. Richards got the job and started the Mare station loft with 20 pair of his own birds.

War Pigeons

An article in the Topeka, Kansas, *Advocate* spoke of the highly regarded messenger service at Mare Island, including this detailed description of the cote.

> On the round-topped hill at the north end of Mare Island, the great naval station of this coast, stands a gaily-painted little cottage which can be seen from any point in the great bay of San Pablo. Inquiring strangers are surprised when they learn that this little house is the home of over 100 finely bred carrier pigeons belonging to Uncle Sam's navy, and that the red and white stripes which decorate the sides are for the purpose of enabling the little messengers to quickly distinguish their home station from a distance.[28]

The article further explained that the birds were to be used as part of a communications network in the event of a war in which the coasts were threatened. This network idea closely followed the type of communications model suggested earlier by Lieutenant Wainwright, a system that would continue to be at the forefront of future threats. The birds, said the article, would carry messages from the fleet to their lofts, including Mare Island, where telegraph and telephone connections with adjacent cities and with headquarters at Washington were available.

> The pigeon loft at Mare Island is considered a model one. It is a neat building, two stories high, with wire-screened windows as well as regular glass sashes. On the first floor, the breeding and nesting boxes of the winged messengers, and here the walls are covered with little boxes like post office delivery. In each box is an earthen bowl, where the birds deposit their eggs and hatch their young. The squabs are tenderly cared for by the skilled attendant in charge, and grow very rapidly to full size. As soon as they are able to fly they are taken to the room on the second floor, which is the general living quarters of the working birds and is fitted with rows of shelves and perches.
>
> When quite young, each carrier pigeon is marked by a small aluminum ring, which is slipped on the leg. This has stamped upon it U.S., the station and the number of the bird, so that he may always be identified. During the past six months, many birds have been taken to sea from the Mare Island loft and nearly all have brought their messages safely home, thus demonstrating their great value in time of war. Although there are many lofts for homing pigeons on this coast where the birds are trained for land service, the Mare Island loft is the only one where the training is exclusively for sea service, and if these wonderful little messengers, by their timely warning, should some day save our fair coast from an unexpected attack by a foreign foe, we shall certainly be grateful to our feathered friend of the naval service.[29]

On the East Coast, the Portsmouth Navy Yard was picked as the northern most site for a Navy pigeon loft. The pigeon cote at the Portsmouth Navy Yard was built in September 1897. Portsmouth resident, William Wetzel was appointed keeper, and he began the training of his

Chapter 2. Pigeons for Sea Duty

51 birds right away. The first transmission of official information from ships at sea with Navy birds had already occurred farther south, on September 3, 1897, when a pigeon carried a message from the flagship, *New York*, 65 miles off Cape Charles, Virginia, to Norfolk Yard in 90 minutes against the wind. The 40 miles between Saco, Maine, and the Portsmouth Navy Yard were made by 17 birds a week later.[30] The Portsmouth loft was up and running, its birds not to be outdone by those from another station. A few weeks later, four pigeons were released from Admiral Montgomery Sicard's fleet in Boston. They traveled to the Portsmouth station at 34 miles per hour, giving the position of the fleet.

According to an article in the August 11, 1989, *Periscope*, the Portsmouth pigeons, once trained, were to be part of a joint experiment with the U.S. Lighthouse Service, where pigeons would be placed in cotes at several lighthouses along the coast. Ships were to send pigeons to lighthouses, and those messages relayed to the Navy Department by telegraph. The article also spoke fondly of the birds' growing appearances in the area. "For the people of Maine and New Hampshire, the Navy Yard homing pigeons became a familiar sight, especially when they landed at private homes."[31] When pigeon #7136 accidentally landed at the home of Melville J. Pride of Stroudwater, Maine—maybe the bird was tired, or

Pigeon cote at Portsmouth Navy Yard, 1899. The standard red and white stripes painted on the sides and top were easy for pigeons to recognize (courtesy Maine Historic Preservation Commission).

Pride's yard simply appealed to it in some way—a message attached to the bird requested that it be brought to the Naval Shipyard. Which Mr. Pride was happy to do.

The Newport, Rhode Island, Naval Training Center was a logical place to host a Navy pigeon loft, as the training station not only held a strategic location on the coast of Rhode Island, it also had already experimented successfully with homing pigeons nearly 10 years earlier, when Commander Higginson took birds out on the flag ship USS *New Hampshire* during training for enlisted men. The USS *Constellation* (with its pigeon cote still a top the capstan) had by this time docked at Newport permanently, also as part of the training program. Master-at-Arms, 1st Class Daly, was the full-time keeper and must have had former experience with pigeons, probably as a member of a pigeon racing club. In this case, the Navy was lucky to have one of its own able to manage a loft. Other stations had to hire keepers from private lofts, a more costly and time-consuming measure. Master Daly managed 64 birds, and the cote thrived.[32]

The Brooklyn Navy Yard had become a major ship building yard and industrial site, with shipways, huge construction sheds called ship-houses, dry docks, railway tracks and power plants. In the 1890s, a small ferry boat plied between the mainland of the navy yard and Cob Dock, a 19-acre artificial island initially built with cobblestones thrown from ships that had used them as ballast. Cob Dock was separated from the main navy yard by Wallabout Channel. The island was home to an ordnance storage area, firing range, coal storage and the USS *Vermont*, a receiving ship for newly enlisted sailors. In July 1896, the Brooklyn Navy yard pigeon loft was built on Cob Dock with an initial population of 60 pigeons. According to the *Brooklyn Daily Eagle Almanac*, by 1901, the numbers of birds had grown to over 200, and they were used to carry messages to the yard from outgoing ships.[33]

Norfolk Navy Yard was the 5th installation chosen for a pigeon base. Norfolk began as the Gosport Shipyard, founded in 1767, a prosperous naval and merchant facility for the British Crown. It became a local, then national base for campaigns against pirates who plagued merchant ships. Gosport built special ships to hunt them down, small swift schooners that later became known as the mosquito fleet. After the Civil War, the yard, now the Norfolk Navy Yard, grew into the nation's preeminent repair facility and a coaling port to support the new steel Navy. Its strategic location and preeminence won it a pigeon station.

In early 1896, Rear Admiral George Brown, commander of the

Chapter 2. Pigeons for Sea Duty

base, wrote Henri Marion a letter stating his wish that the Norfolk loft be a model station for all others, and also a central station that would include a breeding program. In a letter to Secretary Herbert, Marion summarized this desire, graciously stating that although he wished to keep the breeding program and experimental station at Annapolis, he understood the value in establishing a central station at Norfolk due to the large number of ships coming and going.

> As the Norfolk loft is to be a permanent one and is desired, on account of its central location to be one of the most important stations, it would be admissible and more economical to place all available means at the disposal of Admiral Brown with the view of making the Norfolk loft the central station of this service, as it has many advantages in the way of training the birds on outgoing vessels.[34]

A naval base was established at Key West in 1822 when Matthew C. Perry sailed the schooner, *Shark*, to Key West and planted the U.S. flag claiming the Keys as U.S. property. The base, built a year later, served initially as a station for fighting pirates and stopping illegal slave trade. The mosquito fleet made Key West its home base for pirate hunting. In 1895, the Navy bought the property to construct new coal sheds to increase its capacity for the coaling of ships using the naval station facilities.

The Army, which had been at Key West since 1831, had already flown homing pigeons from the site, including from Havana, Cuba, to Key West, so it was logical to start the service again, particularly with its strategic location so close to Cuba and the Gulf of Mexico.

Lieutenant Charles Harlow, an officer on special duty in Washington, D.C., and assigned to assist Henri Marion, personally oversaw the building of the loft at Key West. Harlow wrote an interesting memo to Commodore Chadwick at the BOE, about the Key West cote, which was finished on April 10, 1896. It's clear from the memo how serious Harlow was about establishing strong and viable lofts. His assignment in Washington as an intelligence officer for that year implies that he might have had special interest in developing the birds as an intelligence tool for the Navy. For whatever reasons, he was meticulous in selecting a site for the Key West loft. It had to look toward the sea, he stated in the letter, with as little view as possible of the surrounding land, and its influences. The loft also had to be angled so as to provide the best shelter from violent gales. He included details of the cote's placement, its dimension and a description of his solicitation of steamship lines and schooners departing from, and arriving at Key West to help train the birds. He stated the cote was well-established under caring and enthusiastic keepers.

Harlow then offered general suggestions for the pigeon service, focusing on careful training and feeding of the birds. He explained, for example, that pigeons at all lofts should be trained only from the sea, making flights over open water, or along the shore; that the Annapolis stock should be used to start the sea training; that the birds should be kept from eating local food, in this case, Key West corn; that all other types of rock pigeons should be removed; that the lofts should be painted alike; that a code of rules should be printed; that the service should have a view to ultimately using lighthouses and lifesaving stations as secondary pigeon stations; and that the Navy's methods of training should be highly confidential.[35] The secret nature of Harlow's thoughts on training again points to early thinking about using homing pigeons as couriers of intelligence.

It was a busy time for Professor Marion, who became the lynch pin of the entire undertaking. Both he and the BOE were flooded with letters from fanciers offering to sell birds to populate the government lofts and from keepers looking for a position.

In October of 1896, Henri Marion patented a new type of message holder for the Navy's pigeon messenger service. Until that time, messages were placed in quills and these quills attached to a bird's tail feather. But the quills could slip off and messages lost. A message wrapped round a pigeon's leg or jammed inside its leg band was equally flimsy. Marion's invention, a small, light aluminum case with a detachable clasp, attached directly to a pigeon's leg. The bird was not bothered by the capsule, and the messages were secure. He received a patent on October 6, 1896, and the BOE made orders for them to be sent to the six Navy yards with cotes. This invention improved reliability enormously and would become a model for message capsules around the world. Professor Marion had no idea how important his new capsules would be.

The first part of 1897 saw more shipments of birds and equipment to various lofts. The Brooklyn Navy yard served as a focal point for the building and shipping of cotes and birds. It began to build cotes for use on board ships, including the armored cruiser, *New York*, the battleship, *Texas*, and *Fern*, a gunboat. Perhaps earlier experiments on using ships for home lofts had encouraged more trials with building on board cotes and hatching birds from them.

In the spring of that year, Lieutenant Harlow, who had spent time at the Brooklyn Yard, was detailed to organize summer training of birds from torpedo boats, small swift ships that could carry pigeons out to sea quickly for trial runs. It seems that no type of naval vessel, from

Chapter 2. Pigeons for Sea Duty

battleship to harbor monitor, would be without a contingent of homing pigeons. From simply steaming, to observing, scouting or engaging in battle, there would be no situation on any naval vessel for which pigeons would not be ready to carry vital information.

To further improve the U.S. Naval Pigeon Messenger Service, naval attaches working abroad were harnessed into action, directed to turn from their duties at embassies, to report on points regarding the care of pigeons in France, Italy, Germany and England. Their reports were to include: the general description of cotes, size and color; the feeding of birds; number of birds in a loft; number of nesting boxes and kinds; breeding; kinds of traps; how messages are attached; how far birds were flown offshore; and if special ships were detailed especially for this work. These findings from countries with well-established pigeon messenger services added much to the knowledge base Marion sought in working toward the best service in the world.

Securing information on European pigeons was capped off by a personal trip by Professor Marion to Belgium, the sacred bastion of homing pigeons. Marion spent the month of September 1897 there, studying all aspects of pigeons. He reported on the primary military homing pigeon station at Antwerp, loft structure, message attachment, types of homers used, breeding, mating, training, food, water, and hygiene. In his report, he also mentioned that some of the birds secured for Navy lofts had been actual participants in *Manoubia*, or descendants from them, and would be valuable additions to birds already bred at U.S. naval lofts. He suggested increasing the efficiency of Navy lofts by fostering competition, as was done in Europe, at various stations with results reported periodically to the Navy Department. He also advised that the best keepers be promoted, and the whole system supervised by a competent inspector.

In this report, Marion again recommended that additional lofts be established at points not more than 200 miles apart, so that a complete pigeon post could operate along the Atlantic Coast, either at more naval stations, or at lighthouses, light-ships or life-saving stations. He added that naval militia might be used at the new stations, which would render invaluable service in time of war or peace. "The whole Atlantic coast would thus be connected and constant communication had any time from a fleet of patrolling the coast, without the need of any of the ships being detached to convey information."[36]

In September, the first official government manual for the care and training of homing pigeons was published. Compiled from various sources, it was put together by the BOE and published by the

Government Printing Office. The manual contained detailed directions on cote construction, traps, nesting boxes, water, food, baskets for transporting birds, breeding, diseases, hygiene and keepers' logs. The training portion of the manual stressed the importance of flying birds constantly over water so they would grow accustomed to flights from ships.

This handbook was more than the first effort to make the care and training of Navy pigeons consistent throughout the country. It was the first manual on the care and training of homing pigeons for any branch of the military.

Out of more than a dozen proposed, only six Navy lofts were up and running as the decade closed. But with the acquisition of excellent birds, the invention of Marion's message holder, plus Lieutenant Harlow's careful plan to train birds from all kinds of naval vessels, as well as the first official manual for the care and training of birds, the Naval Pigeon Messenger Service had been launched.

Would it be in time? In 1897, the United States felt the first overseas threat tickle its shores since the War of 1812.

Chapter 3

Put to the Test

We need go no further than the present differences existing between the United States and Spain taken in connection with the state of affairs in Cuba, to see the great benefit our government would derive from a homing pigeon messenger service... —F.H.S. Morrison, President of the National Federation of Homing Pigeon Fanciers, 1898

The Spanish-American War was reluctant in coming. Cuba had long opposed Spanish rule, and the Ten Years War, from 1868 to 1878, ended with Spain still in control of its colony. The revolt garnered sympathy in America. Hundreds of Americans traveled to Cuba to fight for her freedom, while others supported the rebellions because they owned land in Cuba or had invested in the island's sugar and tobacco products. In October of 1896, Spain sent General Valeriano Weyler to quell the uprising. Weyler forced peasants into concentration camps, burned farms, destroyed crops and killed resistors. Even when more than 200,000 people died in the concentration camps, President Grover Cleveland remained against going to war. Instead, he tried to negotiate a settlement, but to no avail.

The press, led by New York newspapers, *The Journal*, owned by William Randolph Hearst, and *The World*, owned by Joseph Pulitzer (both of whom employed homing pigeons to carry news), used half-truths and sensationalism to sell papers and stoke public opinion. This yellow journalism outraged segments of the U.S. public, and calls for action rang throughout the country.

When William McKinley became President in March of 1897, he, too, tried a peaceful approach to the conflict. Nothing worked. Newspapers continued to thrum the public with news of Spanish brutality, and senators appealed to McKinley and Congress to act. Talk of war with Spain began to simmer.

From the start of his administration, McKinley acted to strengthen the defense of America's coastlines, improving on the armament and fortifications begun by the Board of Fortifications some ten years earlier. That October, Secretary of Navy, John D. Long, appointed a board, headed by Commander John Schouler, to consider establishing a Coast Signal Service for naval defense to be manned by the State Naval Militia. The recently organized, all volunteer militia existed in 15 states as reserve units. The volunteers came from various educational and social backgrounds. They had little or no seagoing training but were committed to serve. They were mainly trained to defend America's coast, by guarding mines placed in harbors and serving as crew on defense vessels, like the heavily armed ironclad monitors. As signal station operators, they would take charge of all lines of communication, including establishing subsidiary stations and preparing plans to connect all stations with telephone and telegraph systems of the country. It would prove a massive communications effort. The board also suggested that the Treasury Department cooperate by offering its life-saving stations, particularly those that could be put in telegraphic communications with headquarters.[1]

Homing pigeons were considered an important part of the Coast Signal Service early on. Here is where they gained traction. In a memo to Secretary Long regarding communication from ships at sea to the signal stations, Commander Schouler echoed Wainwright's sentiments. "Considering the importance of receiving information from a distance beyond the range of visibility, there seems to be but one method which has already had sufficient success to warrant the board recommending it as the best method for communication from a fleet, scouting vessels, or picket boat at distances ranging from 10 to 50 miles, with a possible extension to 100 miles—the homing pigeon."[2]

Later that fall, the impracticality of using life-saving stations for pigeon lofts became clear, and lighthouses were suggested as a replacement. In a memo to the BOE, Captain W.S. Schley, Chairman of the Light House Board, explained that lighthouses could be key locations for the lofts as they were at strategic points off the coast. Unlike life-saving stations, the tall buildings that formed parts of a lighthouse structure would be easy for the pigeons to see, and boats to train the birds were already in place. Plus, lighthouses had a proven record with pigeons. All over the world, lighthouse keepers used homing pigeons to communicate with the mainland. The main purpose of maintaining a flock was to get help in case of an emergency, such as the need for a doctor or equipment, or to report storm damage or a shipwreck. However, since the pigeons required constant training, the keepers were allowed to send

Chapter 3. Put to the Test

personal messages to their families. Beyond exchanging information, these family pigeon-grams became a source of comfort and renewal for isolated lighthouse tenders.

In the United States, as early as the mid–1800s, keepers at several of the offshore screw pile lighthouses (lighthouses built on stilts anchored to the sea bottom) of the treacherous Florida reefs sent messages to lofts in Miami or Key West via pigeon post. Farther north, Boon Island, Maine, keeper, William C. Williams, relied on pigeons in the 1890s to bring him news from friends and family ashore. (Supposedly, the pigeons delivered to Williams news of the end of the Spanish-America War.)[3]

That same fall, the *United States Army and Navy Journal and Gazette* reported on the Naval Pigeon Messenger Service used in exercises of the North Atlantic Squadron. Assistant Secretary of the Navy, Theodore Roosevelt, summed up the cruise, including the pigeon flights, as more than satisfactory. Another *Army and Navy Journal and Gazette* article detailed flights of birds that were released from the squadron off Hampton Roads to fly to the Norfolk Navy Yard. The birds carried messages stating the whereabouts of the ships and what kind of exercises were done.

> On Friday of last week, a pigeon bearing a message was dispatched from the flagship, New York, at sea, 65 miles E.N.E. of Cape Charles. The message was as follows: "Squadron—New York, Brooklyn, Iowa, Massachusetts, Indiana, Texas, Maine—approaching Southern drill ground and will probably anchor. Puritan in sight. Lieut. C.H. Harlow." The bird covered the distance to Norfolk in about an hour and a half, flying a part of the time against the wind. On receipt of the message at Norfolk it was telegraphed at once to the Navy Department at Washington. A few hours later a second dispatch was sent stating that the squadron had anchored, but that the weather was too heavy for target practice with the great guns. Since Friday, several other dispatches have been rapidly and successfully transmitted in this manner. The Department is very enthusiastic over the success of this first experiment with carrier pigeons on the squadron, as it is believed that this means of communication may prove of the greatest practical value in a time of actual hostilities. The only previous use of the carrier pigeon in carrying news from Navy ships have been limited experiments on practice ships at Annapolis. Two other messages were received this week via Norfolk. The first was as follows: "Ship New York, 3 p.m., Sep. 7, 50 miles from Norfolk. Assistant Secretary is on board: Iowa engaged in witnessing great gun exercise with service charges. Brooklyn and Massachusetts will follow. Sub-caliber exercises will follow. Search and night signal exercises to-night."
>
> This was the second message: "ship New York, 9 a.m. Sep. 8, southern drill grounds, 50 miles from Norfolk. Comdt. Norfolk Navy Yard. The squadron getting underway for evolutions before Asst. Secretary, who remains on Dolphin, very

War Pigeons

successful target practice by Iowa and Brooklyn yesterday. Searchlight last night and attack on drifting target, by six and one-pounders with aid of four searchlights. Weather hazy. Light airs from East; seas smooth." Excellent time was made with the last message, it having been received at the Navy Department in one hour and fifty-four minutes from the time the pigeon was released at sea.[4]

Pigeons appeared to fit into the squadron's exercises seamlessly. Yet, the service they provided continued to be viewed as experimental.

Early in 1898, McKinley sent the USS *Maine* to Cuba on a friendly fact-finding mission—and also as a means of escape for Americans working there, if needed. On February 15, 1898, the *Maine* mysteriously blew up, killing 260 crew members. (Pigeon aficionado Lieutenant Richard Wainwright was on board but survived.) Yellow journalism flew rampant, popularizing anti–Spanish sentiment characterized by the famous slogan, "Remember the Maine, and to hell with Spain."

America cried out for war, as did many politicians and the country's outspoken Assistant Secretary of Navy, Theodore Roosevelt. Roosevelt supported the theory that the U.S. should build a strong navy able to extend its power across the ocean where it could defend U.S. interests at a safe distance. Also, if the Navy were to be a world power, he believed that bases needed to be established at various locations such as Cuba, Puerto Rico and Hawaii. He wanted to oust foreign control from the region. While Secretary of the Navy, John D. Long summered in New England, Roosevelt stayed in the Washington heat that year, putting together a playbook to deal with Spain.

The organization of the coast signal stations sped up. A memo from the Bureau of Navigation to the BOE suggested placing signal stations, complete with pigeon cotes, at no less than 21 lighthouses along the Atlantic seaboard, Gulf of Mexico, and the northwest coast.[5] The radii of the birds' flights would intersect with one another so as to form a complete circuit around the coast. A message, theoretically, could leave Alaska on a pigeon, and be transmitted via pigeon relay around the United States until it reached the coast of Maine.

Arrangements were made for the construction of signal stations and their occupation by signalmen whenever the final word was given. Naval militiamen would be ordered to man the stations and trained in the use of signals, including flags and lights, as well as telegraphy. The War Department ordered 3000 homing pigeons to be put in training with birds from cotes at the six Navy yards as well as from private lofts. Messages were to be written on thin rice paper inserted in Henri Marion's light, water-tight message-holders.[6]

Chapter 3. Put to the Test

As discussion of war continued, homing pigeon clubs from around the East offered their pigeons for the government to use. The effort echoed a similar sentiment less than 30 years earlier at the Siege of Paris, where clubs had donated their birds to connect Paris to the outside world. The heroism of those birds rallied the cry once again. It would come twice more in the history of the birds' service to the United States.

A letter dated March 18, 1898, to Secretary Long, from A.T. Berry, Secretary of the prestigious Boston Homing Club showed how highly Berry regarded his birds and the capable courier service he believed they would bring to fighting the war.

Dear John D. Long, Secy

I take this method to call your attention to my Homing Pigeons who were flown from Cruisers Columbia and New York when tried out. They are the same birds used by the Boston Journal at that time and have records of 300 and 600 miles.

As far as I know this is the only case that homing pigeons have performed successful from over water, out of season, … the wind blowing 36 miles per hour against them.

They are available for the use of the Government in case of war to fly to Boston.

Respectfully,
(signed) A.T. Berry[7]

The President of the National Association of American Homing Pigeon Fanciers, E.F. Baker, followed soon after with his own letter to Secretary Long offering not only his birds, but all of birds belonging to the association.

April 9th, 1898

The Hon. J.D. Long,
Secretary of Navy, Washington, D.C.

Dear Sir:--

As the President of the National Association of American Homing Pigeon Fanciers, I in behalf of the said Association offer you the services of our homing pigeons for the benefit of the navy in case of war.

I would be glad to furnish you with the exact number and locations of lofts in Baltimore, Philadelphia, Fall River, and some of the Western States, as well as the New England states. The birds to be furnished to your government free of expense other than the general transportation expense.

If you think the matter worth considering, I would be glad to go further into the details for the benefit of your Department.

I am Very respectfully yours,
(signed) E.F. Baker[8]

War Pigeons

On April 9, Captain Caspar F. Goodrich, in charge of framing the Coast Signal Service, received orders to establish the system of coast signal stations for national defense according to previous plans. It became clear that the country felt threatened.

Two days later, on April 11, McKinley approved war with Spain. Then, final orders were issued to establish the Coast Signal Service for national defense. When completed, the organization had eight districts in which were 36 signal stations, manned entirely from the State Naval Militia. A total of 18 officers and 210 men and thousands of pigeons.[9] Photographs of all Spanish war craft were given to each station. The Coast Signal Service had nearly the entire coastline from Maine to Texas under observation for the approach of an enemy vessel or suspicious craft.

New York's naval militia were among the first to establish pigeon lofts in conjunction with the Coast Signal Service. They had already begun training runs from ships earlier in the year, and were anticipating races with their Navy Yard counterparts. The militia also began a public relations push to let people know what the birds could do. Few segments of the public knew much about homing pigeons and their skills. According to the *U.S. Army and Navy Journal and Gazette*:

> The State of New York is the first to cooperate with the Government in this work, having recently established a cote on board the U.S.S. New Hampshire, foot 23rd street, East River, New York City, where there are at present twelve pairs of breeders, presented by the Navy Department from the cote at the Brooklyn Navy Yard; also another at Buffalo, N.Y. This will cause a spirit of rivalry in flying these birds, between the Naval Militia and the nearest Navy Yard, and the Naval Militia will not rest until they have broken some of Uncle Sam's sea records, though this will be very hard to do, especially that of the Brooklyn cote, under the management of Mr. Howard Carter, who is an expert on the breeding and training of homing pigeons and has his birds in splendid condition for breeding all records from the fleet at sea. The longest distance flown was from the U.S.S. Texas and U.S.S. Annapolis, from 150 miles at sea, the speed being thirty-two miles an hours, against a strong northeasterly breeze. Mr. Carter had made as high as fifty-seven miles from shorter distances. He will exhibit twelve of these pigeons under his care at the annual Poultry and Pigeon show to be held at Madison Square Garden Feb 1 to 5; also some original messages that have been carried from the ships at sea to the Brooklyn cote during last summer.[10]

Homing pigeons were every bit as ready as the volunteers to do their part. America's first war birds, strong and well trained, would take to the skies at any moment desired to carry information from ships to the signal stations, whether they be messages about the Spanish fleet, an emergency on board, or a change in strategy.

Chapter 3. Put to the Test

The use of homing pigeons in war preparations reached the ears of Congress. On April 18, 1898, Eugene Hale, a republican senator from Maine, presented to the 55th Congress, a paper prepared by F.H.S. Morrison, president of the National Federation of American Homing Pigeon Fanciers. In it, Morrison pushed the advantages of the Federal government using homing pigeons, particularly at a time so near war. While admitting that telegraph and telephone technology had reduced the need for pigeon couriers in the commercial arena, he believed that in time of war,

> when commercial systems are disrupted, and when, by the very nature of things, our modern means of communication are extremely unreliable, and if maintained at all is at an enormous expense, the homing pigeon is once again called into use. With a well-equipped pigeon messenger service available, a government conducting war upon its own territory, or upon a territory not too far removed, is absolutely independent of the telegraph and telephone systems, and can, at comparatively little cost, maintain regular communication with its land and water forces, thus making it possible for the innocent birds to become such potent factors in the affairs of nations as to render them indispensable."[11]

Morrison lamented that the government had not pushed the idea of a pigeon messenger service more, despite interest from some agencies. He suggested that many departments—War, Navy, Signal Service, and Light-House Board—would benefit with feathered couriers, and at a reasonable cost. With pigeons included in the communications plans of these departments, the result would be "...the most perfect service in the world, and at the same time, a service which would be maintained at less expense to the General Government than any such service in existence."[12]

He pointed out several wars involving England and the United States, in which pigeon services might have had an impact.

> Take for example, the Afghan war, the duration of which was about two years. During this war about 200 miles of telegraph wires were laid. The expenditure was enormous, and yet the service was unsatisfactory, the reason being that every few days the wires were cut by the natives. The territory in which the war was conducted was such that it could have been completely covered by a pigeon service at comparatively no expense and the service thus obtained would have been more effectual and more satisfactory that the one which was obtained by the telegraphic system. The same thing could be said of the Zulu and the Ashantee wars.
>
> During the late civil war, when the State of Virginia constituted the great battlefield, a well-equipped pigeon service in the city of Washington would have been the means of making it a comparatively easy matter to communicate with the Federal Government within a few hours from almost any point in the State. Those

War Pigeons

who are posted upon the inconveniences caused in many cases by delay can fully appreciate the great value that such a service would have been.

Upon our western frontier during the trouble with the Indians great loss of life and property could have been avoided by establishing pigeon posts at various forts which constituted the strongholds of the western division of the Army.[13]

Morrison further submitted that in the present situation with Cuba, Consul General Fitzhugh Lee, with a basket of Key West homing pigeons at his headquarters in Havana, would be independent of the cable as a means of quick communication with Washington, D.C., and that a pigeon service would play no small part in a war with Spain.

Many pigeon fanciers agreed. During war preparations, they made sure the government knew homing pigeons were available for use in communications beyond coast signal stations. On April 23, 1898, Mr. Baker sent Commodore Royal B. Bradford, now Chief of the BOE, a list and locations of private lofts at the Government's service. He even went so far as to help strategize communications by suggesting the territory birds from each loft could cover:

> Birds in Baltimore could take care of the Chesapeake Bay and on the Coast 100 miles south of Cape Henry and as far north as Sandy Hook.
> The birds in Philadelphia can very easily take care of the points from the Delaware Breakwater to Boston.
> The Fall River birds can take care of the Atlantic Coast in the New England territory.

Birds were donated from Baltimore; Philadelphia; Wheeling, West Virginia; Cincinnati; Trenton, New Jersey; Shamokin, Pennsylvania; and Fall River, Massachusetts— about 500 in all.[14]

The offer came with bragging rights—that many of his club's birds had flown, in fair weather, up to 500 miles in a day. But also with a condition—that the birds should not be cooped up longer than 10 days, not released in foggy or stormy weather, or in bad winds, unless utterly necessary.

On April 25, President McKinley declared war on Spain. The Navy was ready. Built in steel, the Navy could send battleships, monitors, cruisers, a ram, gunboats, and torpedo craft to meet the Spanish. The U.S. fleet could also draw support from American merchant ships and private yachts. In addition, shipbuilding and repair yards were nearby. And, U.S. forces were much closer to Cuba than were Spain's. All told, the U.S. had an overwhelming advantage in the conflict.

The war did not last long. In the Pacific, Commodore George Dewey, stationed in Hong Kong, steamed to Manila Bay in the Philippines. On

Chapter 3. Put to the Test

May 1, in a morning encounter, Dewey destroyed the anchored Spanish fleet, costing America only a few wounded seamen. This first major battle of the Spanish-American War ended colonial rule in the Philippines.

In the Atlantic, Commodore William T. Sampson gained control of the Caribbean by the end of June and blockaded Spanish Admiral Pascual Cervera's fleet at Santiago Harbor. A force of 17,000 troops assembled in Tampa, Florida, under the command of General William Shafter. One section of that force was Colonel Leonard Wood's First Volunteer Calvary, better known as the Rough Riders, led by Theodore Roosevelt. The troops headed to Cuba at the end of May. At the end of June, the 5th Army Corps under General Shafter landed east of Santiago and established a base of operations. An indecisive win by the Spanish against the 5th Army Corps resulted in Spanish troops regrouping to Santiago. With Spanish forces isolated by marines and Cuban rebels at Guantanamo, the Americans, on July 1, took the fortified village of El Caney, and swept San Juan Hill. Admiral Cervera led his squadron from Santiago harbor on July 3, trying to escape along the west coast of Cuba. His ships were sitting ducks, coming under strong fire from U.S. guns. Shafter then laid siege to Santiago and forced a surrender on July 17. The Santiago campaign was concluded, and Cuba was free from Spanish rule.

The government's pigeons, flying as the Naval Pigeon Messenger Service, operated primarily between ships off the East Coast heading to Cuba and mainland ports. As well as official messages, many birds flew private notes. Some of the messages birds brought back to Baltimore lofts were from Hampton Roads, announcing they had arrived at that port. Several were from officers on board ships heading for a convoy going to Cuba to their families in Baltimore.

And this one from Commander John Davis to his wife: "This note is brought by pigeon, and it will interest you and the children to know that the bird comes 200 miles outside Cape Henry. Sailed yesterday morning and had to wait 36 hours in Chesapeake Bay for my convoy. All goes well. Great deal of love to you all."[15]

During the spring and summer of 1898, magazines, journals and newspapers from around the world published articles about homing pigeons in the war. One article from a July 1898 *Hawaiian Gazette* pointed to the use of Marion's new message holders patented just two years earlier, and that the professor likely was heavily involved in delivering the birds to various lofts and ships. The article also mentioned that at the start of the war, the Navy had made inquiries into the use of pigeons being trained at the six navy yards. Together with donations from pigeon clubs, the Navy had a good number of trained feathered couriers on hand. An elite few had even accompanied Admiral Sampson on his flag ship, *New York*. A May 1898 issue of *The Press*, a weekly in New Zealand, included this about the potential homers:

> It was not until Professor H. Marion, of the Naval Academy, established a loft (six years ago) that the attention of the government was drawn to the importance of homing pigeons in such a crisis as now exists. Says the *Baltimore Sun*, a well organized pigeon service will be invaluable in case of war with Spain, bringing the ships on duty in the gulf around Cuba in telegraphic communication with headquarters at Washington through the stations at Key West, which will be put into commission at once. Professor Marion has received an order from the department for 1000 quills [probably his capsule] used in sending messages, designed by himself. By the aid of the Homing pigeon, ships on blockade or scout duty would be enabled to keep their stations, report movements of the enemy and follow him up. Without these messenger facilities, ships might be compelled to leave their stations and run for port in order to communicate the shore.[16]

The Hawaiian Gazette mentioned homing pigeons used on torpedo boats out of the cote at Key West, site of naval headquarters, and on ships leaving San Francisco for Manila.

> As soon as hostilities were expected to break out between the United States and Spain, the Navy Department immediately made inquiries about the pigeon service and found that a large number of rapid, accurate pigeons could be placed at its disposal. The birds were taken to Key West, which is only ninety miles from Havana, and located in Lieutenant Harlow's cote there. They were taken out from this cote to sea and released time and again and always with the greatest success. Scarcely ever did a pigeon fail to return to its home. In the torpedo flotilla which was equipped to match Spain's flotilla means were provided on every boat for the accommodation of the Homing Pigeons. It is asserted that the Navy Department will use 10,000 Homing Pigeons for service during the present war with Spain, to carry messages from the fleets to stations on shore. The Manhattan Homing Pigeon Club has loaned the government 2000 of their birds for this purpose. A cote for Homing Pigeons was out aboard the US Flag Ship New York, a few days before her departure from the New York Navy Yard, and stocked with twelve of the best birds bred at the New York loft. These birds are to be used by Admiral Sampson in transmitting messages from shore to the ship, and from the ships of the fleet, when out of signaling distance by semaphores and flags. They are to be trained to fly by sign only as the ship is constantly changing position. They are expected, however, to carry messages from fifty to 100 miles to the USS New York, these flights being over water. Homing pigeons have already been used to some extent in the war. It is not generally known that the second Manila expedition had pigeons aboard on leaving San Francisco. One of these was liberated off the Farallones with a message to General Merritt. The bird was picked up in Watsonville by a small boy. It had on one leg a tin tag stamped "IIU22." To the other was attached the usual little tin case containing a blip of paper, on which was the following mes-

Chapter 3. Put to the Test

sage: "General Merritt, San Francisco. We are passing the Farallone Islands at 4:45; smooth sea; cloudy; ships are in prescribed formation. We are making eleven knots instead of ten, and I believe we can maintain this speed. Admiral Dewey should be notified accordingly. (signed) GREENE."[17]

(Watsonville, CA is south of San Francisco, about 87.5 miles from the Farallon Islands.)

Ten thousand birds were never used, but had there been more time to train the Navy homing pigeons, they might have been truly tested in the Spanish-American War. It appears that the Navy department had every intention of using pigeons to carry messages as part of the Coastal Signal Service and to convey information from fleets at sea to home ports. In a few cases, successful trips were documented, and probably many more unknown or undocumented flights were made using pigeons from the six Navy yards and private sources. Though sporadic and short-lived, the Naval Pigeon Messenger Service had proved itself capable of sea duty.

At the start of the war, the Army was not so well prepared as the Navy. At the time of the sinking of the *Maine* on February 18, 1898, the regular Army included less than 30,000 men, backed up, at least on paper, by an untrained and poorly equipped militia of about 115,000.[18] The president issued a call for 125,000 volunteers. The Army Signal Corps quickly grew from a handful of officers and men to over 1300 personnel, organized into 17 companies, including one balloon and a field telegraph train. Their communications effort focused on cutting underwater telegraph cable lines off Santiago that connected Cuba with Spain, and then establishing cable communication between American forces arriving in Cuba and Washington. After Shafter's troops landed, the signal soldiers built land lines to complete the circuit between the front and Washington. The land expedition depended on wire communication with flag signaling between coast stations and Sampson's fleet. The Corps also strung telephone lines along the line of advance and nailed hand-cranked telephone boxes to trees right up to the front lines. This was the first conflict in which the U.S. Army used telephones. A Signal Corps balloon was taken to Cuba where, despite some mishaps, it provided some aerial reconnaissance.

Although Dewey had control of Manila Bay, that was not the case for the city of Manila, and the Commodore requested the Army's help to secure the city. Several forces of men sailed from San Francisco to the Philippines in the summer of 1898, among them the First Colorado Infantry, a state volunteer regiment. The Colorado regiment sailed from

War Pigeons

San Francisco on the *China* on June 15, 1898, under the command of General Francis Greene. According to Geoffery Hunt's account, *Colorado's Volunteer Infantry in the Philippine Wars, 1898–1899*, the troops released homing pigeons from the ship to keep General Merritt in San Francisco abreast of their progress across the Pacific. An article in the *Hawaiian Gazette* also mentioned pigeons being used to carry messages back to shore, although the distance from which they flew varies with the reports. One bird's arrival was documented, and the message forwarded on to Washington.

> San Francisco, Cal. June 21, 1898
> (Received 7.50 p.m.)
>
> ADJUTANT-GENERAL, *War Department, Washington, D.C.*:
>
> Dispatch from General Greene received by carrier pigeon which left the ship 40 miles at sea gives his opinion that the sea speed of 11 knots instead of 10 knots can be maintained by that fleet. Possibly Admiral Dewey should be notified accordingly.
>
> Merritt, Major-General,
> Commanding.[19]

In conjunction with the fleet, Major General Wesley Merritt landed in the Philippine Islands with a force of about 11,000 men and attacked the defense of Manila. A Signal Corps unit arrived a few weeks later. Here, the Signal Corps communicated with Commodore Dewey of the fleet with wigwag flags to correct naval gunfire and mark the position of advancing infantry. They also strung telegraph lines. There is no mention of the use of pigeons by the Signal Corps although embedded newsmen sent their reports to Manila from the front lines via pigeon. The city quickly fell on August 13, 1898.

Although the Army's communication mode of choice during the war was telegraph, with some telephone and flag use, there are indications that pigeons were used in a few instances. Beyond ships leaving San Francisco for the Philippines, they flew from the Army hospital ship, *Relief*, which served as a floating hospital off Cuba during the Spanish-American War. Small boats carried wounded and sick soldiers from shore to the ship, which was one of the most modern hospital ships of its time. The *Relief* even boasted an x-ray machine. Pigeons released from the *Relief* likely headed to Key West, perhaps with a message about needed supplies.

At the conclusion of the Spanish-American War, communications arose as an issue warranting attention. During the conflict, there had

Chapter 3. Put to the Test

been a tendency to make strategic decisions at Washington instead of in the field, and while intra-fleet communications were sufficient, rapid communications between various squadrons and the Navy Department was inadequate. Also, communications between the Army and Navy had been unsatisfactory during joint operations conducted along the south coast of Cuba.[20]

The need for better communication encouraged the Navy Department to look more closely at using wireless telegraphy, and officials began to follow the results of radio tests in Britain and Europe with growing interest. The past several years had seen wireless signals travel across greater and greater distances, including over bodies of water. Guglielmo Marconi had, a year earlier, established a radio station on the Isle of Wright. He set up an antenna 130 feet tall outside the Royal Needles Hotel, and despite howling seas, signaled that station from a transmitter on a ship 20 miles out. A Russian scientist, Alexander Popov, equipped a coastal radio station at Kronstadt on Kotlin Island just west of St. Petersburg, and on the Russian Navy cruiser, *Africa*, with wireless apparatus and began to experiment with signaling at sea. Over the next two years, he would relay information over nine kilometers of water.

In July 1898, off the coast of Ireland, far from the war in which the Americans had been engaged, the Kingstown Sailing Regatta took place. The Dublin's *Daily Express* newspaper arranged to have the races observed from a steamer, the *Flying Huntress*. The steamer served as a movable sending station for Marconi radio messages which described the events as they happened. When news arrived at Kingstown, it was telephoned to the Dublin newspaper. *The Express* was able to print full accounts of the races almost before they were over, and while the yachts were far beyond the range of any telescope. This made a sports event the first public broadcast.

By now, the intrepid Marconi, had sent wireless signals across water several times and was operating a wireless link from the Isle of Wright in the English Channel to Bournemouth, about 40 kilometers away. He spent the remainder of 1898 and 1899 demonstrating longer and longer paths of transmission, culminating in the first international radio message sent in 1899, from a wireless station at Wimereux, France, across the English Channel to England.[21]

That year, while the Navy continued to populate lofts and train birds, encouraged by the success of pigeons in the Spanish-American War, several demonstrations in the United States brought the potential of wireless closer. In April 1899, First Lieutenant George O. Squire of the

War Pigeons

Army Signal Corps transmitted radio signals between Fire Island Lightship and Fire Island at the approach to New York Harbor, a distance of 12 miles. His success was quickly followed by two more. Squire established wireless connection between Governor's Island and Fort Hamilton in New York Harbor, then between Fort Mason and Alcatraz in San Francisco.[22]

Then, James Gordon Bennett, one of the first American newsmen to use homing pigeons to gather news, invited Marconi to report the 1899 America's Cup Race between the yachts *Shamrock* and *Columbia* for the *New York Herald*. Marconi agreed and erected an antenna mast on the lawn outside the Navesink lighthouse in Highlands, New Jersey, at the entrance to New York Bay. The Secretary of the Navy sent several naval officers to observe the workings of the Marconi system during the yacht races. A lack of wind dragged out the races from late September to October 20. But eventually, results were successfully reported with Marconi equipment.

Around this time, Commodore George Dewey was returning to the U.S. in the USS *Olympia* following his triumph at Manila Bay. He had cabled the Navy Department that he anticipated arriving in New York on September 30. While waiting to cover the yacht races, Marconi boarded Dewey's flagship, the SS *Ponce*, and reported the Commodore's progress with wireless via the station he had set up at Navesink.

A naval parade was held in honor of Dewey, and from on board the SS *Ponce* a naval officer radioed this message:

> Bureau of Equipment, Washington, D.C.
> From Steamship Ponce, underway in Naval Parade via Navesink Station.
> Mr. Marconi succeed in [opening?] telegraphic communication with shore at 12:34 p.m. Experiments were a complete success.
> /S/ Blish, Lieutenant USN[23]

This was the first paid ship-to-shore radio message and the first official U.S. Naval radio message. The *Ponce* transmitted about 2500 words on the first day at an average speed of 15 words per minute. The longest distance between messages sent and received was about 17 miles.

Nothing—neither mechanical nor feathered—could compete with the speed of radio waves. Lieutenant Commander G.W. Denfield, one of the naval officers sent on board the *Ponce* as an observer, said in a report to the Secretary of the Navy that the equipment worked under all conditions of weather, which was not the case with any other mode of communication[24] The potential of this new type of communication

Chapter 3. Put to the Test

for maritime purposes impressed both the public and government and resulted in an increased effort by U.S. scientists and engineers to develop wireless.

Further tests on naval ships had mixed results, and the Navy did not immediately buy Marconi's equipment. An excerpt from the 1900 annual report of BOE Chief Bradford commented on the Marconi System of Wireless Telegraphy, concluding that further tests were needed. "After a series of trials lasting over a week, in the port of New York and at sea off the Highland Lights, the board made a favorable report on the usefulness of the Marconi system. The only serious defect found is commonly known as 'interference'" which he briefly described:

> When signals are being transmitted from one station to another, as between the USS *New York* and the Highland Lights, for instance, and another vessel comes within signaling distance and attempts communication with the Highland Lights, then the signals from the two ships become confused, and the receiving station on shore is unable to distinguish between them. Mr. Marconi claimed that he could overcome this defect, but did not do so. It is said that he has since perfected apparatus which will, in a measure, accomplish this result.
>
> Notwithstanding this defect, the board recommended that Mr. Marconi's system be adopted for further trial in the Navy. ... After a careful study of the Marconi system, the Bureau is convinced that its chief value is for use at sea, for the purpose of communication between ships and between ships and shore stations.[25]

Ironically, similar phrasing just ten years earlier described the potential value of using homing pigeons at sea.

In 1901, an event took place that changed how the entire world communicated. Marconi sent three dots, Morse code for the letter "s," across the Atlantic Ocean from Prudholm, England, to St. John's, Newfoundland. It took only a matter of seconds for the three clicks to travel 2000 miles.

A year later, Bradford's annual report included this passage:

> At the request of the Bureau, the Department in April last ordered a board for the purpose of considering and reporting upon the advisability of discontinuing the homing-pigeon service used for the transmission of messages from distant points and substituting in lieu thereof some system of wireless telegraphy. After various changes in its membership the board reported in May to the effect that the homing pigeon service should be discontinued as soon as some system of wireless telegraphy is adopted. In the opinion of the Bureau, the pigeon service should be discontinued at once, since it does not appear to be of any practical use at present, nor has it in the past developed any great promise of success in naval operations.[26]

By 1902, all new Navy ships had provisions for installing wireless, and the Naval Pigeon Messenger Service's fate was sealed.

War Pigeons

With the inevitable adoption of wireless in the fleet, the Naval Pigeon Messenger Service ceased to exist, and the birds were auctioned off. Articles similar to this one from a farm journal appeared in newspapers and magazines around the country. The article directed private fanciers to the birds being sold at the original six Navy yards and stations chosen to host the first lofts. Only six years earlier, these yards had been busy building lofts and populating them with the swiftest carriers of messages through the air. Now, instead of wings, they were making room for wireless gear.

> Sale of homing pigeons belonging to the U.S. Navy—there will be sold at the navy yards: Portsmouth, N.H.; Brooklyn, N.Y.; Norfolk, Va; Mare Island, Cal; Training Station Newport, RI; and Naval Station key West, Fla; all the homing pigeons belonging to the Navy and now at the several yards and stations above mentioned, about 67 of breeders and about 900 fliers in all. The birds at each station will be offered in pairs of breeders and small lots of fliers and bidders will have the option of bidding for part or all at any one or more stations. The sale will be for cash to the highest bidder by sealed proposals to be opened at 12 o'clock noon, December 31, 1901 at all the yards and stations on the Atlantic Coast, and January 11, 1902 at the Navy yard, Mare Island, Cal. Schedule showing number and kind of birds at each station and containing form of proposals and terms of sale will be furnished upon application to the Commandant of the several yards mentioned. JOHN D. LONG, Secretary of the Navy.[27]

The sale of Navy homing pigeons to fanciers from each of the six original lofts totaled $182.22.[28] It seems a paltry sum for the birds' stellar service at sea.

Henri Marion and the naval officers and pigeon fanciers who had helped him establish the first official pigeon messenger service in this country, must have been devastated. In just ten years, their dream of a winged messenger service on the east coast of the United States equal to the vast network in Europe, went, literally, into thin air. The matter of pigeons for sea duty disappeared.

Henri Marion continued to teach French and Spanish at the Naval Academy. He died in 1913 and is buried at the Academy cemetery. Although he never realized his dream of a fully feathered naval pigeon messenger service, he did live long enough to witness the beginning of the rise of homing pigeons into legend. For the role of pigeons in the U.S. military was just getting started. In 1903, another type of bird flew the skies, one made of wood and cloth and powered by an engine. Shortly after planes took to the air, the U.S. military trained pilots to fly them, accompanied almost always, by homing pigeons.

Chapter 4

Into the Breach

Carrier pigeons alone carried messages silently, swiftly and directly... —Lt. J.J. McAtee, R.F.

While the Navy had sold its pigeons and closed its lofts, the raising and racing of pigeons proliferated in the United States. In 1909, two organizing bodies had merged into one, the American Racing Pigeon Union, and by 1916, the organization had 1652 members in several dozen clubs around the country.[1] Newspapers continued to report on race results, and new journals such as *The American Pigeon Journal*, the *American Pigeon Keeper*, and *The American Racing Pigeon News*, were available to enthusiasts with information on both fancy breeds and racing homers.

There was still no official government-funded pigeon messenger service in the early 20th century. Communications work focused on improving telegraph and telephone technology and developing radio. Radio had many advantages over visual, wire and cable systems. It was not limited by darkness or fog. It could go where wires could not, for example, ship to ship, and ship to shore in a matter of seconds. Both the Army and Navy set up their own laboratories to further develop radio.

In Europe it was a different situation. Despite improved communications technology, the start of the World War I saw both Entente and Central Powers using homing pigeons. Telegraph or telephone wires might be cut or tapped. Wireless could be intercepted, and atmospheric disturbances periodically interrupted transmission. On the battlefield, it was sometimes impossible to use runners, flags or dogs to convey information. The Belgians, French and Germans recognized early on the value of homing pigeons over electricity. The birds were light and easy to carry, were affected only by the worst weather, and could not be intercepted except by a bullet or a hawk. Each of these countries had forces of pigeons to draw on. Not until 1916 did Britain send pigeons to the Front, fueled by the country's fanciers. About 100,000 birds, donated by patriotic breeders were offered to the Pigeon Service, and by the Armistice, it is estimated that about 9000 to 10,000 British war pigeons actually served.[2]

While pigeons in Europe were flying regular missions over land and sea with clockwork precision, the U.S. Army Signal Corps found an opportunity to give them another look on home territory. It had been nearly 30 years since their successful trials with pigeons at the Army's Key West barracks. This time, the Signal Corps flew them in the Mexican Punitive Expedition.

The expedition, lead by Brigadier General John J. Pershing, was directed by President Wilson to hunt down Pancho Villa and stop his attacks. Villa and his marauders had been raiding and killing along the U.S.-Mexican border for months. The hot-headed revolutionary had aligned and then realigned himself with various leaders, but had parted ways with the current head, Venustiano Carranza. When President Wilson recognized Carranza as the legitimate leader of Mexico in 1915, allowing him to use railroads in Texas, New Mexico, and Arizona to outmaneuver the Villistas, Villa felt betrayed and sought revenge. On March 9, 1916, he led a deadly raid on Columbus, New Mexico, and adjacent Army Camp Furlong, killing 24 Americans.

Pershing set up his base at Camp Furlong and with 12,000 men, swept into Mexico to find Pancho Villa. The Signal Corps unit accompanying Pershing faced barren, dusty and mountainous land, and weather that changed from deathly hot to icy cold. To stay in communication with Camp Furlong as Pershing marched deep into Mexican territory, the Signal Corps employed a number of technologies. They relied heavily on telegraph, field service buzzer (telephones that transmitted Morse code), heliograph and flags. Wireless wagon sets at Columbus and Colonia Dublán, Pershing's forward headquarters 400 miles into Mexico, proved too heavy to keep up with the fast-moving cavalry, so most messages were sent via wire. For the first time, the Corps utilized airplanes to gather information and fly it back to Camp Furlong. The 1st Aero Squadron, an eight-plane force of JN-3s, struggled over the mountainous terrain and through high winds on 90-horsepower engines, but accomplished some scouting runs and carried messages back and forth to the cavalry patrols, and from Mexico to Columbus.

Even though the Army had not yet trained pigeoneers nor created a pigeon messenger service, the Signal Corps flew pigeons briefly during the expedition.[3] While other technologies were susceptible to the prevailing bad weather and mountainous conditions, the pigeons were not.

Chapter 4. Into the Breach

However, the birds were vulnerable to a lack of pigeoneers at Camp Furlong to care for and train them, and they had too little time to acclimate to their surroundings, time needed to use visual, sound and smell cues to form that all-important map. Without those key components, the pigeons were not reliable couriers.

Although Pancho Villa avoided capture, the raids stopped, and Pershing's force returned to the United States in February 1917. The expedition gave General Pershing and his Signal Corps valuable experience in using new and old communications tools available to them, including pigeon messengers. This knowledge they would soon use in the looming war.

Americans watched the Great War rage with mixed feelings. Some saw it as a remote event, having little to do with them. President Wilson wanted to stay out of war, and support for a neutral position was strong. Others felt that the U.S. would eventually become involved, and that the country should be prepared. Advocates, including ex-President Theodore Roosevelt, believed that U.S. needed to build up its military. The U.S. held a traditional aversion to maintaining a large peacetime army, and had no peacetime conscription, as was common in some European countries. Wilson was not interested in readying the regular Army, believing that the National Guard would prove adequate in the event the U.S. did become involved.

When the Germans sank the passenger ship, *Lusitania* in May 1915, opinion shifted, and a new Preparedness Movement began in cities around the country, proclaiming the need to strengthen naval and land forces. Both civil and military advocates wanted to sell Americans on the idea of preparedness as essential to national security. Rallies and parades, movies and posters aimed to sway the public toward a military escalation.

Starting in 1913, military instruction camps had been created for college students, and after the sinking of the *Lusitania*, more were built. New York citizens received government funds to set up a military training camp in Plattsburg, with more than 1000 enrollees. Other states soon followed suit.

Acts of Congress expanded preparedness. The National Defense Act of 1916 authorized an increase in the strength of the Army and National Guard. The Naval Act of 1916 provided for the construction of battleships, cruisers, destroyers, submarines and auxiliaries. The build-up began, and not just of military personnel and machines.

With the word out about the need for reliable couriers, pigeon

War Pigeons

fanciers around the country did their part, breeding and training pigeons as fast as they could. In a 1916 *New York Times* article Vermont fancier, Cyrus F. Wicker, made a plea to the public to breed these valuable birds:

> And you, reader, may take part in such a nation-wide scheme of preparedness by raising and training our own homing pigeons and holding them ready for the service of the military authorities in time of war or of your community in time of peace. ... Perhaps not this year or the next, but some time your pigeons are going to be useful to your country or community, and meanwhile, by introducing an intelligent and living wireless into your own home, you are busy preparing.[4]

Wicker went on to point out that the airplanes used in the recent Punitive Expedition would have better served their purpose of ferrying messages if they had carried along a basket of pigeons and sent several with messages from the planes. Wicker even boldly pronounced that pigeons might have been the key to Villa's capture had the Army been more aware of their abilities and used those skills to their advantage. The Vermont fancier's lack of awareness of the Signal Corps' attempt to utilize pigeons in the expedition suggests that the birds were few and their flights not publicized.

In the fall of 1915, Germany had ceased submarine warfare against American shipping, but they resumed their attacks in early 1917, and more merchant and passenger ships sank to the ocean floor. Loss of American lives mounted. Then, British cryptographers intercepted and deciphered a German telegram offering Mexico U.S. territory in return for joining the German cause. Enough.

On April 6, 1917, the U.S. declared war on Germany, and the country mobilized for war. The American Expeditionary Force (AEF) combined units from the regular Army, Marines, various State National Guards and the new National Army created from volunteers and draftees. Two million troops eventually went to the Western Front and another 200,000 naval personnel to European waters.

When the U.S. entered the war, the country had no organized pigeon force—the Navy's birds had been sold off 16 years earlier. But civilian pigeons were ready, and civilian pigeon experts were ready. They were just waiting for the call. The call came, and what resulted was an unprecedented joint effort between military and civilian organizations. In June 1917, General John J. Pershing, head of the AEF, and now in Europe, requested the mobilization of military homing pigeons. By late summer, the Army had found two men to head the pigeon service, both military and both pigeon fanciers—David C. Buscall and John L. Carney,

Chapter 4. Into the Breach

a veteran sergeant with the Signal Corps living in Pittsburgh. They were both commissioned as lieutenants in August 1917. Under their direction, birds from around the country were purchased for $2.00 each, with many more donated. Pittsburgh involvement didn't stop with Carney. The 300 members of the Pittsburgh chapter of the American Racing Pigeon Union offered not only 10,000 of their award-winning birds, but also their services as trainers and builders of lofts.[5]

During the summer of 1917, the Army started training pigeons and pigeoneers at 110 camps and posts around the country, with the Pigeon Breeding and Training Headquarters at Fort Monmouth, New Jersey. Every regular Army, National Army, and National Guard camp in the country was equipped with lofts and pigeons procured from private fanciers. Lofts were also set up at 22 aviation camps, 10 lofts on the Mexican border, nine in Panama, two in Hawaii, and 15 at coast defenses on both sides of the country.[6]

Training the homing pigeons was straightforward. At first, young birds, squeakers a few weeks old, were trained to fly to stationary lofts. On each outing, they were released from points farther and farther away until they could fly home from over 100 miles out. As important as training the birds in these early stages was teaching men to handle them. The majority of pigeoneers recruited had backgrounds in

New pigeoneers at the Great Lakes Naval Training Station, learning how to release a basket of pigeons, ca. 1918 (courtesy NARA).

War Pigeons

World War I Signal Corps officer inspects one of a flock of pigeons he is raising for the Army (courtesy NARA).

raising and racing pigeons. Even the mechanics who maintained the lofts and vehicles that pulled them preferably had some kind of pigeon experience. Those who did not, were taught the intricacies of the job. A sense of trust between bird and keeper was important, and to promote this, keepers were encouraged to spend time getting to know their birds and handling them.

Besides hawks, these first military pigeons faced a human adversary—civilians who shot pigeons-in-training en route back to their home lofts, thinking they were a nuisance. It became such a problem that the American government levied heavy fines for shooting military homing pigeons, stating that the death of each military pigeon at civilian hands hurt the war effort. Congress passed a law in 1918 that included a maximum penalty of $100.00 fine and six months imprisonment for shooting a government pigeon.[7] This rather severe penalty—$100.00 in 1918 would be worth about $1800.00 today, plus jail time—shows the importance the government began to place on the role of homing pigeons in the military.

Chapter 4. Into the Breach

Advanced instruction focused on training the birds to fly to mobile lofts, as these vehicles would be the pigeons' homes at the front. An innovation of World War I, the mobile lofts were self-contained homes on wheels, with nests, food and fresh water. They served the same function as stationary lofts, but with the added challenge of being moved about, often every week. Training birds to home to mobile lofts started with changing the position of the lofts little by little, gradually increasing the distance the lofts were moved. The birds learned to recognize the shape of their loft and markings on the roofs, and were able to return to them, even when released miles away. Once pigeons had completed mobile loft training, they were ready to go to war.

In late October, Lieutenant Buscall, six non-commissioned officers, 800 pigeons, 12 mobile lofts and a supply of feed boarded the *Agamemnon* for France.[8] Colonel Edgar Russel, Chief Signal Officer for the AEF, was waiting in Paris. He had established four new organizations within the Land Section of the Signal Corps, one of them being a pigeon service. Russel sent Buscall and a few of his men to study British stationary lofts as well as mobile lofts active at the front at Vimy Ridge in Northern France. When Lieutenant Carney arrived in France in early December with more officers and pigeons, he and Buscall continued their education in live pigeon messaging by observing combat operations at French stationary and mobile lofts. By early spring of 1918, the American Pigeon Service had been organized and entered the war with 10 mobile and one stationary loft, 652 pigeons and resources for 20 more mobile lofts.[9]

> The first American pigeons to enter action, however, were housed at the French stationary loft at Cornieville. Those pigeons, under the training of Sergeant Lewis Swanker of Lakewood, Ohio, entered the front lines at three trench posts with stations of four pigeons each. Two days later on March 17, 1918, "Gunpowder," a black check hen bred by Herman Moser of Aurora, Illinois, delivered the first American pigeon message from the trenches of the front to the headquarters of the 26th division at Boucq. "Gunpowder" was followed by a second pigeon, the black pied hen, "Pretty Baby," carrying a carbon copy to ensure delivery in case the first bird went down.[10]

Into the breach American pigeons flew.

Pigeons traveled to the front in wicker baskets attached to the backs of soldiers, dogs and horses, and also via motorcycle. The baskets contained small corselets suspended from the inside walls of the basket by elastic. Birds were securely fastened but could move around without being injured en route. Food, message tubes, and an instruction card were sent with each bird. Messages were to be written "in the open,"

War Pigeons

Soldier writing a message to be transmitted via homing pigeons, ca. 1918. Note the two pigeons resting inside the basket, held secure and safe in specially made vests (courtesy NARA).

or encoded, on thin paper and placed into metal capsules on their legs. Units in the field released the birds which carried their messages to the division or corps mobile lofts. There, pigeoneers removed the messages and relayed the contents to the rear headquarters. The Signal Corps marked each pigeon to show what loft it belonged to in case a bird accidentally flew to the wrong one.[11]

At the front, American forces used both British and American pigeons. Their speed, consistency and ability to home, even to mobile lofts, made them especially useful compared to other existing communications available to the Signal Corps. With opposing forces laying face-to-face in trenches sometimes barely a hundred feet apart, flags, lamps and heliographs were confined to areas behind the lines. Radio sets lacked some important abilities such as fine tuning, and telephone and telegraph lines could be intercepted or cut. Pigeons proved themselves as the most reliable couriers over and over again.

The feats they performed through gas and firestorms are legendary. Writing on the military value of the Homer, J.L. Carney said,

Chapter 4. Into the Breach

World War I soldier on horseback with a basket of homing pigeons, ca. 1918. During that war, pigeons were carried on the backs of soldiers, mules, horses and dogs (courtesy NARA).

In the Argonne Forest where probably the bloodiest battle of the war was fought, a battle the duration of which ran into months, the racing pigeon played a most heroic part.

Barbed wire entanglements, machine gun nests, and Boche-filled trenches that honeycombed the scrubby woods from end to end made this pivotal point a Gibraltar. Nothing could live above ground and the trenches and shell holes were filled with dead and wounded. Time after time the attack was on and almost as often repulsed. Division after division was thrown into the line to face the most deadly of modern weapons, the machine gun. With small artillery firing incessantly, high explosive shells dropping everywhere and the gas attacks on hourly, there was little wonder that man-made lines of communication should wither and break.

Into the breach went the little racing pigeon—the most gallant bird the world knows. And they came through—came through with messages of weal and woe; came through when shattered troops were crying for aid—when every other line of communication had failed.[12]

Homing pigeons fought beside American soldiers and Marines in France, and their record is impressive. During the Aisne-Marne

War Pigeons

Offensive, 72 birds carried 78 important messages; in the St. Mihiel Drive, 90 messages were delivered; in the Meuse-Argonne Offensive, 442 birds delivered 403 messages safely, sometimes arriving mutilated or dead.[13] A number of homers performed feats which have not been publicized, and they remain unknown.

The reliance on each other during trench warfare surely deepened the bond between soldier and bird, and pigeoneers took every measure to keep their birds safe. In response to gas attacks, special covers with air filters were placed over baskets of pigeons. A storm bag was also developed to protect the birds during bad weather, as mud caked on a pigeon's feathers, hindered its ability to fly.[14]

Along with their rifles, Marines in World War I entered combat with pigeons inside wicker baskets strapped to their backs (official Marine Corps photograph, 127-N-528828).

So vital were the birds that pigeoneers risked their own lives to save them. On November 10, 1918, just one day before the armistice, the Black 92nd Division was engaged in local action when German shells struck a building being used as a communications center, as well as a munitions dump in an adjacent building. Military police ordered an evacuation of the area, due to continuous secondary explosions from the burning dump. However, a 92nd Division pigeoneer would not leave his birds behind. Defying the order, he crept into the damaged and smoldering communications building amid more explosions. He found his birds and got out safely.[15]

Sometimes pigeons worked with other animals to get their message through. The unswerving determination of the animals was heroic,

Chapter 4. Into the Breach

Harley-Davidson motorcycles saw action on the front lines, leading convoys, dispatching messages and transporting personnel. Some were mounted with sidecars that converted to stretchers or gun batteries. This 1917 model was outfitted with a pigeon carrier, probably used to ferry birds to the front (courtesy Wheels Through Time Museum).

as described at Thiaumont, France, where a small French garrison, taken by the Germans, then back again by the French, was being bombarded to dust.

> Once the brave little French garrison was being shelled to pieces by a German battery. Wireless and telephones to the rear were shattered. The garrison commander knew the location of the battery which was doing the damage, and if only he could get word back to the French artillery! He sent up his last pigeon. Like the others, the bird was shot down immediately. Then the garrison waited—waited for death. The commandant gazed with his glasses longingly towards the French part of France—the French lines. He turned pale. He could scarcely believe his eyes. Across a terrain of bursting shrapnel, where high-explosive shells detonated so rapidly and so thickly that their smoke entwined and floated off like fantastic ghostly devil waltzers; there, where nothing should live, something was living! A black-looking object was moving. It would dart across the open fields, disappear into a shell hole and then then reappear. It came nearer and nearer, and the whole garrison gazed upon it in a sort of unbelieving horror. The thing was bewitched,

War Pigeons

else how could it live and move in such a place. As it drew nearer the glasses showed it to be a dog with something on its back. Breathlessly, the little handful of French poilus watched and prayed, and, when the animal dashed into the redoubt, they saw that he carried a small basket. In it were two homing pigeons.

The commander wrote his message twice, telling the location of the death-dealing German guns, and dispatched both pigeons at once. Like tiny white geysers, they rose straight upwards, poised an instant and flew. Shells screamed at them, buckshot from choke bore shotguns whizzed thousands of tiny bullets at them; a gas shell whistled its way by them, but failed to explode at the proper time. Again the little garrison prayed and again the god of battles decreed that the dumb friends of man should prevail over the battle din which man had made! Again, the living traversed a space where no thing could live (man thought). Both birds reached French artillery headquarters. The great German batteries were silenced.[16]

Above the broil of the battlefield, American pilots flew observation and attack sorties, and with them, pigeons. The Signal Corps began testing airplanes at Fort Meyer, Virginia, on August 20, 1908, in a Wright Flyer and formally accepted this airplane as "Airplane No. 1," in 1909. Four years later after taking part in maneuvers in Texas, the Chief Signal Officer designated the assembled men and equipment the First Provisional Aero Squadron. It was later renamed the 1st Aero Squadron, December 8, 1913, the first military unit of the U.S. Army devoted to aviation. This was the squadron that flew messages in the 1916 Punitive Expedition.

When war broke out in Europe in August 1914, the 1st Aero Squadron represented the entire tactical air strength of the U.S. Army. It counted 12 officers, 54 enlisted men and six aircraft.[17] By 1916, the Aviation Section called for two dozen squadrons, seven for the Regular Army, 12 for the National Guard divisions, and five for coastal defense, plus balloon units for the field and coast artillery. By the time the U.S. entered the war, all 24 squadrons had been formed.

Although earlier flights took place, it was September 1917 before an Air Service attached to the AEF was officially established. Up until this time, no airplane in America had ever mounted a machine gun, and there was practically no knowledge of radiotelegraphy and telephony, photography, bombing equipment, lights for night flying, clothing, compasses used in flying or other aviation instruments known to the aviators of Germany, England and France. France gave American aviators both lessons and planes. The first squadrons arrived in April 1918, and by October and November 1918, a total of 45 American squadrons were at the front lines, most of them fighters and observers. Balloon companies were also in service. Allied squadrons fought over St. Mihiel and allied aviators helped stop the German Offensive at Argonne-Meuse.

Chapter 4. Into the Breach

Army airman with 90th Aero Squadron, 82nd Division, about to release a homing pigeon over Ourches, France, July 15, 1918 (courtesy U.S. Army Signal Corps).

The Army Air Service used pigeons to relay intelligence messages from observation flights as well as to report the location of downed fighter planes. A few pilots had stateside experience with pigeons, including those who had trained at Fort Lewis, Oregon. This Army base, south of Tacoma, Washington, had opened in 1917 and was one of two west coast pigeon training sites. The other was at Ross Field in Arcadia, California. Second Lieutenant Ray Delhauer, an experienced pigeon fancier from California, was recruited by the Signal Corps to head Camp Lewis' pigeon program. He had served with Pershing in the Mexican Punitive Expedition and was likely one of the handlers who had tried to use pigeon couriers in that conflict. Two years later, as commander of the camp's pigeon program, he supervised two pigeon lofts and ran a training course for soldiers in the use and care of pigeons.

During large-scale training at the camp, pigeons carried messages between the field and headquarters. In the first field exercise, Captain Charles Z. Sutton released a pigeon to send back intelligence on "enemy forces." It was released at 4500 feet and reached headquarters in a few minutes—much faster than if Sutton had chosen the other courier option, dropping his message to a horseback rider below.[18]

Civilians expressed a strong interest in the pigeon program, so as New York naval militia had done at the start of the Spanish-American War, the Camp Lewis pigeoneers took their birds to local events. They answered questions about the birds and how the messenger system worked, and perhaps allowed a few children to hold them. Then the pigeoneers released the birds, and before the crowd of upturned heads, the pigeons circled a few times and flew straight for their lofts at the camp.

As Captain Sutton learned, pigeons could be released from planes at an altitude of up to 8000 feet and 100 miles from home. With good training, the release distance could reach 200 miles, and the altitude raised to 15,000 feet.[19] The military was starting to comprehend what superpowers the birds possessed.

Whatever the altitude, care had to be taken when releasing a bird

Close-up of pigeon being released from a plane over Ourches, France, July 15, 1918 (courtesy U.S. Army Signal Corps).

Chapter 4. Into the Breach

World War I pilot releasing a pigeon from a typical Allied float plane, ca. 1918 (official U.S. Navy photograph).

from an airplane, because the sudden blast of wind upon release could not only injure a birds but strip its feathers off. The Air Service developed a standard protocol for their release, later detailed in an Army manual, *The Pigeoneer, Student Manual for All Arms*. The directions were explicit, and must have taken practice, preferably on the ground first.

1. PREPARATIONS BEFORE STARTING ON A FLIGHT
 a. See that the birds are in their box.
 b. Fasten the message pad on the top of the box.
 c. See that the lower half of the message capsule is attached to the bird's leg.
 d. Place the upper half of the message capsule in the clip provided on the box.

2. PREPARING A MESSAGE (one hand required)
 a. Write the message on the pad which is fastened to the top of the box.
 b. Fold the message blank to the proper size to fit the capsule; detach it from the book and roll it; then insert it in the upper half of the message capsule.
 c. Take the message capsule in the hand, open the side door of the box, and reach in and insert the upper half of the capsule into the lower half which is on the bird's leg. Close the side door.

War Pigeons

3. RELEASING A PIGEON

a. Open the door of the box with the right hand and place the hand over the bird's back with the four fingers over the bird's left wing and the thumb over its right wing with the bird facing along the forearm toward the body. Bring the bird close up to the side of the box.

b. Using a gentle downward movement to the vent, bring the wings and tail together with the thumb and index finger close up under the vent and as close to the body of the bird as possible, leaving the bird down in the cockpit where he will be protected from the propeller blast.

c. Notify the pilot of the ship, by some prearranged signal, such as tapping him on the back, that you are ready to release the bird. The pilot should throttle his motor to idling speed and "float" his ship. It is not necessary to stall the plane. The speed should be about 70 miles per hour.

d. When the pilot has throttled the ship raise the right arm to about the height of the head holding the bird well over the side of the ship. Then swing the arm down and release the bird at the bottom of the swing. The plane of the arc described by the hand should be about 30 degrees out from the side of the ship. Use considerable force, but do not squeeze the bird. The force with which the bird is thrown down will cause the bird to clear the tail of the ship while the force of the wind striking the bird when he is released is thus reduced.[20]

Except in cases of emergency, the manual discouraged releasing birds from aircraft at night, in fog, or in very bad weather. However, it reassured the aviator that in such a case, the bird might find a safe place for the night, then resume its way home at dawn.

By the end of the war, thousands of pigeons had died on the battlefield or were horribly mutilated. Yet, they had gotten 95 percent of the messages through to their destinations. If they, themselves, were not heroes, their efforts were heroic. Gratitude showered on both the birds and their handlers, from privates to generals, from ordinary citizens to heads of state. Returning pigeons were paraded alongside soldiers as heroes of the war.

A few whose feats were recorded by Chief Signal Officer of the AEF, George O. Squire:

N.U.R.P. # 615, black check hen
(Named—Cher Ami)
Delivered 12 important messages from the Verdun front to loft at Rampont. Average distance 30 kilometres. Average time, 24 minutes. Returned on last occasion with leg shot away, message tube containing important document hanging by tendon. Missile which carried away leg, also passed through breast. Wonderful vitality of bird enabled it to recover quickly. In this seriously wounded condition number 615 flew 40 kilometres in 25 minutes, being liberated at 2:35 P.M., arriving loft at 3 o'clock. Point of liberation Grand Pre.

Chapter 4. Into the Breach

U.S.A 18–16374, black cock
Sire: 6445 Grizzle C
Dam: AU16D 8153 BCH
(Named—President Wilson)
Leg carried away by missile while carrying from Verdun front to loft at Cuizy, during operations American Army during November. In this sector bird also worked from tanks. During St. Mihiel operations Number 16374 especially distinguished because of splendid work from tanks when all other communications failed. Also worked from airplanes.

AU19–D-4084, red check splash cock
(Named—The Mocker)
Eye destroyed by shrapnel while working from Beaumont front in St Mihiel sector during operations American Army. Bird had carried many important messages.

USA 18568, red check cock
Sire: 1 Blk C C
Dam: AU17BX 417 R C H T. Thomason
(Named—The Poilu)
Severely wounded head and neck while carrying message from Verdun front to headquarters Cuisy. Distinguished for splendid work from tanks to Ourches, during St. Mihiel operations American Army.

U.S.A. 17314, red check cock
Sire: AU16D RCC Zimmerman Delmotte-Osman
Dam: Tgl 23161 Blk c w f hen H Weaver
(Named—Kaja-Boy)
Head severely lacerated by shrapnel while carrying important message from post near Pont-a-Mousson, in Toul sector during operations of American Army.

USA18–19079, black check hen
Sire: AU16G 9911 BCC A.H. Licht Grooter-Delmotte
Dam: 34 Blk C H Robt Trapp Wegge-Grooter
(Named—Blanchette)
Carried important message from advance Centre Information 90th Division, on Verdun front, November 3, 1918. Four birds on post, other three killed by shell which also killed two pigeoneers in charge of birds.

USA—16891, red check hen
Sire: AU16H 8787 RCC E.L. Miller Osman
Dam: AU16C 331 Blk C Spl H
(Named—Petite Rosette)
Working from extreme advance post, Third Corps, First American Army, carried message announcing the capture of Hill 287, one of the hardest positions to overcome on the entire front. This bird carried many important messages during Verdun operations and was commended by commanding-general for splendid service.

USA 15539, black check cock
Sire: AU17K 2577 BCC
Dam: AU17CF 256 BlkCh C.J. Sachs Trenton Gitz

War Pigeons

(Named—King Bloomfield)
Carried important message from Third battalion, 111th Infantry, 28th Division, when troops crossed Vesle River. Distance from Fismette to Igny-de-Abbaye, 16 kilometres. King Bloomfield flew this distance in 11 minutes.

USA 18—16757, black check cock
Sire: AU13 9156 Blue C
Dam: Au13 13442 BCH
(Named—Lord Adelaide, later named Cuisy Bill)
Severely wounded while working from trenches to loft at Cuisy. Carried several important messages during November operations. During St. Mihiel operations, American Army, this bird received special mention for splendid services rendered in carrying messages from tanks.

USA 15705, black check cock
(Named—Reliable)
Carried many important messages during Chateau Thierry drive between Vesle River and Igny-de-Abbaye: also during Argonne Forest drive in Verdun sector specially distinguished for flight of 20 kilometres in 21 minutes, when troops surrounded and in desperate need of assistance. All other communications had failed. Reliable arrived in time to secure needed relief and was instrumental in enabling American troops to drive back the enemy.

USA 15360, black check cock
Sire: PB 4869 BCC
Dam: AU17D 2608 BCH
(Named—The Premier)
Flew 22 kilometres on October 13, 1981, from Argonne Forest carrying very important message from beleaguered troops. Flight made during heavy rain and fog. Also worked during Chateau Thierry drive of American troops carrying many important messages from posts on Vesle River.[21]

An accounting of World War I birds would not be complete without mentioning Kaiser. Born in Germany in 1917 as 17-0350-47, he was assigned to the Imperial Army engaged in trench warfare at the Argonne Forest. When men of the 28th Infantry Division overwhelmed the Germans in October 1918, along with soldiers and equipment, half a dozen German pigeons were captured, among them young 17-0350-47, whom the dough boys nicknamed *Kaiser*. Just a month later, the war ended, and the Signal Corps returned home with distinguished American pigeons as well as captured German birds, including Kaiser. After the POW birds were paraded around, they settled down at the Signal Corps Pigeon Center at Fort Monmouth. Kaiser became a breeding bird and enjoyed a good life at Fort Monmouth. He did his part to supply many squeakers for the U.S. Army, sending his offspring to serve in World War II. As he aged well beyond the lifespan of normal homing pigeons

Chapter 4. Into the Breach

(around 15 years), he was continually celebrated. The children at the fort's nursery school held a birthday party for Kaiser when he turned 31. On account of "serving" in two world wars, the American Legion gave him memberships at their First Retread Post NO. 667 in Los Angeles, in August 1948. Kaiser then went to Washington, D.C., to celebrate the inauguration of President Harry Truman on January 20, 1949, as part of a Signal Corps exhibition. On Halloween night, 1949, Kaiser passed away at his Fort Monmouth home at age 33. He outlived the real Kaiser, many wives, as well as any other pigeon that had served in the First World War. According to military historian Frank Blazich, "The progeny of his great-great-great-great grandchildren, sold to the public when the army disestablished the pigeon service in 1957, remain in lofts across the United States, undoubtedly still producing racing champions."[22]

* * * * * *

Although the Navy's pigeons found themselves landlocked as radio became standard equipment on board ships, they grew more important than ever when Navy pilots began to fly. In both successful experiments and real situations in the Spanish-American War, the Naval Pigeon Messenger Service had laid crucial groundwork that established homing pigeons as invaluable communication modes in Navy planes and lighter-than-air craft.

In 1908, the Navy detailed Lieutenant George C. Sweet and naval constructor William McIntee to observe a test of a Wright airplane at Fort Meyer, Virginia. They were so impressed with what they saw that the Navy extended an invitation to the Wright brothers to attempt to launch one of their planes from a battleship. The Wright brothers declined, but on November 14, 1910, a Glenn Curtiss pilot, Eugene Ely, flew off a platform built on the bow of the cruiser *Birmingham* at Hampton Roads, Virginia. The flight's success, plus the competitive interest of the U.S. Army in using aircraft for their own scouting ambitions, spurred the Navy to request money in the 1911–1912 Naval Appropriation Act for aviation procurement.

The Navy's first aircraft was ordered on May 8, 1911, marking the official birth of U.S. Naval Aviation. The first naval aviation camp was established near Annapolis, Maryland. Two Curtiss float planes were sent to the camp, followed by a Wright airplane and a small group of naval officers hoping to learn to fly them. Early planes were made of pieces of spruce wood glued together, with wings of fabric stretched in place, sewn, and then made taut with cellulose paint. Struts and bracing wires gave structural strength. The planes looked, and probably felt, hardly sturdy enough to fly.

In October 1913, the Secretary of the Navy established a Board of Aeronautics to plan the future of the naval aviation. The board's first action was to relocate the Greenbury Point air detachment from the Annapolis area to Pensacola, Florida, where good flying weather was available year around. On January 20, 1914, the first naval air station (NAS) was put into operation with the arrival of the Greenbury detachment. This year also marked the start of World War I.

By this time, naval radio had developed to a point where ships were no longer out of communication once they sailed over the horizon. Dozens of high-powered shore radio stations allowed direct contact with ships. Wireless transmitters were mounted on more than 1000 ships and became instrumental in the war's anti-submarine warfare.[23]

But radios were still crude, vulnerable to weather and cumbersome. And, while wireless gave squadrons or individual ships a new tool to navigate through hostile seas, especially to arrange for fuel and other supplies, it also broadcasted, or answered, calls from other ships or shore stations, and was likely to reveal her presence to an enemy vessel in the area. Interception was also possible with the heliograph, telephone, and telegraph. "Carrier pigeons alone," said J.J. McAttee, a naval officer and pigeon fancier, "carried messages silently, swiftly and directly to the parties for whom they were intended, and enemy bullets dispatched to interrupt their flight seldom stopped these faithful couriers."[24]

Knowing that homing pigeons were proven couriers over both land and sea, Great Britain had created the Naval Pigeon Service in 1914. This organization was established even before the British Army saw the value of homing pigeons on the battlefield. British submarines and mine sweepers carried baskets of pigeons to communicate with bases in case of an emergency, or if out of range of their radio equipment.[25] Pigeons were then used in surface ships that hunted for U-boats. Before the convoy system was adopted to protect shipping, German U-boats attacked every type of commercial ship off the British Isles, from steam liners to fishing boats. The U-boats were a formidable weapon. They could travel underwater two hours, carrying 35 men and 112 torpedoes. In the first few years of the war, U-boats sank hundreds of allied merchant ships and passenger vessels, including the *Lusitania*, which had on board 1,960passengers and crew, 1,193 of whom perished.[26]

Toward the latter part of 1916, the British Admiralty battled U-boats off the British coast with secret "Q ships," commercial vessels

Chapter 4. Into the Breach

such as steamers, colliers, trawlers and schooners, that hid guns under fake smokestacks, tarps and other gear. Posing as benign merchant vessels, these disguised ships would lure U-boats within range and then fire on them. Because radios were expensive and not always available, pigeons often went with smaller Q ships to carry messages to shore. More than once they saved lives. A well-known incident involving the *Nelson* was just one example of the pigeons' worth. In August of 1917, the *Nelson*, an armed fishing smack skippered by Tom Crisp, was fired upon by a U-boat. The *Nelson* was badly damaged, and Crisp nearly disemboweled by the attack. Dying, but still conscious, Crisp ordered that the ship's papers be thrown overboard. He then dictated a message to be sent to port via the smack's four homing pigeons, the smack having no wireless. "Nelson being attacked by submarine. Skipper killed. Jim Howe Bank. Send help at once." One of the pigeons, Red Cock, made it to his loft on shore, and the survivors of the *Nelson* were rescued.[27]

An article in a 1919 *The Ohio Farmer* suggested that many pigeons were used on board naval vessels during the war, especially on ships that patrolled coastlines. "By every navy engaged in the war they [homing pigeons] were used for scout duty along coasts, and were carried by practically every scout boat operating in European waters."[28]

While homing pigeons served on ships with and without wireless, most of the documentation cites them as used mainly in naval aircraft. From early planes, communication was primitive and difficult. A pilot had to land, or signal with colored lights or by dropping weighted notes. While airborne, he received instructions from strips of white and black cloth laid out in an open field, according to a prearranged design.[29] Wireless sets were large, heavy, and unreliable, and would not fit on board aircraft easily, so many pilots refused to carry them.

At the start of America's entry into the war, the Navy's air strength consisted only of 48 officers, 239 enlisted men, 54 training planes, a couple of balloons, one dirigible and a naval air station at Pensacola, Florida.[30] So pilots trained in the United States, then went overseas to England, Ireland and France and learned to fly their seaplanes, conducting mainly anti-submarine patrols off the coasts of those countries. Beginning with the arrival of the First Aeronautic Detachment in June 1917, the U.S. Navy established air stations at 21 bases in Ireland, England, France and Italy. At this time, General John Pershing was in England en route to Paris, to his command of the AEF.

Off the coast of England, convoy and antisubmarine patrols became crucial along important shipping lanes that bordered the coasts of Great

War Pigeons

Britain. But once a plane left England's coast and headed into the North Sea, there were no landmarks to indicate where the pilot was. The pilot of a plane flying over land could locate his position by railroads, villages, rivers, roads and other landmarks visible on the landscape. Over the ocean, he had to steer entirely by compass, never diverting attention from the instrument. The slightest deviation from a fixed patrol path could result in running out of fuel and crashing into the water.

As reconnaissance and anti-submarine patrols increased, loss of pilots and crews became a dire problem. Aviators whose planes went down in the water found their wireless sets, if they had them, flooded and useless. Unless an aircraft was seen falling into the sea, there was little hope of rescue. The Entente speculated that since homing pigeons had been trained by military pigeon messenger services, including the U.S. Navy's, to fly over water from ships, they might be able to help save lives of men stranded on the water, many miles from shore. They were so right. Homing pigeons were recruited as part of air crews and taken into planes wherever they patrolled. On large bombers, they were caged in the front cockpit, and on seaplanes, a specially designed container was installed on the floats. If a plane's patrol area was more than 30 miles out to sea, at least two pigeons were carried on board.[31]

Most of the pigeons used for these sorties were from military and private lofts in Belgium and France, with some from England, and they were delivered to the U.S. Naval Air Service in August 1918 at the air stations from which they flew. Records show that about 700 pigeons were stationed with American Navy pilots. Some 10,995 messages were delivered in one year from U.S. Naval patrol boats and planes operating off the French coast, and 219 were from seaplanes down at sea.[32]

The swift-flying pigeons were of immeasurable value where seaplanes were forced to land on the ocean, or in carrying messages from planes where it was impossible or undesirable to use wireless. Despite the normal challenges in training the birds, as well as the fierce weather—wind, fog, sleet, rain—that many faced in flying their routes, only 11 feathered couriers out of more than 800 went missing in action.[33] A remarkable achievement.

Joe Cline, a U.S. Navy pilot serving in France, explained how naval aviators used the valuable birds at the St. Nazaire naval station:

> We always had carrier pigeons with us. There was a Frenchman who controlled the pigeon loft with the carrier pigeons. I got to know him pretty well. I used to give him cigarettes and gum. One of the older pigeons was named Nancy, and every time I'd go out on patrol, he'd give me Nancy, because she would always come

Chapter 4. Into the Breach

home. We had two pigeons in a little basket. Any time we had a forced landing, or sighted a submarine, we'd write a note and put it in a little vial on the pigeon's leg, giving them our location, what our trouble was, how we were—and then Nancy would beat it for Le Croisic. When she went to the pigeon loft, she went through a little slot that rang a bell, then the pigeon master would go up and get the note.[34]

Distress messages were written on onionskin paper and inserted in a small aluminum capsule (probably Henri Marion's invention) attached to one of the bird's legs. The pigeon was then set loose to find its way back to its loft. To ensure birds would clear the plane when thrown, Navy pilots used the Army's system for releasing a bird.

Tales related by aviators about their lives being saved by a pigeon elevated the birds to almost supernatural status. Story after story tells of men being rescued; of pigeons making it home even after badly shot; of birds dying of exhaustion but getting the message through. Lieutenant James McAtee, an American officer and pigeon expert, wrote:

> At a certain seaplane station in Flanders early one morning a pigeon was seen to dive from the clouds and enter its loft hurriedly. The piece of thin tissue paper inside the small aluminum cylinder on its leg was at once unrolled, disclosing the following message: "Shot down, Potvin, 10 miles NNW Nieuport; One Hun down and my tanks are shot; French torpedo boat destroyer on its way. Send fighters. Graham."
>
> At the seaplane station this meant that Flight Lieutenant R. Graham, who had left that morning on special patrol work, had encountered enemy aircraft; that a seaplane had been shot down, whose pilot was Flight Lieutenant Potvin; that a German machine had also been shot down; that shots had pierced his own [fuel] tanks; that a French torpedo boat destroyer was approaching and that more fighting seaplanes were needed at once. Five minutes later another pigeon homed with this message: "Shot landed OK; down 10 miles NNE Nieuport. Potvin. I shot one down but he did not crash. My tanks are not good, cannot climb. French torpedo-boat destroyer on its way. Send more fighters quick. Graham."
>
> Eighteen minutes later a third pigeon homed with a message from another member of the patrol which read: "Am shot down, hit in tank radiator, [my observer] Rogers dead. I am unhurt. Please send help at once. Paine." Seven minutes later a fourth pigeon homed with this message: "Machine turning over to port; have jettisoned everything. I am on wing tip, sea is calm. Machine is seemingly steadied, nothing in sight. I think machine will float for a long time. Land bus just made one circuit, but I don't think he saw me. If my machine sinks will swim to buoy close by. Rogers was killed instantly, wound in head. Paine."
>
> Two seaplanes were sent to guide a French torpedo boat destroyer to the scene. They located the damaged Short [plane] eight miles from Nieuport. They had just reached it when a German submarine and four German torpedo boats destroyers arrived, and shortly after a French motor lighter, and a small craft zigzagging madly to avoid the courtesies of the German submarine.
>
> Flight Lieutenant Graham reached home safely with his machine which was

taken in tow by one of the patrol vessels. Flight Lieutenant Potvin was killed by his fall.

That ends the story, which happened in a half hour, and the blood and tragedy of that half hour was swiftly conveyed by these wonderful pigeons.[35]

John Staub, an American pilot who flew patrol missions out of Killingholme, England, wrote about his narrow rescue. On October 1918, Staub was first pilot on a four-man reconnaissance seaplane. He had just ended a long patrol and was about to return to Killingholme, when his aircraft suddenly went into a dive. Staub narrated:

> The plane plunged straight down—righted itself—plunged again—then slammed sideways into the sea. The sickening sound of cracking struts and tearing wings left little room for doubt that we were in trouble. We climbed on top the wrecked hull—wondering how long it would float under the weight of two motors, a few Lewis guns and ammunition.
>
> Suddenly, I heard a frantic shout, "The pigeons!" A dripping wet basket was quickly brought topside and opened. Two of the birds were dead. The last one was wet and chilled and barely alive—but it was our last hope of being rescued. We wrapped the bird in a dry woolen muffler and kept it as warm as possible. Within a half-hour the pigeon had somewhat revived. By this time, the sky was becoming dark and ominous. I decided not to wait any longer. I wrote a brief message and sealed it in the aluminum cylinder attached to the bird's right leg. Then, gingerly carrying the little fellow, I climbed to the highest point on the hull, and tossed the gutsy messenger into the air. The pigeon immediately dropped toward the water—but, promptly pulled up—skimming the waves—rose slowly as it gained strength—and disappeared into the twilight.

Meanwhile, at the homing pigeon station near Killingholme, night was approaching. A cold mist was falling, and a raw wind began whipping up angry waves that hammered the rocky coast. A British pigeon handler on duty recalled:

> It was teatime, and several of us were sitting in the mess room chatting around a roaring fire. One of the fellows told the story of a Portuguese naval officer who had mistaken a gift of pigeons for a dinner treat....
>
> Before anyone had a chance to comment on the veracity of the story, a bell sounded, announcing the return of one of our pigeons. I hurried to the loft. Huddling in a corner was a very wet, and shivering light blue pigeon. I carefully detached the capsule, put the bird in a basket, and quickly brought it to the warm mess room.
>
> The message was removed and smoothed out flat. The men gathered around me as I read it aloud: "Machine wrecked and breaking up south-east of Rock Point. Send boat!" A moment later, the boys on watch grabbed their ponchos and were out the door. I could hear the put-put of the motorboats as it plowed through the heavy surf and headed out to sea.

Chapter 4. Into the Breach

John Staub and his crew still clung to the struts of their wrecked and sinking seaplane. As night arrived, the wind increased and strong waves began pounding with a vengeance at the fragile raft of wood and cloth. Staub narrated:

> We were soaking wet and chilled to the bone. I was so cold that my fingers were numb and I could not feel my feet. Just as we were about to abandon all hope of being rescued the faint sound of a motor was heard. We shouted as loud as we could, guiding the boat to our location.
>
> Upon our safe return to the station, I noticed a small basket resting alongside a fireplace—and on top, a tired blue pigeon—nonchalantly preening its feathers.[36]

Ensign Kenneth R. Smith was stationed at Le Croisic, just south of Brittany on the coast of France. On a mission to search for German submarines, he lost his engine, and he and his crew pitched into the ocean.

> At 11:30 a.m. on Wednesday, 22 November 1917, we were notified that an enemy submarine was operating in our sector. I was assigned the search mission, and was enthusiastic at the prospect of engaging the enemy.
>
> I promptly selected my crew—Frank Brady as observer and W.M Wilkinson, mechanic and gunner. This was to be our first war flight, and we were skeptical about carrying live bombs. The only instructions we received had been given to us by a French officer who was not very fluent in English.
>
> We took off at noon. The weather was miserable—foggy, with a high sea running outside the breakwater. I headed in a southeasterly direction, and, within minutes lost sight of land. I had an improvised map, but it was not in a wind-proof case. This omission made navigating difficult, as none of us had any experience in reading this kind of map, or flying by dead reckoning. Furthermore, the air was very bumpy. And, it was only by snatching a glimpse of the seascape now and then, that I was able to figure out where I was going. We were running against the wind, and it took about 30 minutes to reach the vicinity where the submarine was last seen. I circled the area for about 20 minutes, then flew due west for about an hour. We still had not sighted the U-boat, so I decided to turn back and return to base.
>
> I was flying low, and had a good view of the high waves and white-caps. The fog was lifting, and I decided to make use of a strong tail wind. The thought had no sooner crossed my mind, however, than the motor began to sputter and miss. I kept flying straight—trying not to lose any more altitude. Suddenly, the engine quit. But, just as I was about to land the machine on the water, the motor came on—wide open. The quick burst of power caused the plane to strike the water at high speed. We bounced off the crest of a wave. I promptly shut off the power. The aircraft stalled and splashed. We hit so hard that I could hear the wood frame crack.
>
> Wilkinson checked the motor, but could find nothing wrong. I cranked the engine. She started up and began to run smoothly. We got rid of the bombs to lighten the load. I throttled the motor to full power for takeoff, but it skipped, popped and died. We tried several times to lift off the water without success. By this time—after pitching around in the waves for more than an hour—all hands were seasick.

War Pigeons

Just before dark, I remembered that we carried two pigeons. I released one of the birds with a message giving our estimated position, and asking for help. During the evening, the turbulent sea increased in violence, and we began to ship water. Watches were set for the night—one man bailed while the others slept.

At daylight, the last pigeon was set free. I was very skeptical about trusting our lives to a couple of young birds—but realized that this was war, and we made up our minds to pay the price if necessary. I added a few words to this last message—that I hoped were not over-dramatic—"Please tell friends we were game to the end!"

About noon, an airplane and dirigible were sighted on the horizon, but our prospects of being rescued were dashed as they turned around and headed north. I decided to try and taxi to a landfall, but we could not make much headway against the strong winds and high seas. My only choice was to get the machine off the water. Once again, I revved the motor to full power. The plane banked sharply to port. The left wind collapsed, and we slammed at an angle into the water. Seams opened in the hull, and the motor was dislodged from its mount.

In order to keep the aircraft balanced, one man had to stand out on the right wing while another bailed. Sleep for any of us was out of the question. I began to doubt if we could ride out the night. The physical and mental strain was beginning to tell on us. Out situation was desperate. The moans and groans of the plane—as each wave smashed against her hull—was nerve-racking. My throat was sore—like when I first had my tonsils out. Swallowing was extremely painful. We had no food or water—our thirst was aggravated by salt that kept crusting our lips from sea spray.

We managed to remain afloat throughout the night, but by morning, the broken left wing was splintering. Each time the plane rolled, mangled struts punched against the hull—threatening to tear a hole in the fabric. About noon, we cut the damaged wing adrift. The right wing now acted like a sea anchor—swinging us broadside to the swell. Our plight immediately worsened as the hull began to ship more water. We spent the rest of the day trying to cut loose the engine and the remaining wing.

Then, about dark, when our morale was about as low as it could get, Wilkinson sighted an object approaching from the south. From this distance it appeared to be the periscope of a submarine. We were helpless, and there was nothing I could do about it. We would either be picked up or blown out of the water. In our weakened condition, we did not care one way or the other.

You can imagine our relief and joy when a French torpedo boat came into view. One of the little pigeons had returned to its loft, and search craft had been sent out to find us. Within 15 minutes, after being rescued, the crushed hull of our seaplane finally sank.[37]

Such rescue stories became legendary, uniting man and pigeon again and again.

Besides helping to rescue downed airmen and sending emergency messages back to bases, pigeons sometimes simply led the way home. "There is a case on record," wrote Lieutenant McAttee in *Country*

Chapter 4. Into the Breach

Gentleman, "where one of our pilots while patrolling on the French coast completely lost his bearings when his compass was out of order. After aimlessly wandering around for some time, he thought of the two pigeons he carried. He accordingly liberated the birds and followed them in their flight which brought him back to his station."[38]

One of the most accomplished and celebrated American Navy birds was Peerless Pilot. He was stationed at Pauillac, France, at one of the American air stations, and began carrying messages for naval aviators at only 15 months old. In the last year of the war, alone, Peerless Pilot delivered nearly 200 messages from planes patrolling over the Atlantic Ocean.[39]

Navy pigeon Skipper, who operated at U.S. Naval Station, Brest, France, 1919. Skipper once delivered a message from 400 miles at sea, a stunning accomplishment (courtesy Naval History and Heritage Command).

While U.S. Navy pilots aided Allies in Europe and Britain, they also flew patrols in the United States, hunting for German submarines, which had begun to cruise the American coast, looking to sink merchant ships. A string of air patrol and training stations, complete with a pigeon force, stretched from Coco Solo at the Panama Canal, to Chatham, Massachusetts, to provide anti-submarine escorts for ships and to search for U-boats. Upward of 900 trained birds were operating in connection with sea patrols as part of the naval air service. Besides carrying emergency notices, the pigeons who flew with pilots from these bases also carried messages not desirable to send by wireless, which could be intercepted. Only two of these stations were at original locations of Professor Marion's homing pigeon messenger service, one at Hampton Roads, Virginia, the other at Key West.

To accommodate the new pigeon wings, a manual was written for the care and training of newly arrived pigeons at six to eight weeks old at the lofts of the naval air service. Updated from the 1896 version, the 1918 manual detailed every aspect of maintaining a successful loft at an

War Pigeons

Celebrated Navy pigeon Peerless Pilot being released in France in World War I. Neither the altitude nor the cold bothered Peerless Pilot or any other pigeon messenger (courtesy Naval History and Heritage Command).

air base, from construction and cleaning the building, to feeding and exercising the birds, how to hold a bird, put on a band, train them, and make reports and inventory. The actual method of release from an airplane was detailed in the Army's *The Pigeoneer, Student Manual for All Arms*. With the astounding effectiveness of the birds in both delivering messages and saving lives, the manual emphasized that a vital part of being a loft attendant was to bond with each bird in his loft. "...to know their birds well and help them overcome any fear or timidity. Emphasize that he's their friend, that they will receive food, water and other comforts through him."[40]

At the North Island flight school near San Diego, Lieutenant Alfred K. Warren, pilot and pigeon officer, explained the birds' role in training pilots.

> Our means of communication out there were pigeons. A little later on when we got some Curtiss HS-2L flying boats and went flying out over the Pacific Ocean to give some of our students some aerial navigation, we would take a crate of three homing pigeons along with us. I had the great responsibility of having command of

Chapter 4. Into the Breach

all of the homing pigeons, and I was the so-called "pigeon officer." We would take these three pigeons out in this crate, and if anything happened we would write a message and put it in a cylinder attached to the pigeon's leg and toss the bird over the side and hope he would get back in. It was a pretty efficient system. I only know of one or two birds that did not get back in.[41]

Lighter-than-aircraft (LTA)—airships and balloons—were manned by Navy pilots in World War I and they, too, carried pigeons. After fixed wing aircraft became a component of the Navy, interest in LTA surged, the Navy feeling that in coordination with seaplanes and surface craft, airships would provide the best protection against submarines. They could cover more territory and stay aloft longer than fixed wing aircraft, and with their ability to hover, LTAs could more readily detect the presence and position of submarines than faster-moving planes.

Sixteen B-class airships were built in the United States from 1917 to 1918 at four different companies. On the eastern seaboard of North America, LTAs operated out of nine naval air stations, some as trainers, others helping to patrol and defend the eastern coast of the United States against submarine threats.

Instruction in the LTAs occurred at many of the naval air stations, but concentrated at Akron, Ohio, Pensacola, Florida, and Rockaway, New York, where pilots trained in dirigibles, free balloons and kite balloons.[42] Kite balloons were large oval-shaped balloons, stabilized with fins and a tail. Beneath the bag was a basket in which observers were stationed. The balloon was connected to a towing ship and used mainly in convoys to spot submarines.

Many pilots who trained in the B-class ships, went on to serve at American naval air stations in Europe, flying European made airships. Some pilots trained at British and French air stations, but the mission remained to escort ships and deter U-boats off the coasts of Great Britain and France.

While on patrol off the east coast of the U.S., airships carried, along with Lewis guns and bombs, a lot of emergency equipment such as radio transmitters and receivers, flashlight and flares, signal pistols with red and green cartridges, life preservers, emergency rations and water, aircraft signal books and local charts, photographic equipment—and pigeons.[43] Homing pigeons had the same mission in LTAs, as in planes—to report on sub sightings, convey other patrol information, or bring emergency notices home. Earlier stories of survival and rescue at sea must have convinced the airship personnel to not leave home without a basket of the feathered lifesavers.

War Pigeons

The majority of naval patrols in airships saw very few encounters with German subs, but their presence deterred many U-boats from attacks. The role of airships, complete with complements of pigeons, only increased in importance during the next world war.

Chapter 5

More, Farther, Faster

> *Numbers of naval aviators undoubtedly owe their lives to these birds, and no plane is now allowed to leave a station unless it contains two or more carrier pigeons.* —Hearing Before the Committee on Naval Affairs of the House of Representatives, 1921

The success of pigeon messengers in the Great War was so profound that the Army, Navy and Marine Corps set up centers to breed pigeons and train both birds and pigeoneers. Other government agencies as well as private companies, some likely inspired by the military's success, employed pigeons in many aspects of American life. During this time of peace, pigeons were not short of work.

The Signal Corps' strength, like other branches of the Army, was greatly reduced after the war and many of its signal training camps shut down, including the Signal School at Fort Leavenworth. Camp Vail, New Jersey, was assigned the new location for the Signal School and became a permanent Signal Corps post. In 1925, it was renamed Fort Monmouth. The fort also housed the Signal Corps' Pigeon Breeding and Training Center. While many birds were sold after the war, some, including breeding pairs donated by the British Pigeon Service, returned home to Fort Monmouth. *Cher Ami* and other particularly heroic birds were housed in a special section called Churchill Loft. Retired from active duty, they were used for breeding due to their exceptional homing abilities, speed and aptitude. The Army also retained a few lofts along the Mexican border, in the Panama Canal Zone, and at several camps and air stations. By 1927, the Signal Corps maintained about one thousand birds in 16 lofts in the U.S., the Canal Zone, Hawaii, and the Philippines.[1]

At Fort Monmouth, the level of training accelerated during the interwar years. The center trained pigeons to fly farther and faster and paid special attention to teaching pigeons to fly at night, a skill that involved specialized care and instruction. To help train them for speed

War Pigeons

Typical pigeon lofts at a naval air station, ca. mid–1920s (official U.S. Navy photo).

and distance and to hone their homing instinct, the Army pigeoneers entered their birds in races. Some were civilian races set up by pigeon racing clubs. Others were against Navy birds, which probably proved as exciting and competitive as the Army-Navy football games.

Birds stayed on duty at Army bases around the country. At Brooks Airfield in Texas, the Army Balloon and Airship School included pigeons in their training programs. In free balloons, pigeons were the only means of communication. During training runs, the balloons sometimes landed 200 miles from home base. Pigeons were released every 30 to 60 minutes while the balloons were airborne, with a final bird released near the location of a landing.[2] This way, the balloonists could be picked up quickly, saving them a long walk to the nearest telephone. The pigeons were also carried in case of an emergency. The school was closed in 1922, but Army pigeons found other peacetime work.

In 1919, birds from the Army loft at Ft. Sam Houston, Texas, were taken on board an Army relief train that steamed to Corpus Christi, Texas, where a hurricane had devastated the area, killing a hundred people. The birds were released from the storm-damaged city, carrying the first news of conditions and of reestablishing communications 150 miles back to Fort Sam Houston. For several days, these pigeons were the sole source of communication.[3]

Chapter 5. More, Farther, Faster

Florida National Guard Signal Corps trainees with homing pigeons, ca. mid-1920s. After World War I, National Guard units were among many organizations that included pigeons in their communications plans (courtesy State Archives of Florida).

In another instance, an Army truck with 18 men drove to the top of Mt. Wilson in Los Angeles County from Ross Airfield. While returning to base, the truck went off the road, killing one man and injuring others. Although the men called for help via a nearby telephone, they also sent a couple of pigeons with a message as to their plight. Both pigeons and phone messages got through to Ross Field Headquarters and help was sent. The pigeons may have been released as a real-time training exercise, but their arrival would have offered a sense of security and the knowledge that should telephone not be available, their wings were.[4]

Also in California, Army pigeons flew fire patrols with the Army Air Service whose pilots reported to base by sending their reliable homing pigeons. After the war, the Air Service was looking for ways to find work for its airmen and to maintain public awareness of its worth. Colonel H.H. "Hap" Arnold, then commander of the Army Air Service on the West Coast, had met by chance Coert Du Bois, a U.S. district forest ranger in a San Francisco bar. They shared a mutual interest in aviation, struck up a conversation and put together a plan so spot forest fires from the air. Their start-up program was approved by the Department of

War Pigeons

Agriculture and the military, and soon air patrols began over the Cleveland National Forest, and the Angeles and San Bernardino Forests in California. The first patrol planes were Curtiss JN-4D and JN-4H models. Crews in the earlier 4D models could report only by dropping messages or landing and then telephoning. The pilots of these planes soon discovered a much more efficient and tried-and-true method—pigeons. If a fire were spotted, a bird was released to fly to headquarters with the urgent message.[5] The homing pigeon messenger service was grounded a month later when de Havilland DH-4s replaced the jennies. The de Havilland's more powerful radios eliminated the need for feathered couriers.

After the war, the 90th Aero Squadron, which had served at the St. Mihiel and Meuse-Argonne Offensives, demobilized with an attachment assigned to border patrol duty at Eagle Pass Airfield, Texas. The Mexican revolution had not yet concluded, and border skirmishes and

Aerial shot of a homing pigeon being tossed from the bow of a Navy seaplane above the Potomac River. Airman is being careful to toss the bird down and away from the engines, ca. 1920s (courtesy Naval History and Heritage Command).

Chapter 5. More, Farther, Faster

Releasing a homing pigeon from an airplane, ca. 1920s. Birds were tossed from different parts of the plane, depending on the type of plane and number of aviators on board (courtesy Naval History and Heritage Command).

violations continued. Flight "A" of the 90th squadron arrived at Eagle Pass in August 1919 with de Havilland DH-4 aircraft. One of the pilots flying observation missions along the border was a young Jimmy Doolittle (later to gain fame in World War II as the leader of the daring bombing raid on Tokyo). As an engineering officer, Doolittle led a mission in 1921 into Mexico to find a downed aircraft. Lieutenant Alexander Pearson, while attempting a transcontinental flight, had lost first oil pressure, then all power engine. He made a forced landing in a Mexican canyon near the Rio Grande, about 250 miles southeast of El Paso. Pearson survived and made it out, but the plane, according to government policy, needed to be destroyed so its technology would not fall into foreign hands.

When Doolittle reached the plane, he found it repairable. However, the engine needed a replacement motor. Radio didn't work in the canyon, and the pilots were far from a phone or telegraph office. Fortunately, Doolittle had brought along homing pigeons. He sent a message via pigeon back to the air base ordering the necessary parts. Soon the parts were delivered by parachutes and the repairs made. Hacking a 400-yard airstrip from the canyon floor, Doolittle piloted the plane home himself.[6]

Pigeons had served with the Marine Corps during the war, and the Corps maintained a small flock of its own homing pigeons at its Quantico barracks in Virginia. It was run by the Signal School. "The Signal School, operated by the 87th Company, conducts two courses, one in radio and one in telephony, each lasting six months. The 87th Company also operates the battalion radio station and the pigeon loft where homing pigeons are bred and trained for carrying messages."[7]

Homing pigeons being handed to a pilot before he leaves on a training flight from NAS Anacostia, February 1919. All Navy planes had to carry pigeons as part of the crew (courtesy Naval History and Heritage Command).

The Navy was just as enthusiastic about maintaining a force of pigeons as the Army and Marine Corps. After the war ended, the U.S. naval air stations abroad were closed, and some of the pigeons that had served alongside navy pilots were shipped in 1919 to the naval air station in Anacostia, D.C. Two years earlier, the Navy had received permission to use a parcel of Army land at the junction of the Anacostia and Potomac Rivers as a test site for their new seaplanes. NAS Anacostia was commissioned on January 1, 1919, with a contingent of nine seaplanes.[8]

The station boasted the largest pigeon school in the country. Impressed, even inspired, with the birds' service in the war, the Navy

Chapter 5. More, Farther, Faster

Female homing pigeon sits on eggs in a nest bowl at Naval Air Station, Anacostia, aware that a squeaker has just hatched (courtesy Naval History and Heritage Command).

intended to establish a dependable pigeon messenger service as a means of communication between aviators and their bases. As well as verification of radio messages, World War I had proven the birds to be critical in the event of a forced landing at sea or on isolated land—the difference between life and death.

Chief Quartermaster and long-time pigeon fancier, Henry Kubec, was in charge of training both birds and their handlers at Anacostia. Kubec taught would-be naval pigeoneers all about pigeons, their habits, health, disposition, how to care for them, breed, and fly them. The men trained six to 12 months and were then sent to other naval air stations that maintained pigeon lofts. Pensacola, Florida, Hampton Roads, Virginia, San Diego, California, Miami, Florida, Key West, Florida, Montauk, Long Island, Rockaway, Long Island, Chatham, Massachusetts, and Bay Shore, Long Island, had all built pigeon lofts as part of the revived pigeon messenger service.[9] The majority of the stations had about 60 pigeons each. Becoming a pigeoneer wasn't easy. Nearly

War Pigeons

Young pigeons in flight training, released from a boat on the Potomac River, about a half mile from their loft at NAS Anacostia. The handler is most likely Chief Quartermaster Henry Kubec, in charge of pigeon training at that station (courtesy Naval History and Heritage Command).

half the students failed Kubec's final exam. "...lacking the sympathetic understanding and patience needed for success."[10]

The 300 pigeons housed at Anacostia were by and large better students. Their rigorous training included being tossed from seaplanes flying from the station. "As many as 100 [birds] can be put in an F-5-L type seaplane and liberated at any altitude up to 10,000 feet," said Kubec. "Birds taken aloft in a plane must do so once a month to keep the birds acquainted with atmospheric conditions and to become accustomed to the roar of motors."[11] To foster their development as swift couriers, Kubec and his students also entered their birds into local civilian pigeon races, garnering many prizes. One bird flew the 1923 National Concourse Race of 110 miles at an average speed of 2,240 yards per minute, more than a mile a minute.[12] Another Anacostia bird, only a year after the program began, won a race against Army and Department of Agriculture birds, flying nearly 63 miles per hour.[13] The Navy gained a reputation for being a keen competitor.

Chapter 5. More, Farther, Faster

The pigeons at Anacostia became more valuable than Henri Marion would have imagined. The lofts were sunny and airy and had electricity and running water. A hospital stood ready if any of the birds grew ill. At night, armed guards patrolled the grounds. Only the most cosseted thoroughbred racehorses received care equal to that of the birds of the Anacostia pigeon wing.

With a new manual issued to all Navy pigeon lofts, a Quartermaster rating of "Pigeon"— Q.M. (P)—in place, a main breeding and training center at Anacostia, and a new appreciation for the birds' value, a cutting-edge naval pigeon messenger service thrived.

In 1921 a Hearing Before the Committee on Naval Affairs of the House of Representatives emphasized the vital role of homing pigeons in the Navy Air Service and the policy that no plane leave the ground without them.

Carrier pigeon communication service has been developed enormously. Navy pigeons have won 75% of all races in which they have been entered in competition

Key to a military pigeon's health and performance is cool, fresh water for bathing. This pan is on top of a loft, but many lofts were equipped inside with running water bathing systems, ca. 1920s (courtesy Naval History and Heritage Command).

with the Army pigeon service and various pigeon clubs throughout the country. The Navy has assisted breeders of carrier pigeons in selecting the breed of pigeon for building up swift and reliable fliers and birds of great endurance. The Navy breeds its own pigeons and a most successful strain of birds with respect to the qualifications above outlined is now being bred at the naval air station at Anacostia. Numbers of naval aviators undoubtedly owe their lives to these birds, and no plane is now allowed to leave a station unless it contains two or more carrier pigeons.[14]

By 1926, the Navy's pigeon service consisted of 12 lofts and about 800 birds. The San Diego Naval Air Station bred and trained pigeons as did the North Island base. The Coronado (CA) Historical Society makes many references to the use of homing pigeons by Army and Navy aviators in the 1920s at the latter base. A 2014 blog entry by Bruce Linder summarized some of the Society's information:

> Just as North Island had become a national center for radio experiments, it was also one of the Armed Forces' largest centers for carrier pigeons that populated at least four pigeon lofts situated along the western edge of the base. Carrier pigeons came into some renown during World War I for their use in carrying battlefield messages. They were especially useful for aviators who were forced down and needed to send their position back to their units. Planes began to routinely carry pigeons held in small containers either on the wings or tucked behind the pilot's seat. From 1918 to the mid-twenties it was basic policy for every Army or Navy aircraft of LTA craft to carry pigeons.
>
> Pigeons at the North Island Pigeons Station probably numbered more than 200. They were exercised daily and carefully bred. Training for North Island pigeons started with short flights from parks in Coronado back to the station. Once the fledgling birds had that routine down, longer flights were attempted and included pigeon races with private pigeon clubs throughout Southern California.[15]

In the 1920s homing pigeons made a short stint back at sea duty. The USS *Langley*, a converted collier, was commissioned in March 1922 as the Navy's first aircraft carrier. Built on the stern, between five-inch guns, was a pigeon loft, the idea being to train the birds to return to the ship from aircraft sent off the deck. Experiments with them were largely unsuccessful, probably due to a lack of careful training from the *Langley*. As long as the pigeons were released a few at a time for exercise, they returned to the ship, but when the whole flock was released while the *Langley* was anchored off Tangier Island, for example, the pigeons flew back to the Norfolk Navy Yard. Early plans for the building of the *Lexington* and *Saratoga* included compartments for pigeons. The suggestion was later scrapped.[16]

Navy birds also served with firefighters. In the Northwest, the U.S. Forest Service borrowed Navy pigeons to use as couriers between fire

Chapter 5. More, Farther, Faster

A group of thirty-four planes rests on the flight deck of the USS *Langley* stationed at Pearl Harbor, 1928, while a flock of pigeons rests in a loft at the stern under the flag (official U.S. Navy photograph).

lines and headquarters in mountainous regions.[17] From 1919 to 1921, the Forest Service used pigeons and equipment borrowed from the Navy to convey messages from firefighters at the front to headquarters in northwest states, including Oregon and Idaho. The pigeons were especially effective in mountainous regions, where travel was difficult. In one instance, a ranger took two birds to the scene of a fire and released one to call for help. When the crew brought the blaze under control, the other bird was sent to cancel the call. As a means of certain and quick communication, the rangers found nothing more effective.

Navy birds went on many official government excursions. In 1925, Donald E. Macmillan headed an expedition to the Arctic. Navy birds specially selected and trained for difficult conditions in the frigid North were chosen to accompany the expedition. The plan was to have them fly with pilots in seaplanes exploring the land by air in case there was an accident to one of the planes. Unfortunately, during their first flight from their loft at the Etah home base, only four birds returned from the 20 sent out. It was thought the others were killed by arctic falcons.[18]

In the summer of 1926, the U.S. Geological Survey conducted an aerial survey of southeast Alaska, organized by the Navy. Since Alaska was far from an air base, a tender was needed to serve the planes and provide supplies for the base. They outfitted a former minesweeper, USS *Gannet*, on loan from the aircraft carrier, *Langley*. However the *Gannet* couldn't quarter both her own crew as well as the aviation personnel, so she was accompanied by a covered barge, 110 feet long and 40 feet wide. This barge was outfitted with sleeping quarters for the aviation crew, a galley, a shop for the care of the plane motors, a photographic laboratory where film could be developed immediately from a mapping flight, radio equipment, hot and cold showers and a barber shop.[19]

The barge, referred to as the Pigeon Roost, also supported a pigeon loft on the upper section of the roof line. (Perhaps the pigeons had come from the *Langley* before the lofts were turned into officers' quarters.) Although the expedition had radio sets, they were heavy and bulky. Radio communication at sea level in mountainous areas was erratic, as the mountains trapped the passage of radio waves. Since the expedition planes would fly at high altitudes, sometimes up to 15,000 feet, the load needed to be as light as possible. A much better means of communication were homing pigeons. The pigeons went with pilots of the amphibious Loening planes during the surveys, to be released in the event of a mishap. Other than in standard trials, the pigeons were never needed for an emergency. Just once were they used to report a delay in a plane's arrival.

Only two of the three Loenings assigned to the survey were used for mapping. The third was equipped with a radio and a pilot and stayed on the beach, ready to take off to search for any plane that failed to return to base within 45 minutes of its schedule. All planes carried emergency

Chapter 5. More, Farther, Faster

rations for five days, guns, ammunition, fish tackles smoke flares and homing pigeons in case of a forced landing.

The expedition flew for 90 days and photographed 10,000 miles of southeast Alaska, generating 17, 280 negatives. The information gathered from these photos stimulated several industries in the region, including forestry, mining and especially fishing.[20]

Yet another government agency, the Civilian Conservation Corps (CCC), found a use for homing pigeons, this time with the all African American Company 2923-C. The CCC was created to employ young men between the ages of 17 and 23 in paramilitary work camps where they took on various conservation projects. The camps, started by Franklin Roosevelt, were administered by the U.S. Army. Government agencies, such as the National Park Service and U.S. Forest Service, located suitable camp sites, chose work projects and supervised them. In California, the CCC built roads and trails, protected stream beds and planted trees, but one of their main responsibilities was to prevent and fight fires. Hundreds of lookout houses and towers were built, one of the biggest projects being the Ponderosa Way firebreak and truck trail, which spanned nearly 800 miles down the length of the Sierras. Company 2923-C at Camp La Cienega in the Cleveland National Forest was one of the camps that regularly responded to fires. They became famous for their firefighting skills, in part because they were the first to use homing pigeons to help them communicate. Raised by firefighting foreman Charles L. Hayes, the homing pigeons lent a distinct advantage as they were able to rely messages directly from the fire lines back to the base camp when other means were not practical. Working under foreman Hayes, the company enrollees built the lofts, raised the pigeons in the camp then trained them to fly from fire areas to fire-suppression camps.[21] No doubt the pigeons helped Company 2923-C maintain a highly distinguished record.

As they had nearly 100 years earlier, before the military had considered feathered messengers, pigeons continued to be a boon to U.S. businesses, both large corporations and individuals. In the 1920s, California Sperry Flour Company salesmen used pigeons to carry orders from bakers to the company loft near the warehouse. Sperry truck drivers took pigeons along delivery routes, and if a customer wanted an additional order, the driver attached a message to a pigeon and released it to fly back to its warehouse loft. By 1929, there were 15 active lofts in the Sperry system, with nearly 300 pigeons ready to fly for the company.[22]

According to an article in the *San Antonio Express*, June 7, 1931, at least one Texas oil company put homers to work to carry messages between drilling camps and headquarters. John F. Camp, for example, had an office in San Antonio and oil wells in McMullen County. Since the camp was far from a telephone, he employed pigeons as messengers. The birds, explained the article, saved on gas and tires and "made communication possible when dirt roads were impassable."[23]

The Express Newspaper Company itself started its own pigeon express to save time. The company, which published a morning and evening paper, wanted a faster way to get action photos from sporting events to the newsroom. "Photographs of the stirring football game between the University of Texas and Louisiana State University held in Austin came, literally, as the pigeon flies," exclaimed the *Express* in 1938. "Twelve homing pigeons, trained and tested for many months, flew high above the traffic between Austin and San Antonio, to shatter speed records and journalistic precedent in Texas, while delivering pictures of the game for reproduction on deadline for the street edition of the Sunday issue."[24] The paper was only the second in the south, after the New Orleans *Times-Picayune* to employ a bird delivery service.

In the late1930s, Joel Parker, an enterprising young pigeon fancier from Manasquan, New Jersey, built a business sending his smooth, sleek Stassart and Bastin pigeons out with commercial fishermen and deep-sea anglers. Ship-to-shore radios were bulky and expensive, with short ranges. The fishing fleets that took Joel's birds sent messages back to shore announcing the size of the catch that day, their estimated arrival, or calling for help after an engine failure or unexpected bad weather. Joel earned enough money to fund his college education. After college, he served in World War II as a tail gunner. His pigeons served in the war, too, as messengers in the Army Signal Corps.[25]

Even an airplane company saw the value of homing pigeons. In 1920, Aeromarine began America's first official international airmail service between Key West, Florida, and Cuba using flying boats bought from the Navy. The company also inaugurated America's first scheduled international passenger service, and replaced cumbersome radio sets with seaworthy pigeons to carry messages during flights. (Rumors persist that if a pilot lost his bearings, he would release a bird and follow it home to Key West. It wouldn't be the first time.)

Between the world wars, reports of Navy and Army pigeons in civilian races and of their success in businesses and other government activities, kept their role as important communications tools in the minds of the public and the military. From aiding firefighters to flying messages

Chapter 5. More, Farther, Faster

for a flour company and helping a young man go to college, there seemed to be no end to the benefits received from employing homing pigeons. That they maintained visibility in the eyes of the military and public proved invaluable, as barely 30 years after the war to end all wars, homing pigeons would be called up again.

Chapter 6

A Call for Champions

> *Our men gave first consideration to the birds. In Africa, if there was but one cup of water available, the birds drank before the men.*—Lt. Charles A. Koestar, U.S. Army Pigeoneer

World War II was a mobile war, fought on four of the globe's seven continents. Reliable and swift communication would prove paramount to success. The advent of World War II brought to the armed forces vastly improved radio and other communications technology, including FM radio, portable and mobile radio equipment, radar, walkie-talkies, radio facsimile equipment, and teletypewriter circuits. The Navy had built the world's biggest radio tower, and the Army Air Service had developed long-range, medium-range, and short-range air-to-ground and air-to-air communications. The globe was starting to shrink.

Despite these mammoth leaps in technology, American armed forces still maintained flocks of pigeons as supplemental and emergency communication. In fact, populations of military pigeons were exploding. By the time the Japanese attacked Pearl Harbor on December 7, 1941, both the Army and Navy had dozens of breeding and training centers across America. The pigeon center at Fort Monmouth, New Jersey, now managed 20 lofts, under the command of Sergeant Major Clifford Poutré.[1] A census of all racing pigeon lofts had been taken, as well as a commitment from pigeon owners to work with the government if needed. A law against keeping or killing government-owned pigeons was passed. It was similar to the one enacted during World War I, with the same punishment—a fine of $100 and /or jail time. Pigeons had become serious government business.

Realizing that another world war would demand more pigeons than were currently being bred and trained at military facilities, the Office of the Chief Signal Office issued on January 9, 1942, a call to civilian pigeon fanciers for young healthy birds.[2] The Army offered to buy each bird for

Chapter 6. A Call for Champions

Sailor releasing a pigeon from a Navy Yard Patrol boat on a training flight over the water (courtesy U.S. Naval Institute)

$5.00, about half the market price, but hoped some would be donated. The only qualification for a feathered recruit was that it could fly 200 miles. The Army wasn't disappointed. Fanciers from around the country contributed offspring of champion fliers and sometimes even the champions themselves. Some outstanding birds had won races that had covered more than 600 miles in a day, at speeds up to 60 miles per hour. These birds, bred from winning families of pigeons, became the parents of war pigeons, birds that, beyond death, would not fail in their mission. They arrived at the Signal Corps by the thousands.[3]

The Signal Corps Pigeon Service bred pigeons and trained them, along with pigeoneers, at several bases, including Fort Monmouth, New Jersey, Fort Sam Houston, Texas, Fort Benning, Georgia, and Camp Crowder, Missouri. The aim was to breed the fastest, strongest birds with the best homing instinct. While a World War I pigeon could fly about 200 miles in one flight, the goal for World War II birds doubled that distance. Under Poutré, the Signal Corps had the know-how. New manuals detailed everything about military pigeons from breeding them to treating injuries, along with a training program that emphasized kindness and patience. According the War Department's Technical Manual for the homing pigeon,

> The pigeon is highly sensitive and responsive to treatment. Of great importance in this respect are kindness, firmness, and calmness of the personnel handling it, and the reward given the pigeon for good performance. The pigeon prizes its home, and every effort should be made to increase the attractiveness thereof by proper loft construction, management, and the maintenance of buildings and grounds.[4]

A reliable pigeon courier took about eight weeks to train from the time the chick hatched. At four weeks, the squeaker was taken from the nest and placed in a mobile loft, as these moving coops would be a pigeon soldier's home for the duration of its duty overseas. Mobile loft training was similar to that used in the previous world war. For two to three weeks, the loft was moved daily. The bird flew short distances, three times a day for several days so it could learn its bearings and memorize the color and shape of its loft. In combat, the loft would move often, so recognizing a certain type was paramount in the bird's training. By the eighth week, when the bird had built up enough stamina to fly for an hour, it was trained to fly 50 to 60 miles, and then farther. If successful, the pigeon was considered combat ready.

In August 1942, the Pigeon Breeding and Training Center was transferred to Camp Crowder, Missouri, with a detachment retained at Fort Monmouth. Camp Crowder became the country's largest pigeon breeding and training center, with about 12,000 pigeons maintained at its peak under the command of now–Major Poutré. While in charge of the Camp Crowder center, Poutré became renowned for training pigeons to home to mobile lofts and to fly at night.[5]

Chapter 6. A Call for Champions

Thousands of pigeon recruits were trained. Fort Sam Houston, Texas, and Fort Benning, Georgia, were supplemental breeding bases, each with about 5000 pigeons. Fort Meade, Maryland, was home to the 281st Signal Pigeon Company with about 4500 pigeons, and the 828th Signal Pigeon Replacement Company housed 6000 pigeons. Later the 281st Signal Pigeon Company was transferred to Fort Jackson, outside Columbia, South Carolina. Camp Claiborne, Louisiana, was home to the 280th and 283rd Signal Pigeon Companies.[6]

Over the course of the war, the U.S. Signal Corps Army Pigeon Service trained a total of 54,000 homing pigeons, and used 36,000 overseas.[7] About 12 signal pigeon companies served all over the world with American soldiers and airmen, delivering messages at every theater of operation. The mission, according to the U.S. War Department, was clear: "to provide pigeons as a means of signal communication to armies, corps, divisions or task forces and to ensure reliable communication by these birds at all times and under all conditions."[8]

Nearly all types of Army units had use for pigeon messengers. The birds carried map overlays, particularly valuable during combat. They transmitted reports from patrols and recon units, they carried messages from airplanes to their headquarters or to combat commanders, from amphibious units to headquarters, from airborne infantry and parachute troops to their rear echelon, when radio silence had to be maintained, and when other modes of communication failed.

Homing pigeons performed their duties in climates and over terrain impossible to negotiate any other way. In mountainous areas, for example, laying telephone or telegraph wire was arduous and time consuming. The range of radio sets was short, and dead spaces in radio reception were another problem. In jungle operations, visual signaling was often impossible, and use of runners slow and hazardous. Poor roads hindered message delivery by vehicle.

Homing pigeons were effective on the battlefield partly because of their natural physical characteristics. They are robust and resilient and when trained properly, exhibit almost supernatural qualities. Trained well, an Army pigeon flew far and fast, over 100 miles up to 60 miles per hour. They flew easily at altitudes of 30,000 feet without any deleterious effects. Even at 35,000 feet, when the air crew wore oxygen masks and heavy clothing against minus 45-degree temperatures, the pigeons simply fluffed up their feathers. Light rain didn't slow them because of a protective coating on their feathers, called bloom. Extreme cold didn't bother them either, due to a high body temperature of around 107 degrees, Fahrenheit. Nor did the heat. Pigeons were released in temperatures as high as 120 degrees in the shade. Well suited to desert warfare, they possess a transparent third eyelid to protect their eyes from sand and dust.[9] Where couldn't they serve?

Beyond these extraordinary physical attributes, pigeons possess a high intelligence and persistence, qualities that make them extremely reliable for carrying messages. As Major Poutré once said, "Pigeons are highly intelligent ... we breed for intelligence first of all. Intelligence and stamina. Speed is not important.... What we want is a bird that will get back, one that won't get flustered, one that is intelligent enough to be self-reliant."[10]

Even to the most skeptical soldier, and there were many, the homing pigeon quickly proved its capabilities. Ninety-nine percent of messages sent by pigeons during tactical operations were delivered. And they did this at speeds averaging 37.5 miles per hour, and up to 50 or 60 miles per hour, over distances up to 100 miles, sometimes farther.[11] They had to be reliable. The direction of a battle and the lives of many people rested on their abilities.

The benefits of using homing pigeons depended heavily on their health and well-being. If pigeons were hungry, thirsty, sick or uncomfortable, they did not perform at their full potential. Like racehorses, military pigeons had to be maintained in perfect physical condition. The military recognized this fully in World War II and paid close attention to their welfare.

With that in mind, World War II saw veterinary care for Army signal pigeons for the first time. Two key concerns emerged with the inclusion of veterinary care: one, the health of the bird was extremely important, and preventative care should be offered; and two, a pigeoneer needed to have a role in the veterinary care of his birds. A change from the early 1920s when it was believed that pigeoneers should not help a sick bird recover, a pigeoneer's knowledge of medicines and simple procedures, such as sewing up a wound, saved many birds, some of whom recovered to fly again.

In 1941, for the first time in the Signal Corps' history, a Veterinary Service officer was assigned to Fort Monmouth Pigeon Breeding and Training Center. The Veterinary Service assisted in the care, feeding, housing and transporting of pigeons and had enormous impact on the success of the pigeon service. These veterinarians studied pigeon diseases, inoculated birds and quarantined them when necessary. World War II also saw the development and wide use of vaccinations for

Chapter 6. A Call for Champions

pigeons, particularly for pigeon pox, a common illness. Overseas, the Veterinarian Service focused on a healthy feed supply, clean water and housing. "A balanced feed and good feeding practices were essential to the well-being of the signal pigeons and had a direct bearing on their homing proficiency."[12] Not only did the feed need to arrive clean and dry and without infestation, it had to contain the right vitamins. Clean water was recognized as vital to a pigeon's health. The lofts, they recommended, should be clean and airy and remodeled, depending on the climate.

The Signal Corps Pigeon Service of World War II was highly organized and efficient. Each of three combat platoons in a signal pigeon company was organized into a headquarters section, breeding section and four combat sections. The combat sections normally operated six lofts and were responsible for the continuous training of birds, preparing them to be transported in containers, and relaying messages that arrived at lofts to the proper authorities. Containers carried two or four birds, and crates had a 10-bird capacity. Pigeoneers were also responsible for parachute equipment and message capsules.[13]

To ensure that the complex process of using pigeon couriers ran smoothly and effectively, most pigeoneers chosen for the job had previous experience caring for them. According to the Signal Pigeon Company Field Manual, pigeoneers also needed specific personality traits: "...dependability in his duties, kindness so his birds gain confidence and trust him, patience, neatness to maintain an attractive comfortable loft for the birds, and a power of accurate description, able to observe details readily and accurately in order to note and learn the characteristics of individual pigeons."[14] For most pigeoneers, these traits were already there. Pigeoneer Jerome Pratt believed, "Pigeoneers were a different kind of soldier. Their morale was above average because they were doing a job that had been their hobby in civilian life."[15]

Whether from a stationary or mobile loft, homing pigeons provided one-way communication from front lines to the rear. Pigeons were usually double-tossed—one bird carrying the original message, the other a duplicate. The lofts were established as quickly as possible so that signal pigeon officers could settle, or train, their birds to fly to a new location, distribute them to combat units, and forward messages received. If a message taken from a bird could not be delivered promptly in person, the pigeoneer transmitted it via telephone. Secret messages were entrusted to pigeons, as silence was ensured if they were intercepted.

During World War II, about 12 American pigeon units were activated. The European theater saw the most, with the 277th, 278th, 282nd,

War Pigeons

A soldier recovers two pigeon cages dropped by a nine-foot parachute from a Stinson L5 airplane during maneuvers at Hunter Liggett Military Reservation, California, March 1944. The birds belonged to the 283rd Signal Pigeon Company and were being used to test the practicality of pigeon messaging in difficult terrain (from the collection of The National WWII Museum).

284th, 285th, and the 2nd platoon of the 280th units serving. The other platoon of 280th served in the China-Burma-India theater; the 279th in the Central Pacific, the 1st platoon of the 281st in the SW Pacific, and the 209th and provisional 6681st in the Mediterranean. Pigeon units also went to New Caledonia, Ladd Field in Alaska and the Caribbean Defense Command (including the Panama Canal Department). Several signal pigeon companies trained in the U.S. with the Army Air Service. Some of these companies became known for their expert night flying, although in combat this was not often practiced.

Those birds going to certain locations such as Panama, faced an unusually large danger from hawks. To those pigeoneers, *The Pigeoneer, Student Manual for All Arms* suggested trying an ancient deterrent, whistles. Pigeon whistles, also called pigeon flutes, originated in China over 1000 years ago and were used in many Asian countries to scare away winged predators as well as create haunting music. Weighing only a few grams, they were carved from small gourds, pieces of horn, reed

Chapter 6. A Call for Champions

tubes, or bamboo pipes. A whistle was attached to the bird's tail and as it flew, the rush of air caused the whistle to sound, startling the hawk or falcon. The whistle, according to the manual, could be left on the bird, as it caused no discomfort and did not interfere with breeding. It needed to be removed only once a year when the pigeon molted.[16]

The 828th was organized as a non-combative unit and remained in the U.S. with a sizable mission. It was to supply pigeon communication at home in case of an emergency, as well as to train replacement personnel. The 828th also field-tested new equipment, instructed other branches of the service and trained officers and enlisted men as combat teams for special overseas missions. Some of these specialists were assigned to the Office of Strategic Services (OSS) to work behind enemy lines, along with homing pigeons. Captain Morris Y. Lederman headed such a team in Burma, and Lieutenant John A. Webb in China.[17]

Personal accounts relate the heroic accomplishments of World War II pigeons. In his memoir, Jerome Pratt, then a Lieutenant Colonel, served in the 285th Signal Pigeon Company assigned to Headquarters, 12th Army Group in Europe. He arrived in England on August 11, 1944, a couple of months after D-Day, and described in his book the use of pigeons in that invasion. He explained that what took place pre-invasion had been very secret, with pigeons playing an important role in collecting information that made the landings in Normandy a success.

> The English fanciers loaned their lofts and birds to the American pigeoneers to support the First U.S. Army in the invasion of the European continent. These civilian fanciers of Plymouth had already established quite a war record in support of the Royal Air Force from 1939 to 1942. Their pigeons had made about 10,000 war service trips with bomber commands.
>
> Many of the flights were over distances of up to 160 miles. The longest flight was from 220 miles out at sea. Some of their birds had gone with secret agents to France, Belgium and Holland; twenty of them brought back very important messages.
>
> On D-Day, 80 of 600 civilian loaned pigeons from Plymouth accompanying the invasion forces were strapped to the chests of U.S. paratroopers that jumped among the enemy troops that momentous morning in the hours of darkness. Only four of the 80 birds came home to England and none carried messages, but three of the four were covered with the blood of their paratrooper partners. It is assumed the others perished with the troopers as they were intercepted by the overwhelming enemy forces. Four other Plymouth based pigeons brought back messages from the Normandy beaches that day.[18]

Pratt included an account, written sometime soon after the war by H.C. Woodman of the British National Pigeon Service, of one famous

War Pigeons

pigeon, Mary of Exeter, who was part of an English volunteer force such as those from Plymouth. She flew some missions with American forces, and her story casts a keen light on the singular toughness of homing pigeons and the undeniable bond with their handlers.

Mary was a black check hen with a shiny aluminum bracelet on her leg. Born early in 1940, Mary, as a youngster, flew all the race points to Darby. She flew during the year of her birth nearly one thousand miles and won several nice prizes. Showing signs of dogged courage, Mary was enlisted in the Exeter Group on the National Pigeon Service lines of defensive communications. Her beat was from Taunton to Exeter but often she was transferred to fly from Plymouth to Exeter. To test Mary's flying capabilities during 1941, she was released one morning in Perth, Scotland, 392 miles away and flew the long distance home to Exeter that same day. One day during 1942 after being released with a message from the United States VIII Corps, she failed to return to her loft. Had she deserted? No, on the fourth day she dropped into her loft covered with blood. She had been attacked by a Perigrin Falcon and her neck and breast had been badly ripped open. Her owner, now very attached to Mary, cleaned her wounds and put seven stitches in her little body. Three months later, fully recovered, Mary was once more winging her way across the moor with her messages strapped to her leg.

Two months later, Mary was missing again. This time for three weeks. One evening, just before dark, she turned up at the loft. How she had reached home was a mystery. She had been shot under the wing. Four pellets were taken from her wing and side and once again Mary was stitched up to go back to the beat again. But bad luck still dogged her. Came the Exeter blitz and a 1,100 pound delayed action bomb fell on the doorstep of her master's house, so Mary, said the Vicar, with some thirty other service pigeons were evacuated to a safe place. Some safe place! The very next evening Jerry dropped a bomb outside the garage where Mary and her pals had been billetted.

Nineteen of them that night were killed on active service. Mary, who was in one of the baskets, was thrown clear and was found early next morning at the loft none the worse for her experience but very nervous.

Back on the service beat, Mary again failed to come home. Ten days later she was reported to her owner by the police. She had been picked up by a farmer in one of his fields. When Mary was brought to the loft, the master had tears in his eyes. Once again a perigrin had swooped to kill her. By some miracle Mary had escaped the cruel killer, but not before the perigrin had torn her open from head to keel, from the gaping wound across her breast hung her crop. The master once again bathed her wounds, pushed back the crop and stitched her up. By now, she had 22 stitches in her body and her owner found to his dismay that not only had she a scar eight inches long but that her neck was permanently injured by the talon of the killer. Undismayed, the master who was one of Exeter's finest bootmakers, set to work to make Mary a leather collar four inches wide for her neck.

For a month, he kept her in a cage and fed her by hand so that Mary would not try to bend her neck. After a month, the collar was take off. Mary's head was erect again—a marvel of surgical ingenuity.

Now that the wars are over, Mary does not have to fly the weary beat over Dart-

Chapter 6. A Call for Champions

moor, graveyard of some many grand service pigeons, prey of the falcons and of guns. Mary is now proudly exhibited by the master, Charles Brewer of Exeter, at lectures and fetes. Over 100 pounds was collected for the Red Cross by this courageous Exeter pigeon who has suffered for her country's sake like the bravest soldier, with a broken neck and 22 stitches in her little body. A grand girl is Mary.[19]

As part of the Headquarters, 12th Army Group, Pratt's company was responsible for training replacement pigeons for United States and French forces under the group. By February of 1945, his company had personnel and pigeons in five countries: England, France, Luxembourg, Belgium and Germany and had participated in three campaigns in Rhineland, Ardennes and Central Europe.

One of the greatest needs for pigeon communication, Pratt said, was at river crossings, where the battalion headquarters were separated from their regiments. At these points they were without wire communications and maintained radio silence. Usually, the nonstop barrage of artillery fire coming from both sides across the river delayed a foot messenger until dark. But pigeons could fly during the day, arriving with a message several hours, and sometimes a full day, earlier than other means. So vital were pigeons at these crossings, that soldiers carried them across the rivers in anything they could sling around their bodies, from ammunition bags to sugar sacks.[20]

When the 12th Army Group entered Germany, one of Pratt's priorities was to search for civilian lofts and seize any pigeons found. A few lofts commandeered and birds were flown with Allied messages. In other cases, the pigeoneers clipped feathers on one wing of the birds to prevent them from flying. As the war neared its end, Pratt's company stepped up their mission, and included military lofts, as they believed the Germans would increase their use of pigeons as their other means of communication ceased to operate.

Eventually, Pratt's pigeoneers investigated 2,821 cities and villages, located 1,175 homing pigeon lofts, and clipped the wings of 15,057 birds. They also examined the records of Germany's national homing pigeon organization, which had been active since 1884. They found an astounding 6,500 affiliated local clubs with a membership of 65,000 at the time Germany was taken over by the Nazi Party in 1933.[21]

A diary written by pigeoneer Frank Hauck offers another opportunity to understand what it was like on the front lines with the Signal Corps Pigeon Service. Hauck was part of the 278th pigeon unit that served with the Ninth Army Ground Forces in France, Holland, Belgium and Germany. Unlike many other pigeoneers, he hadn't started

War Pigeons

out raising pigeons. Hauck entered the Army April 17, 1943, and began mechanics school in Gulfport, Mississippi. One morning, he was transferred to a pigeon camp, and that was the end of being an Army mechanic. It was lucky he found pigeoneering to his liking. Corporal Hauck's Operation Log of 278th Signal Pigeon Company Overseas 1st Platoon, traces his journey from Gulfport, Mississippi, in 1943 through the European Theater to the unit's disbandment on October 12, 1945.

Hauck left New York August 11, 1944, on the transport, SS *John Ericsson*. He landed in England and with his company took a land and sea transport (LST) to Normandy. His log from that point to May 1945, gives insight into the challenges pigeoneers faced while moving quickly with ground forces, setting up lofts in a variety of locations and settling their birds, stealing civilian and enemy pigeons, and always, the danger, including sabotage. Rather than relating pigeon activity on the front lines, Hauck notes in short, riveting bursts of detail what it was like for the pigeoneers. Some of his log entries:

September 25–26, 1944
Saw pillboxes that once protected the shore line. Wrecked landing craft all over the beach.

September 26–October 10, 1944
September 26 beached late afternoon (in Normandy). Went to first pigeon area 13 miles from Cherbourg.
Water was choppy and weather overcast. Boat ran up on beach late in evening. Beach was plenty beat up. Was dark when they finally opened the doors and we drove off. Drove up a very rough road to a spot about 10 miles from beach where we set up for night. Left for a campsite near Cherbourg where we set up and got our birds flying. Birds were very stiff and took long time to limber them up.

October 10–13, 1944
Left Normandy early in the morning of 10th Oct. for the front. Drove through Paris morning of the 12th. Camped in forests at night and slept atop of jeep which was very comfortable and dry. Had Naylor and Zink riding with me. Passed through Belgium on 12th somewhere near the Seigfried Line. Passed through Luxembourg.

October 14, 1944
October 14 arrived with convoy in Maastrick, Holland continued to Valkenbourg where we were billeted in Valkenbourg Castle; set up lofts surrounding mote.
It is still raining every day and its miserable and muddy out in the field training the birds. Half of us billeted in half of a hotel in town. This place was just taken and there is still sniping and shooting all night long. Bombs dropped near us one night and almost demolished hotel. Woman who ran hotel was later taken as a spy. We traveled back and forth from castle only during daylight hours.

Chapter 6. A Call for Champions

October 26, 1944
October 26 left Valdenbourg Castle (Netherlands) for Tongeren, Belgium, where we set up our lofts behind a big mansion. Buzz bombs are coming over every 20 minutes here. Can see them very closely as large tongues of flame trail the bomb.

November 9, 1944
November 9 left for Germany Rimburg. Set up loft on roof for our flying pigeons. Had Germans throw shells at us while hijacking their pigeons. Buzz bombs are going off quite frequently. Found a place where people were very friendly so we took 2 rooms on second floor of house. Set up our lofts and put one on small roof outside our window. Front only ¾ mile away as the crow flies. Starting training birds immediately. Found a loft nearby and tried to get these birds but was observed by enemy and got shelled.

December 25, 1944
Battle of the Bulge is on and our front line at Linnich is very thin. A lot of air activity going on every day. Kelley, Schultz and I went for a trailer load of coal today and were caught in a barrage as we were souvenir hunting in a house in Sigguath [spelling] near Gelsenkirchen [Gilenkirchen]. Got out lucky as 5 shells hit all around us and brought down many a house. One shell went through church steeple ½ block away. Paratroopers are now being dropped every nite. Caught 3 spies at the bridge this afternoon … passing as Hollanders…

April 12–13, 1945
Left Herford April 12 for Osterberg on the Elbe. We drove 140 ahead with the tanks. It was a long and dangerous ride. German soldiers are standing around waiting to be taken prisoner. Passed through towns that had no GIs in them yet. The pigeoneers are spearheading. We rolled into Osterberg 1 hour behind the tanks. A Panzer division was bypassed on our way here. They cut our M.S.R. for 3 days which cut us off and we had no supplies coming up to us. Took a house on the outside of town and set up [pigeon lofts].

Opened window one morning just in time to see a jerry plane bomb houses adjoining us. One slug went through my jeep floor.[22]

The work of pigeons in the North African and Italian campaigns is well documented by Gordon H. Hayes in his memoir, *Pigeons That Went to War.* Hayes, a pigeoneer with the 829th pigeon platoon, served in North African, Tunisian and Italian fronts. He arrived in Safi, French Morocco, November 18, 1942. From the start, pigeons were in great demand, as other means of communication were failing, due to shell fire, difficult terrain and sabotage. Sergeant Hayes cites example after example of the precarious flights pigeons undertook to carry messages through intense fighting and severe weather. He emphasized that the recollection of these flights are the only recognition most of the birds would ever receive. Hayes did not hold back. He made clear that the condition of many birds upon arriving home was horrific—lost eyes and legs, torn wings, shrapnel-studded chests. But that many miraculously survived, healed and flew again.

As soon as breeding lofts were set up and birds trained, mobile teams moved into the field. According to Hayes, a mobile combat loft was unlike any other kind of unit in the Army.

It consisted usually of one sergeant and two corporals or privates. The sergeant, most of the time, picked the two men to accompany him. The unit consisted of two mobile lofts, one or two trucks, all the grain the trucks could carry, camouflage cover for the lofts; as well as an arsenal of submachine guns, carbine rifles, .45 automatic pistols, and a 12-gauge shotgun. No beds, tents or food were provided. This unit was called a combat team. These were sent on orders to attach themselves to the designated combat units at the front. They were completely on their own, and the closer to the front the loft was located, the better. For the food supply, the combat team would attach itself to any unit close by, and sometimes there would be only C-rations to eat, the worst kind of food one can imagine. Many times it was spoiled and, in consequence,

Herman Williams, co-trainer of World War II courier Captain Fulton, examining a wound on Captain's head, sustained while carrying a message from the front at Sessa, Italy. Captain Fulton had already been credited with bringing the first news of the surrender of the German 10th and 15th Panzer Divisions in Tunisia, flying 65 miles in 82 minutes (courtesy Holt-Atherton Department Special Collections, University of the Pacific Library, CA).

Chapter 6. A Call for Champions

we developed diarrhea. Gasoline was ever plentiful, though. The Army Engineers always had a pipe line with special attachments and one just went to the line and filled up. We mostly slept on the ground, under the truck, or in bombed houses, and sometimes, if the house was occupied, we just moved in with the family.

The only contact we had with the outside world was through Red Bronson and his "Bronx Express" which delivered replacement squeakers to us. And you can believe every time he came with that truck, the grandiosely named Bronx Express, he took his life in his hands—a prime target for "Jerry," he brought with him all the news from the breeding base and our headquarters.

We were faced at this time by two crack outfits, Mussolini's Black Shirts and Rommel's Afrika Corps, both veterans of desert warfare. The fighting was very intense at times. It was during this time that our pigeons were really being discovered. All of a sudden everyone wanted to use our winged messengers, even the war correspondents wanted them to serve as their "flying post office," for their stories. For them time was money. The first stories out got the headlines. Unfortunately, we didn't have enough pigeons to go around. Every feather that could fly was on duty, and as soon as a bird arrived at the loft with a message, it was hauled back to he front line without so much as a day's rest.[23]

Most of the pigeons were packed in 4-bird containers and sent from their mobile homes to a message center near the front. Each bird had on its leg a snap-on plastic capsule to be filled with messages written on small strips of onion-skin paper. At the message center, the birds were picked up by various combat troops, infantry patrols, forward artillery observers and any other units needing quick communication. These troops carried the pigeons with them until they returned to headquarters or until they needed to send a message from the field. In the latter case, the soldiers followed instructions that came with the birds. A form accompanied every bird that went out, stating exactly where it would return to. For example, these birds were trained to fly to lofts in Béja:

1. These birds will return to Béja.
2. Messages will be turned over to II Corps Message Center which has contact with all the other message centers.
3. Send the original and one or more duplicates to ensure quick delivery of the message; the message and the duplicate to be sent on different birds released simultaneously.
4. Send all radio messages also by pigeons to ensure quick delivery.
5. Never release birds without a message of some kind, so pigeoneers will know the time and place they were released.
6. Please water, but do not feed the birds.
7. These birds are in demand, so make good use of them. They

can be depended upon to deliver highly important and secret messages.

    8. Message capsules are on the bird's leg.[24]

The pigeons became increasingly more valuable, and generally, a bird spent more time out on a mission than in its loft. On a few occasions, Hayes stated, he was forced to move the mobile lofts while the birds were on a mission. When they returned, home was gone. Undismayed, the intelligent couriers would fly around the countryside until they found their own loft, even if it had been moved 50 miles. "This may sound uncanny and incredible," Hayes said, "All the same, it remains a fact."[25]

For some long-range missions, such as invasions, beach landings, or behind-lines parachute jumps, arrangements were made in advance. The troops usually came to the lofts to pick up their pigeons and found them always prepared for any assignment. Hayes and his men took particular pride in their birds. "As good pigeon men, we knew the particular merits and habits of each. When the special agents came to the lofts to select the birds we always tried to choose the most suitable for their particular missions. Our success rate was one hundred percent due primarily to the high quality and champion class of our birds."[26]

There were no veterinarians in Hayes' pigeon platoon, so any surgery was done by the pigeoneers themselves. They knew how to sew them up, set their legs, and take care of any other medical problems their pigeons had. Such was the case of Lady Astor, Sergeant Adam Sampson's swift hen who flew many missions back and forth across enemy lines.

> Lady Astor was donated to the U.S. Signal corps in the fall of 1942, by the members of the Steinway Pigeon Club of New York City. This little blue check hen was sent to the African theater of war and here she was given her first opportunity to do her part for the U.S. Signal Pigeon Corps. She was sent nearly 60 miles from her home loft to a combat unit at the front. The following day she was picked from a small four-bird container and an urgent message was attached to her leg. She was then set free.
>
> Although it was raining heavily, she launched the flight back to her home loft. Then, piercing the silence of the area, a few shots rang out. Bullets riddled her breast. She was torn from her eye to the keel of her breast, her leg was fractured, and half her feathers were torn loose from one wing. This did not deter her. She continued on her mission. After reaching her destination, she alighted on the roof of her loft. Exhausted now, and gasping, she fell to the ground. Here she was picked up, the message was removed and delivered safely. Immediately, her wounds were dressed and she was gradually nursed back to life and perfect health. She was not called upon again for she had done her utmost in winning the war in North Africa, and her handlers were compassionate men.[27]

Chapter 6. A Call for Champions

It was Sergeant Sampson who tended to Lady Astor, setting a broken leg, sewing at least twenty stitches in her body and head, nursing her back to full health.

After the North African campaigns, Hayes' company, now the 209th, went on to Italy, landing at Salerno, just south of Naples on October 1, 1943. The Germans were entering Italy from the north, and Allies fought them from Salerno to Cassino, Anzio, Florence and the frigid Futa Pass, where the Germans were stopped. Hundreds of pigeons were used to carry messages in these campaigns. Germans sometimes captured Allied birds and sent them back with fake messages or maps, suggesting where the Allies should next bomb. Or, they would return a pigeon with a menacing greeting such as this:

World War II combat loft in the Futa Pass, Italy, with birds exercising, despite the snow. The Futa Pass was part of the Germans' last major line of defense along the summits of the northern Apennine Mountains (courtesy Holt-Atherton Department of Special Collections, University of the Pacific Library, CA).

Monday January 24, 1944

To The Americans
36th Division

Here is your pidgeon back. The German troops have enough to eat. By the way, we are gladly looking forward to your next visit by your degenerate lice-infested comrades.

(Signed) The German Troops[28]

War Pigeons

While stationed at Cassino, Hayes experimented with pigeons delivering exposed film. Photos were taken regularly by the Army, but often arrived at Headquarters too late for the fast-moving American troops to find them useful. A faster means of transporting the film was needed, and Hayes had a possible answer—a pigeon express. He developed a special harness made of waxed cord that attached to a four-inch-long cylinder that would contain the film. In test runs, the birds flew easily with the cylinder harnessed to them. On May 24, 1944, he tried it out. A pigeon named Old 17 carried the exposed film, flying from the Cassino front at a swift 50 miles per hour.[29] This was the first time a bird had flown live film in the Italian campaign. The Cassino pigeon express benefited both the Army Pictorial Service, as well as war correspondents covering the campaigns.

In control of central and northern Italy, the Germans had established a series of defensive lines across the country south of Rome, including formidable defense positions, called the Winter Line, outside the town of Cassino. The Allies, including Hayes' pigeon company, advanced on this line between December 1943 and June 1944. The

A camouflaged and partly buried combat pigeon loft at the front in Cassino, Italy, during World War II (courtesy Holt-Atherton Department of Special Collections, University of the Pacific Library, CA).

Chapter 6. A Call for Champions

wintry weather, flooding, mountainous terrain and tenacious German defense made the advance slow, with many casualties suffered by both soldiers and pigeons. But sometimes the news was good.

A company of Gurkhas and British soldiers had made it to the top of Hangman's Hill, just west of Cassino, a key allied position in the campaign, but they were trapped by heavy German fire. For nine days they hid in the rocks. Provisions were dropped by Allies, but the Germans got most of it. Three volunteers, a Scotsman, an Englishman and a Welshman, offered to try to penetrate the German lines to save the men. Each one carried a homing pigeon with a prepared message. The Scotsman was pinned down en route by machine gun fire. His pigeon, Master Brian, flew back with that message. Two hours later, Miss Peggy, arrived with a message stating the Englishman had reached his objective. Twenty minutes later, Just Jerry, released from the Welshman's hands, arrived with a similar message. With information brought by the birds, the Allies laid down a lane of projectiles and smoke bombs that night, and the isolated Gurkhas and Brits passed through the lane of protective shellfire, unscathed.[30]

In World War II, pigeons for the first time served with paratroopers. Pigeoneers were assigned to battalions with paratroopers, and familiarized the jumpers with the handling, care and release of the birds. A updated pigeon vest on the shoulder or chest of each man was standard equipment. The U.S. Army Pigeon Vest, Equipment #PG-106/CB, was specially made for pigeons jumping with paratroopers. Ida Rosenthal's Maidenform Brassiere Company in New York already made silk parachutes for the paratroopers, and she readily agreed to manufacture the pigeon vests. The demure vest designed in the early 1940s was wrapped and laced around a pigeon's body, leaving its head and tail exposed. Attached by a strap to a paratrooper jumping behind enemy lines, the vest protected the bird during its descent from plane to earth.[31] Pigeons also "jumped" by themselves, pushed from a plane in a basket attached to a mini-chute.

Pigeons parachuted into enemy territory as part of espionage work in the war. With a coded message attached to its leg and no way to "talk," even when intercepted, these birds were nearly perfect couriers for spies and agents. In World War I, pigeons were used in secret service work for both the Central Powers and the Entente. So valuable were pigeons to convey intelligence, that when the Germans marched into Brussels in 1914, the Belgians destroyed over 30,000 of their prized birds so they would not be seized by the Germans.[32] In intelligence operations, pigeons were dropped over occupied territory with requests for inhabitants to send them back with reports on German activity. To find sympathizers who would risk sending back information, the British loosed small hydrogen balloons downwind from the British side of the front lines to any area believed to concentrate German forces. The pigeons were released at night, four birds in a basket with a parachute. A device with an alarm clock rang at an appointed hour, releasing the parachute and basket. Patriotic locals could fill in the form, clip it onto a bird's leg and release it early the next morning. Later, a slow burning fuse was substituted for the clock.[33] Attached to each pigeon basket was a questionnaire asking about German presence.

In World War II, pigeons continued to be part of espionage tactics by both Allied and Axis powers. The MI 14 section of the British Military Intelligence upped the game. In 1941, they instituted a secret program known as COLUMBA. Homing pigeons were parachuted behind lines in France, Belgium and Holland, where the program hoped that those who were pro–Allies would report back to Britain on German defenses in their area.

According to a *London Telegraph* article, "Each pigeon came with a miniature spy kit: a bakelite tube to put a message in; sheets of ultra-thin paper and a special pencil; detailed instructions in French, Flemish or Dutch on how to fill in a report."[34]

A questionnaire included with the bird asked for information about military movements, enemy morale, German lodgings, restrictions on civilians, access to BBC broadcasts, and other matters. Even scribbled quickly, the messages not only reported on German presence, but also revealed life under occupation. The notes are poignant, sometimes desperate, but determined and hopeful.

John Douglas Charrot was a navigator who flew on pigeon drops in the operation. An excerpt from his interview appeared in *Forgotten Voices of the Secret War,* by Roderick Bailey, and reprinted in Jennifer Spangler's book, *The World War II Pigeons and The Secret Columba Messages.*

> We had a chute you could use as a toilet, a little chute, and we had these bundles of leaflets. It was usually the rear-gunner's job on the wireless operator's they could tear the string off them and push them down the chute and they would float away. The pigeons we were much more careful about. They had their own little parachute, they were in a little cage made of cardboard and they had food and some water in there, and we used to try and find a nice quiet spot for these so they could be all right. We would drop them and watch them go down and sometimes quite

Chapter 6. A Call for Champions

useful information came back, I gather. We didn't see that of course. But there'd be a little pencil in this cage and a piece of rice paper and they were supposed to get hold of these pigeons you see, write a message and put it round their legs and send them back.[35]

After his retirement, Charrot reported that his squadron alone delivered 39,000 containers of pigeons and 1000 agents. This figure referred to pigeons used by Resistance workers and agents, as well as pigeons who participated in Operation Columba.[36]

Hoorn, in North Holland, was occupied by the Nazis from their invasion in 1940 until May 1945 when the Germans surrendered. This note, returned early in the operation in November 1941, tells MI 14 about a bustling German presence, with good morale.

> Dropped at HOORN, NORTH HOLLAND, on the 7th November. Another two dropped in the neighbourhood, but they were taken to the police; Not much news about the invasion of England.
> There is an oil dump and depot of Rubber Boots in the KRENTENTUIN (current garden, see attached) at HOORN. Air Post on top of the Public Baths and Water Tower.
> The German Morale is good. The Factories in EDAM are being adapted for the manufacture of "Fokker" spare parts. Round it there is...?
> The "Fokker" factories have been well and truly hit.
> Do not drop pigeons in thickly populated areas.
> At SCHOUW on the N.H. (Noord-Holland) Canal a good deal is being unloaded, chiefly cases with grenades, and they are stacked there in depots.
> Some little while ago the auction room of van Zwaag was hit by a bomb, there was no point in that at all. Who did that?
> On the Berkhauten Road there is a ... house, which at the moment is full of Germans. At ALKMAAR they are preparing the barracks at the Westerweg (Western Road) for the winter when the Germans return from Russia, and have won the war over there, ha-ha.
> But Boys, beware and don't underestimate him. Can't you throw any time bombs on the railways to Germany? Much too much goes there, we lose everything, so keep your eyes open. Patriotic greeting also to the Queen [Wilhelmina, in England].
> I sign
> TOON.
> V.[37]

This one from Calvados, July 11, 1941, near Normandy, spoke of trains, a munitions depot, plans to invade England, and hunger.

> We found your pigeon on the 10th July near CHEURES [sic: probably Rouvres, north of Falaise] and sent it off again early on the 11th as we were unable to keep it longer owing to there being Germans in the Commune. They have already destroyed one pigeon found by a woman who gave it up to them.

War Pigeons

> The only information we can give you is that there is a munitions depot in the forest of St. Ohdre near La Huquette.
> The Germans hope still to invade England and their moral is still very good.
> For 8 days past trains have been passing full of men, lorries and M.Gs. These trains are of 25 to 30 wagons each.
> No other news to give you except to beg you to make an end to this as soon as you can before we die of hunger.
> We live in the hope, like many other Frenchman, that Victory is near. Come, dear comrades of yesterday!
>
> No signature.[38]

Initial returns from the first few months of the operation proved valuable. Over three months, 221 birds had been released over Flanders, Normandy and Brittany. Forty-six returned, 17 with useful information. Especially beneficial was that the pigeons brought intelligence so swiftly, within hours of a report being written. This was a unique source of intelligence and highly valued.[39]

This one from northern France was returned via pigeon to MI 14 and the Royal Air Force on October 6, 1941, just three days after the bird had been found. Besides describing the dire situation under occupation, including the writer's grief and anger at the loss of a son killed by the Germans, the reply encouraged the invasion of France, which the writer claimed would not be met with all that much resistance.

> Pigeon was dropped 7 K.M. from the coast (ETAPLES) and was found on the 3rd October.
> No troops in this district.
> A few at MONTREUIL and no doubt along the coast, but no formations—scattered units but many villages are now without.
> Not a single gun or a single tank is seen to go by anymore—no D.C.A. here—about 50 horses with small carts and an equal number of men engaged on transport. Bad morale with regard to what happens in the East. The soldiers returning from leave come back with their head low and talk of the bombing of Germany.
> But their demands are becoming increasingly; cows, one talks of horses (?)
> It is the destruction of the French breeding stock.
> The peasant is requisitioned for more potatoes than he grows and for more grain so that he is left with almost nothing for his own animals.
> Discontent is general and one asks oneself why, with so few troops to oppose you, there is not a landing on the conquered coast. They cannot claim to be able to resist.
> I do not live on the coast.
> I cannot get any information about the sea.
> I do not want any compensation. One does not need that when one serves one's country.
> This is a means for me to avenge myself for my son, whom they have killed.

Chapter 6. A Call for Champions

After the war I would like to replace the pigeons which they have killed, and as I am a lover of pigeons, your one could hardly have come into better hands. I would like to receive some more pigeons to replace those killed.

I come back from a journey. I have only met troops (trucks) in THEROUANNE, AIRE, ARQUES (Luftwaffe).

Farmers complain of the demands for butter and milk for the Co-operative at Verton and would like to see its disappearance. We would rejoice in its destruction, because there they work for "them."

No more radio (they have broken it), but I would know if you receive this. I will tell a reliable friend who listens in.

NO more talk of an invasion of England. They have their hands full with Russia.

All those who talk with me do so with horror. They did not expect such a resistance, and in France neither, so that you are now relegated to second importance. They say that they fear the English soldiers less that the Russians and think that you will not *dare* ever to make a landing. However, if you had good infantry, followed by artillery, to throw on the coast with mechanized units to open the way, you would be surprised. A few scattered soldiers would surrender, the rural French as well as the townspeople will rally to your help and are capable of gibing you considerable assistance. As hunger is increasing the general discontent grows. Just look at the executions in the "Nord"—but a famished stomach has no early—and that movement will increase.

No coal for the winter—insufficient and mediocre bread.

When will the end be.

Munition dump at the forest of LONGVILLERS.

When your aeroplanes pass, they become sullen, sad and follow them with glasses.

Petrol dump at the forest of RECQUES on the COURSE.

An ardent A.B.R. 4th Zouaves (bis)

A very dense telephonic network with the central exchange on the right hand side of the National Road No. 1, going into MONTREUIL, I think it is the 2nd house. At LE TOUQUET the high authorities live in the very best hotels.[40]

As the operation continued, it was managed more and more by organized resistance workers, rather than the British government. The information received grew richer, full of particulars only locals could provide. In addition, reports revealed a growing fragility in German morale.

This report, sent on August 12, 1944, gave extremely detailed information on German troop movement, defenses and ammunition, as well as signs of deterioration in morale.

Dear Friends,

It was with great pleasure that we found your pigeon with parachute in very good condition on the 31st July in the plain of Beauge (Eure et Loir) district CHARTRES. To show our devotion and not forgetting our duty to our Fatherland, we will tell you what we know about the enemy although here it is difficult to move

War Pigeons

about at will on account of the fact that everything has been stolen including our bicycles.

Enemy Defenses. Important Ack-Ack batteries around the town of CHARTRES. Also several searchlights and listening-in posts. Airfield at ETAMPES. Ack-Ack and searchlights at MONDESIR.

Enemy Troops. HOUVILLE LA BRANCHE. German hospital in the Chateau Boville le Comte. Soldiers of different regiments are being re-grouped at OYSONVILLE on the boundary between SEINE ET OISE AND BURE ET LOIR. There are many troops at the Chateau.

Military convoys pass during the night and very early in the morning before six o'clock.

They pass chiefly on the roads from DOURDAN, MONDOUVLEAU, CHARTRES, LIMON, ANGERVILLE, PAARIS-ORLEANS, CHARTRES-ORLEANS. Those routes follow roughly the railway lines. The convoys are only slightly escorted.

Kommandantur and Feldgendarmirie and Gestapo at CHARTRES.
Etat Major at AUNEAU.

The morale of the elderly Germans is fairly low, that of the young ones a bit higher.

Aviation. From the old French aerodromes at CHARTRES, MONDESIR, ETAMPES, bombers of the Junker 88 type depart often in the evening at 8 o'clock at a low altitude in a north-westerly direction.

Works have just been completed 10 kilometres before AUNEAU on the road from CHARTRES to AUNEAU.

In the forest of BARONVILLE there are at the moment fighters which are camouflaged. The types of fighters in this wood have as insignia a yellow flag at the end of the wings and on the rudder.

Many ammunition depots in the forests of Senoches, RANBOUILLET, BAILLEAU L'EVEQUE. There are very important cement block-houses here spaced 500 kilomtres one from the other. They number about 20.

At CHATEAUDUN and at AUNEAU there is a depot of engineering material situated 2 kilometres from the station of AUNEAU.

B.B.C. On account of lack of electric current, we cannot often listen-in. When we can, we do so in the morning about 0330 hours which is much less jammed than at other times. We do not know any jamming stations.

We very much hope that your pigeon will arrive safely and will be happy if you would let us know of its arrival. WE await you impatiently and hope to see you soon to get rid of the dirty Boches who have poisoned our country for 4 years now.

Vive la France et ses Allies.

This comes from a small locality 30 kilometres from CHARTRES and is sent to you by two good Frenchmen of 22 years of age.

(Sgd) Lulu et Riri.[41]

By the middle of 1944, 808 pigeons had returned with intelligence out of more than 13,000 sent.[42] That amounts to only a 6 percent return rate, but the service, Operation Columba concluded, was worthwhile.

Chapter 6. A Call for Champions

As important as the intelligence received from occupied countries, was the hope the birds provided. Under such desperate situations of starvation, loss of neighbors and family, mistrust, fear, anger and sadness, the appearance of a pigeon in a nearby field must have been likened to the appearance of an angel, as Spangler describes in her book:

> Then, you find a pigeon! You have a chance to help the Allies do damage to the Germans. You have a chance to describe the horrors you see and endure. You have the hope of hearing on the BBC that the pigeon made it back with your message. You write. You are no longer helpless. You have thoughts and useful information. But you don't have much time. You must send the pigeon as soon as possible. If a friend or family member sees the pigeon they might report you to the Germans. When it is time, you toss the pigeon into the air. He circles once to get his bearings and then flies toward Britain with your words.[43]

In the European and African Theaters of Operation, pigeons of particular note include Julius Caesar, Yank, Black Magic, Monkey Face and GI Joe. Julius Caesar, a blue check cock splashed with white, flew in North Africa, carrying 44 messages, all in fast time. At the time, pigeons were still being used by the 17th Group Operation bombers flying out of Tunisia on raids to Italy. Just prior to the Allied invasion of Italy, Julius Caesar was taken by bombers and parachuted north of Rome to an intelligence agent. With a secret message about German troop movements strapped to his leg, Caesar flew home, nonstop across 300 miles of the Mediterranean Sea.

Yank, hatched at Fort Benning, Georgia, served in North Africa in the French Moroccan and Tunisian campaigns. In March 1943, pigeoneers at Tebessa, Northern Algeria, were selecting a bird for what would be an extremely important flight. The American 2nd Corps was beginning the famous battle of the Kasserine Pass. The bird picked was Yank, a big, silver red bar male. Yank carried a message on March 17, 1943, with the first news of the fall of Gafsa, flying the 90 miles in one hour 55 minutes in very bad weather, arriving ahead of wire or radio. The message sent March 17, 1943, by David Brown, a war correspondent, read as follows: "Italians started evacuation of Gafsa, only half hour post formal attack underway at 10:00 moving toward El Guetttar. Stop. Americans moved into Gafsa against only light resistance about eleven o'clock. Signed, Brown, Reuters correspondent."[44] Yank's other famous flight was on the following April 1, sent by General George Patton. Intense fighting and bad weather had silenced electronic communication, so Patton released Yank on a stormy 90-mile flight. He arrived at his destination in 100 minutes with information some say saved Patton's life.

War Pigeons

Black Magic, a jet-black cock, was assigned in early 1944 to wind-swept Corsica to work with military intelligence. On March 4, he was ferried by a spy via submarine to the coast of France. A few days later he was released with one of the most vital messages ever carried by an Army pigeon. Black Magic headed directly across the water for his loft in Corsica but didn't quite reach home. A Signal Corps officer found him limping down a street in Bastia, Corsica, with a hole in his chest, but with the highly secret message still in its leg capsule. Black Magic was whisked to a hospital and his wound sewed up. He was restored to health and then relegated to raising more black magic.

Monkey Face, a blue splash cock with an oddly marked face, was considered one of the best pigeons in the Army. He flew sixty-two missions on many fronts including Tebessa, Ferriana, Beja, Tabarka, Matuer and Bizerte, and hauled more messages than any other pigeon during the African campaign. Monkey Face was lucky, he was never wounded. After the end of hostilities in Africa, Monkey Face retired from combat and went to the breeding base at Bizerte. He raised many youngsters, most of them with identical features of their famous father.

GI Joe hatched in North Africa, a blue checked splashed male. He was on duty with the British 10th Corps in Italy when the 56th infantry asked for air support to bomb the German-held town of Colvi Vecchia, October 18, 1943. When British troops unexpectedly took the town, Joe was sent on a life-or-death mission, 20 miles to headquarters to stop the bombing of the town with over 1000 British troops already occupying it. Flying 60 miles per hour, Joe made the flight in 20 minutes, stopping the bombers as their motors warmed up for take off. GI Joe is the only American bird to win the Dickin Medal, awarded to him on November 6, 1946. Retired from active duty by then, Joe made the trip to London from the States by airplane for the presentation. In a regal ceremony in the Tower of London, a British colonel read Joe's citation, a major general hung the medal on him, while a field marshal and an American major general stood by.[45]

In the first ceremony of its kind, GI Joe was again honored on November 14, 2019, at the Rayburn House Office Building on Capitol Hill, Washington, D.C. The Inaugural Animals Medal of Bravery Award Ceremony honored animals that served with the U.S. military during wartime, or a living service animal that has exhibited extraordinary bravery and service to our country. This medal is commensurate with Great Britain's Dickin Medal that has been given out to 71 deserving animals since World War II. (Thirty-two of those were pigeons.) At the

Chapter 6. A Call for Champions

ceremony, six posthumous medals were given to animals, including GI Joe. Tom DeRosa, a handler for GI Joe after the bird retired to Churchill Loft at Fort Monmouth, accepted the medal for GI Joe.

At the war's end, about 1000 birds that flew in Europe and North Africa were considered outstanding fliers, and the Signal Corps planned to keep them in the regular Army. When birds brought from the continent had been consolidated with those on hand in England, there were 1,067 pigeons that shipped home to Camp Crowder. Later, when the Pigeon Breeding and Training Center was returned to Fort Monmouth, most of the pigeons from Europe were housed there. The "heroes," including GI Joe, spent their retirement days in "Churchill."[46]

In the Pacific Theater of Operations, pigeons served in China, Burma, the Central Pacific, and South West Pacific. Many of these campaigns were fought in a jungle environment with treacherous and remote mountains. All messages in these conflicts were sent in duplicate and despite the terrain, rain, fog, hawks, and enemy gunfire, they never lost a message.

The Office of Strategic Services (OSS), the precursor to the CIA, provided intelligence in many Pacific campaigns. The outfit was led by Colonel William Donovan, who had created the OSS in 1941. Detachment 101 of the OSS operated in the China-Burma-India Theater. On April 14, 1942, Donovan activated the detachment for action behind enemy lines in Burma. The first unit of its kind, the detachment was charged with gathering intelligence, harassing the Japanese, identifying targets for the Army Air Service to bomb, and rescuing downed Allied airmen. The detachment relied on support from tribal groups in Burma, particularly the fiercely anti–Japanese Kachin people. Starting in July 1943, small groups or individuals from the detachment were parachuted behind Japanese lines to remote Kachin villages. The Americans then created independent guerrilla groups of the Kachin people, calling in weapons and equipment drops, including homing pigeons.[47] Once established, the groups, called the Kachin Rangers, ambushed Japanese patrols, rescued downed American pilots, cleared small landing strips in the jungle and took on other unconventional missions.

Detachment 101 relied heavily on pigeons for communications from behind lines. The Signal Pigeon Unit consisted of 10 pigeoneers transferred from the 828th and commanded by Captain Morris Y. Lederman. The achievements attained by his unit were remarkable. Coded messages were sent via pigeon across hundreds of miles of jungle in brutal tropical weather and mountainous terrain. In his official report, May 1945, Captain Lederman stated that a loft had been established behind

War Pigeons

Japanese lines in the Myitkyina area. After only 10 weeks in that location, the pigeons returned 225 and 250 miles when released by agents who had parachuted into the vicinity of Mandalay, Shwebo and Maymyo. The most outstanding flights were made near the Thailand border back to the loft at Bhamo, 325 miles.

He further stated, "Pigeons in advanced areas were very valuable with agent operations. During the month of January, nine groups were parachuted in and pigeons either beat the radio or were the only means of contact for seven of these groups. The shortest distance flown was 175 miles, the balance were from 225 to 300 miles. The pigeons had to be held in the jump containers from one to three days."

On one occasion, he recalled, "We have tossed a pigeon 150 miles after eleven days in a location, and although they were resettled pigeons, they made it in six and a half hours. A new shoulder message carrier was developed, and pigeons flew fifty miles with a full roll of negatives.

Out of the hundreds of messages flown, only four were lost and all were from distances greater than 150 miles."[48]

Some remarkable pigeons served in the Pacific Theater: Captain Lederman, a blue check cock, hatched in Burma in September 1944. He flew his first message from a patrol operating 120 miles behind Japanese lines. He was dropped during January, February and March by parachute or taken by jump container, to patrols operating along, or behind enemy lines. Each message carried by the Captain contained valuable information on Japanese troop movements and heavy gun placement. He flew many missions over 100 miles.

When only four months old, Jungle Joe, another blue check cock, was dropped by parachute far behind Japanese lines. During the jump, a radio operator became lost from the rest of the party and believed captured. Without radio, the patrol had no contact with rear headquarters. Jungle Joe was confined for a week in his jump container, a 14 × 4 × 4" bamboo box, while the patrol collected intelligence on the Japanese. On the eighth day, he was released with a secret and urgent message. In spite of being confined for a week, Jungle Joe covered 225 miles in good time, delivering information that helped open up Burma to Allied forces.

Burma Queen, a blue check hen, flew during some of the heaviest fighting in Burma. On one occasion, a group of Allied troops on the border of Burma and Thailand was attacked and overwhelmed by a force of Japanese troops. They retreated, but, fearing capture, they destroyed their radios and codes. A B-25 bomber was dispatched to search for

Chapter 6. A Call for Champions

the weary troops. They were seen, and Burma Queen parachuted into their open arms. She was then released at 6 a.m. and flew 320 miles with important intelligence, arriving at headquarters at 3 p.m. More remarkable was that she was released 120 miles off the course she was trained to fly.

Blackie Halligan served with the 280th signal pigeon company. With 1500 other birds, he was shipped from Louisiana to the west coast and embarked for New Caledonia. With the 132nd infantry, he flew from outposts as far away as 125 miles. He was then sent to Guadalcanal, the first island of the Solomon Islands taken from the Japanese. Blackie was stationed along the Lunga River, and one day arrived at his loft badly wounded, but carrying a message giving the location of some 300 Japanese troops. When word of the bird's feat reached General "Sandy" Patch, commander of the U.S. Army and U.S. Marine Corps during the campaign, the general made a special trip to Blackie's loft to decorate the recovering bird.

* * * * * *

The U.S. Navy also used pigeons in World War II, but to a lesser extent, and mostly on the home front. Along with advanced electronic communication equipment, Navy ships maintained early methods of signaling, such as blinker lights, steam whistling, semaphore, and flag hoisting. However, messaging via pigeon was out. At least on big ships.

During the early days of World War II, the United States became a major source of war material for Great Britain. Adolf Hitler knew this support enabled Great Britain to withstand his nation's offensive. If this lifeline from America could be cut, or reduced to insignificant levels, Britain would be strangled and starved into submission, losing Axis control over Western Europe. Germany's long-range submarines, *Unterseebooten* or U-boats, were just the weapon to attack the transatlantic convoys headed to Britain from U.S. shores.

Soon after the attack on Pearl Harbor, the German Navy began Operation Drumbeat, the campaign of U-boats on shipping off the east coast of the United States. The war had suddenly reached America's shores, and she was unprepared. Merchant ships, unaware of danger, often sailed with their running lights on. The coastline was not yet blacked out, which meant that ships were clearly silhouetted against the sparkling lights of coastal towns. The government, with its hands full supplying ships for battles on two oceans, was slow to establish convoys to protect shipping. They did not have the ships or manpower to pursue the German "wolf packs."

Without coastal convoys, merchant ships presented easy targets. Starting in January of 1942, German U-boats crossed the Atlantic Ocean and scouted the waters off the eastern seaboard and in the Gulf of Mexico. At first the German Navy sent six 500-ton submarines, each of which carried 14 torpedoes and deck guns that alone, could sink a ship.[49] They also planted mines in strategic harbors. Among their prime prey were allied ships off Cape Hatteras and warships entering and leaving Hampton Roads. This region was an essential part of the nation's economy and military. It was the heart of the Fifth Naval District, occupying parts of Virginia, West Virginia, Maryland, and North Carolina, and with jurisdiction 15 miles out to sea during wartime. The region was also home to the Naval Operations Post, Norfolk; the Norfolk Naval Shipyard, Portsmouth; and several Army forts.

The Hampton Roads area became a focus of U-boat attacks. According to James R. Powell and Alan B. Flanders' book, *Wolf at the Door*, "In the first seven months of the operation, the tides grew heavy with the corpses of dead sailors when 585 ships, totaling more than three million gross tons of shipping, were sunk off the East Coast."

In 1942, we had no escorts for those ships. They traveled singly and got knocked off five or six a night down there (Hatteras). People in Norfolk and Virginia Beach did not know about the severity of the sinkings, but people in Hatteras knew about them. On the Outer Banks, they had more and more oil, bodies, and debris coming ashore.[50]

Both the Navy and Coast Guard were anxious to begin anti-submarine warfare missions, but it proved a slow and formidable task. With few Navy or Coast Guard ships available, they turned to civilians for help. In 1941, the regular Coast Guard had formed the Coast Guard Auxiliary and Reserves to expand their capabilities. Members and their boats were recruited to participate in patrols and rescue survivors from torpedoed ships.

Spring 1942 saw improvement in protecting shipping along the coast. The number of vessels authorized for Coast Guard Reserves had increased with 65 cutters, 15 patrol boats and converted yachts, and 14 armed British trawlers. Army and Navy planes were flying out of 19 bases. A Coastal Convoy System was eventually enacted in May of 1942 from Maine to Florida, along with increases in Army, Navy, and Civil Air Patrols.[51]

Hampton Roads finally implemented a U-boat defense network.

Chapter 6. A Call for Champions

A row of pigeon lofts, to the left of the car, provided the Navy with birds for communication. The Woods Hole, Massachusetts, base was one of several small bases established for coastal patrol and anti-submarine warfare (courtesy Woods Hole Historical Museum Archives).

Along with coastal convoys, they used minesweepers, antisubmarine nets and anti-torpedo nets. The defense of Hampton Roads also relied on reconnaissance by harbor pilots, yachtsmen, fishermen and civilian pilots. The multifarious undertaking mirrored the efforts of British Q-ships that had so valiantly fought German submarines in the previous world war. And the motley mix of vessels and planes was up against the same shortage of communications equipment. During the operation, fishermen without radios often sent emergency reports to shore via the only reliable means of communication—homing pigeons.

Homing pigeons became a valuable asset to this defense system, operating off the east coast of the U.S. and in the Gulf of Mexico. From military craft, fishing boats and shrimpers, the birds carried intelligence about the presence of U-boats, downed ships, and survivors. They took off from Coast Guard vessels, small power boats and sailing craft, flying home through storms, fog and freezing temperatures.

By mid–June 1942, 17 skippers and crew with their trawlers were enlisted and put into action. Soon after the fishing boats joined, nearly every offshore boat became involved in the anti-submarine warfare program, an astounding 43 vessels in all. These boats proved to be an important set of extra eyes for the Navy.

However, attacks on merchant ships did not stop. The military responded. Enrollment in the Coast Guard Reserves and Auxiliary skyrocketed. An integrated Army-Navy-Coast Guard "Sea Frontier" defense system was established, including a Coastal Picket Force (CPF). The picket concept called for the use of privately owned yachts rugged enough for both defensive and offensive patrol duty at sea. The first patrols of the coastal pickets began in July 1942. A normal patrol was five days out, two days in, and crews were to report actions of all hostile submarine, surface and air forces. By September 1942, auxiliary flotilla had sprung up in 16 cities, with 480 CPF vessels working the Atlantic and Gulf coasts. Large 50 to 100-foot sailboats were the signature CPF vessels, and while propeller noise forced U-boats to lay silent, a fleet of ocean-going sailboats could cruise silently. Those with Sonar onboard could detect a submarine's running electric motors and report the sub's location.

As on the fishing boats recruited, not all of the pickets had radios. Some carried homing pigeons which were released with messages during the day. They returned to their lofts at Fort Story, according to one picket member, Joseph Kelly, where the Army Signal Corps would collect the messages. "We would release them just before starting in. It was fun to watch them, as they tracked on a radio signal of some kind, what we knew as the proper course from 20 miles offshore."[52]

The weather, more than the enemy, often proved more than most picket boats could handle. Several times, stated Kelly, sailboats were reported missing until they were able to ride out storms and able to radio in. Those that carried homing pigeons used them. In one case, the pigeon's flight through a gale enabled a missing boat to relay its location after it became lost in a storm.[53]

Still, early summer saw German U-boats making their way into the Gulf of Mexico. The Coast Guard had fewer ships and aircraft available to send to the Gulf, but Army and Navy planes from Florida air bases began to patrol the region. Auxiliary Coast Guard patrols operated as well, and by November 1942, the Auxiliary patrol consisted of 137 boats, 126 of which were owned by shrimpers. These shrimpers operated all over the Gulf, alternately fishing, while manning their observation stations. They were ultimately responsible for saving the lives of many survivors of torpedo sinkings.[54] Many were furnished with guns and radios, but again, those boats without radios always included pigeons as part of their crew.

Shrimpers off the south east coast of the U.S. went further than picking up survivors. Some became part of the Office of Naval Intelligence's (ONI) counterintelligence program. ONI created Selected

Chapter 6. A Call for Champions

Masters and Informants (SMI) sections under district intelligence officers to recruit fishermen as informants. Their operation didn't catch any spies, but it did offer some comfort against the threat of sabotage. By October 1942, SMI sections had recruited 586 agents, 200 of them in the Sixth Naval District, with headquarters in Charleston, South Carolina. The ship owners were paid $50.00 to cover installation of radiotelephones, but only 50 boats received them. Otherwise, the Masters reported via homing pigeons which were owned at the time by Navy-operated lofts at Mayport, Florida, and St. Simon's island, Georgia.[55]

Pigeons remained a crucial presence in the Navy's lighter-than-air craft (LTA). At the beginning of the war, Naval Air Station (NAS) Lakehurst, New Jersey, was the only active LTA station operated by the Navy. (Moffett Field, California, had changed hands between the Navy and Army several times, and in April 1942, was returned to the Navy.) The Navy requested in 1940 more stations for anti-submarine patrols of the coasts and harbors of the country, but it wasn't until July 1941, that Congress authorized the construction of eight facilities to accommodate up to 48 airships. LTA facilities were built in addition to NAS Lakehurst and Moffett Field, including at: South Weymouth, Massachusetts; Weeksville, North Carolina;

Pigeon about to be tossed from a Navy nonrigid airship stationed in the U.S. during World War II. From float planes to bombers to dirigibles, homing pigeons were valued crew members (courtesy U.S. Naval Institute).

War Pigeons

Glynco, Georgia; Richmond, Florida; Houma, Louisiana; Hitchcock, Texas; Santa Ana, California; and Tillamook, Oregon.

The semi-rigid airships were advantageous for observation of coasts and harbors because of their ability to slow down and hover over a suspected object. The airships carried radios to warn shore stations and surface craft of danger. But when radio silence was needed, the ship's crew used pigeons to carry messages back to their base. Whenever an airship left on a routine patrol and on a convoy flight, up to six pigeons accompanied the crew. A 1943 Bureau of Aeronautics newsletter article highlighted the importance of homing pigeons as part of emergency procedures in a Lakehurst blimp crew.

> Every time a blimp leaves on a routine patrol, or convoy flight, six pigeons, crated, accompany it. When messages, which incidentally are coded must be gotten to the home base, via pigeons, it means that strict radio silence must be maintained so as not to betray the presence of the craft to enemy vessels. The success of the non-rigids against enemy subs has made the nation blimp-conscious. The day the Japanese attacked Pearl Harbor the Navy had a few blimps and all were based at Lakehurst. While no actual figures can be revealed, it is safe to say that the increased number of blimps and stations is bad news to axis subs. Ordinarily messages are sent in black plastic capsules, aluminum no longer being used. Two of the birds bear a red-colored capsule for use only in emergencies. Thus, when the home base finds a birds with a red capsule that has winged back from the ship, officers know something big is breaking out where the bird was released.
>
> In addition to patrolling to detect the presence of enemy subs the blimp has effected heroic rescues of men stranded on life rafts. When feasible the blimp comes as low as possible and hovers over the raft with ladder for the survivors to be brought aboard. Otherwise, food, cigarettes, first aid kits and the like are lowered by rope and the two pigeons, each carrying duplicate message, wing back to the home station which will arrange to have a vessel pick them up. Of the birds carried on the flight all but two may be used for messages of this type but the remaining two must always be held in reserve for the sending of vital messages in time of actual combat.[56]

An article in the *Orange County Register* in California, recalled the birds at the LTA base in South Tustin, California, home to a fleet of Navy blimps used to patrol the west coast, escort convoy ships to sea and perform sea rescues.

> Birds being trained to carry messages from the air ships when they might be under radio silence or in the event of radio failure at sea of over land, were housed in pigeon lofts at the LTA base under the supervision of four people, two Waves, both holding ratings of Specialist, a Chief Specialist from USNR and a civilian well-versed in pigeon raising.
>
> The chief specialist rating was specially created for pigeon handlers. Once the

Chapter 6. A Call for Champions

birds were acclimated to their home loft, they were boxed in crates and taken on local hops of several miles which ended with their release to find their way home. The length of these flights was gradually increased until the birds could fly back from as far as 50 miles away.

For racing, the usual activity for a pigeon, the birds were trained to fly in a straight line along definite routes. Navy pigeons had to learn to find their way home from a blimp at sea. The birds had a great deal of trouble with this despite their training and after leaving the blimp, they would circle in the air many times before getting their bearings and heading for home port.

Flying over water was most difficult because there were no familiar landmarks. However, after the training, which included being released from a blimp once or twice a week, the birds developed their homing instincts. The only drawback was their fear of flying at night. Pigeons will fly no earlier than a half hour before dawn and no later than a half-hour after sunset.[57]

Another west coast naval air station, Moffett Field, trained its LTA crews to not only rig and pilot blimps, but also to learn the care and feeding of the homing pigeons that stocked each craft. Part of the sailors' training in the 246-foot-long blimps was to launch the birds safely. "Launching the pigeons while aloft was no easy feat. To clear the prop wash of the blimp, a crewman held the bird's wings down and then threw the critter from a cabin window much in the same manner as throwing a football."[58]

Lakehurst, New Jersey, was the last station where the Navy trained pigeons, supplying birds to other LTA stations, Coast Guard Stations and Harbor Entrance Control Posts. From this station, homers accompanied aeronauts in dirigibles, both rigid and non-rigid, and in free balloons. In the dirigibles, they supplemented radio, but in free balloons, they remained the only means of communication with the ground.

In the early 1940s, pigeoneer became a rating for women in the WAVES. At a conference at the Bureau of Aeronautics on September 3, 1943, it was decided that 20 of the 26 enlisted men engaged in the work of breeding and training pigeons could be replaced by women. On October 5, 1943, the request was approved and WAVES were selected and ordered from recruit school to the pigeoneer class convening November 18, 1943. The criteria for selection of women trainees was similar to that for men. She should be experienced in working with birds or animals and able to drive a car in order to retrieve a pigeon who had lost its way during a training session. She needed to have the ability to learn diseases of birds, as well as their treatment and care.[59]

The uniqueness of this rating, or perhaps a love of animals, attracted many trainees, as evidenced by an article in a March 1944 *Philadelphia*

War Pigeons

A WAVES 2nd Class Specialist holds a homing pigeon at NAS Santa Ana, CA (courtesy NARA).

Inquirer. Grace and Knickerbacker Davis related in their article a visit to the Pigeon School at the Naval Air Station, Lakehurst where the first class of WAVES was just completing the six-month course which gave them the Specialist x rating. They were to replace some of the male pigeoneers who would serve outside the country. The article stated that WAVES chosen to become Specialists x required more than passing classification tests during recruit training. "...in selecting WAVES for study at the Navy's Pigeon School, civilian backgrounds in which chicken or pigeon raising, care of pets, humane work, or allied interests had played a more than casual part becoming influencing factors." And "deep love for birds and animals, unlimited patience and determination to learn what makes a homer tick."[60]

* * * * * *

Homing pigeons found yet another role on the home front in civil defense organizations where they became a crucial part of many communication plans. While World War I marked the first time that

Chapter 6. A Call for Champions

organized civil defense was practiced on a large scale in the U.S., the Second World War saw an even greater use of civilian soldiers. The Office of Civilian Defense was created on May 20, 1941, charged with promoting protection measures and elevating national morale. This organization mobilized civilian populations in response to the threat from Axis powers. In particular, they maintained anti-saboteur vigilance.

Among the organizations, the Civil Air Patrol (CAP) patrolled the coast and borders, performed Search and Rescue missions, courier service, cargo transport and forest fire patrol; the Civil Defense Corps, run by the OCD, organized about 10 million volunteers who trained to fight fires, decontaminate after a chemical weapons attack, provide first aid and other duties. A Ground Observer Corps watched for enemy aircraft.

Several wings of the CAP used pigeon messengers. The Alabama Wing, for example, tested the use of homing pigeons to bring back messages from CAP planes on scouting missions. Reported a CAP Bulletin:

> That terse order telephoned at 3 a.m. Sunday routed 35 members of Squadron 461–2, Civil Air Patrol, out of bed and sent them on their first flight training mission as an air patrol unit. Members called from their homes in various parts of the city assembled at operations headquarters Central Park Airport and received instructions to locate an unidentified plane reported to be based and operating in a stated area. Three flights were dispatched on the mission.
> Less than two hours later, Cathryn Stamp, an observer for flight Two and the only girl in the squadron, spotted the craft concealed in a small field and partly concealed by a tarpaulin. About 35 minutes after the discovery, "Big Shot," a large blue male carrier pigeon, fluttered into communications headquarters atop the Birmingham Age-Herald News Building with news of the finding. "Big Shot," is one of the *Age-Herald News* prize pigeons trained by Ray Norman, had a new experience. He was released from an airplane more than 1000 feet in the air with news of the discovery. He performed like a veteran, flying an unerring course to his home loft...
> (It turned out that the plane belonged to Squadron Commander G.I. Alley, Jr., who had concealed it for purposes of the mission.)
> Several other birds were used in the exercise. For years, the newspaper has used them to fly news and pictures. By the slowing down of a plane to a stall, they can be released in the air, with due caution to prevent their being struck by struts or tail assembly.... There may be many circumstances in future CAP missions where radios must be silent and carrier pigeons can be of crucial importance.[61]

A later CAP Bulletin reported similar results with birds used by a CAP Squadron based at the Chicago Heights Airport.

> Recently, 10 birds were released one by one from a CAP plane at 2500 feet altitude. The plane scooted back to the airport to observe results and all of the pigeons arrived safely at their loft shortly afterwards. A local pigeon fancier lends

birds to the unit whenever needed. Some of the birds have 500 and 1000 mile flight diplomas. Describing the test, Lloyd Reckner, Squadron Communications Officer, was quoted in the *Chicago Heights STAR* as follows:

> It is obvious that in these days of rationing, a radio may not always be available. Our trial proves the homing pigeon a valuable aid in case of emergency. When the experiment first came up, the pilots were in doubt about a pigeon being able to weather the big gust of wind from a propeller. In the trial flight, it developed that if the pilot banked sharply to the left and the pigeon was released at the same time from the window in the right door, the bird would follow the under surface of the right wing, up and away from the ship without any trouble.[62]

Wings from other states followed suit. The Nevada Wing of the CAP found pigeons especially useful in sending back messages from its Range and Mounted Commands on search and rescue (SAR) missions. The Nevada Wing was known for its efficient SAR procedures. Besides the usual air-spotters and ground personnel, Wing Commander Eugene Howell's searchers had a mounted command, several ski detachments, and some vehicles. These "rough riders" numbered about 150 wilderness-wise ranchers, farmers and businessmen who often rode their own horses. They were at home in the roughest and most remote sections of the state. In a usual search mission, the Second Air Force would notify Wing HQ in Reno of their need for help. Sometimes the civilians succeeded after the Air Service had searched and re-searched an area in vain.

Until two-way radio became the standard method of maintaining air-ground contact, homing pigeons were the only reliable communication means between field parties of CAP and Reno HQ. On one mission, Nevada Wing went on a SAR after an Army Air Service transport crashed in the Desatoya Mountains. Searchers removed 11 bodies, but the area was so remote that no telephone or telegraph lines lay within 45 miles, and radio couldn't reach home base. The pigeons got through heavy storms with maps of the area.[63]

Staff Sergeant W.M. Burns, a pigeon fancier in Reno and one of the top trainers for pigeons for the CAP, started working with the birds when they were four weeks old and continued as long as they were used as couriers by the search-and-rescue parties. Special containers were made to carry the birds on horseback or on ski-pack rescue missions.

One of the most valuable things the pigeons carried were photographs, which proved crucial in many remote SAR operations. When a wreckage was partly covered with snow, or in swampy or heavily wooded areas where the terrain could confuse even a trained observer,

Chapter 6. A Call for Champions

the importance of photo enlargement was paramount to finding objects. Air observers would photograph the terrain, then, using a dark changing bag, removed the exposed film from the camera, seal it in a capsule which they would attach to the pigeon's leg. On arrival at Reno, the film was quickly processed and, a few minutes later, enlarged projections of the photos were ready for study.

Because of civilian bombing campaigns in Europe, concern about possible attacks against U.S. citizens became a growing concern. With the OCD created in 1941, corresponding defense councils were established at the local level. These councils practiced defense plans such as air raid drills, blackouts and sandbag stockpiling. The Lansing, Michigan, Civilian Defense Council was likely just one of many that employed homing pigeons in air raid drills, using them to send messages in case other communication failed. They practiced sending messages via pigeons just as they practiced other aspects of the drills.

Close-up of a message capsule used on a Lansing, Michigan, Civilian Defense Council pigeon (courtesy Forest Parke Library and Archives, Capital Area District Libraries).

Lansing Civilian Defense volunteer releasing pigeons during a drill (courtesy Forest Parke Library and Archives, Capital Area District Libraries).

At the start of the war, a massive mobilization of troops, materials and equipment embarked from Fort Mason in San Francisco for the Pacific Theater. Among the ships that passed through the Golden Gate Strait were those that carried pigeons and pigeoneers. The San Francisco Bay Area pigeon fliers were a small, but significant part of

Chapter 6. A Call for Champions

Message center at the Lansing Civilian Defense Council, where a note arriving via a messenger pigeon is being read (courtesy Forest Parke Library and Archives, Capital Area District Libraries).

the effort. Many Bay area fanciers donated birds to the Signal Corps. According to a 2015 California State Racing Pigeon newsletter, one fancier, Glen Hahn, sent a total of 70 or 80 birds to Fort Monmouth as part of the war effort. Another San Francisco flier, Stan Culligan, donated a young blue checker. Later, Stan received a letter from the office of

President Truman, reporting that his bird had served on the front lines of Burma.[64]

Before the war, the newsletter bragged that there were four pigeon clubs in the City of San Francisco: the San Francisco Racing Pigeon Club (SFR): The Mission Boys' Club: the California Club and the West Enders. The West Enders didn't last long, the article explained, because its head, Sashi Natashima, was interred in a Japanese internment camp.

Other fliers were called into various services. Jim Lewis had come to the Bay Area in 1929 and became Secretary Treasurer of the SFR in 1934. After Pearl Harbor, he was selected to head the pigeon communication service for San Francisco Civil Defense Council. Lewis supervised the Civil Defense pigeon loft on the roof of the Marine Club downtown at Sutter and Jones Streets. By January 1944, the San Francisco Board of Supervisors reported that as part of their war effort and in defense of the City:

> We have established a carrier pigeon service, which is probably the first of its kind to be activated by Civilian Defense. The finest racing pigeon stock in the West has been utilized. Fifteen pairs of pedigreed birds, donated by owners, were originally obtained and to date fifty-four birds have been trained for this work. One loft has been installed, and two additional lofts are now under consideration for construction. We are advised that our program can be expanded to cover the entire Bay Area with a speed of communication second only to the telephone network.[65]

The California State Guard, a defense force organized in January of 1941, also used pigeon messengers. The Guard was assigned the mission of guarding lines of communication, facilities and installations, such as the Golden Gate Bridge, water supplies, oil refineries, piers and harbors in California. In January 1942, the *Los Angeles Times* reported that a new State Guard unit had formed in the southern part of the state, made up entirely of homing pigeons—400 of them. In the article the Commanding Officer, Captain Harold Barham, stated "In time of emergency these birds make continued communications possible, even though power lines, radios, railroads and even airplanes may be kept out of operation."[66] The Guard, said the article, was enlarging their pigeon unit, to create a far-reaching network of pigeon messengers. The service's headquarters were at Exposition Park Armory, with stations at Santa Barbara, Glendale, Pasadena, Bishop, Inglewood, Long Beach, San Pedro, Redlands and North Hollywood, with about two dozen birds at each of these posts. This state Guard unit trained their birds every day, sending them to the outlying posts to be returned to the Armory with messages. It was a network honed and ready to go, should attacks on the state continue or increase to the point where other communications systems failed.

Chapter 6. A Call for Champions

Pigeoneers from both the Army Signal Corps and Navy proudly show off their birds in a post-war Memorial Day parade in Ludlow, MA, 1948 (courtesy Chrysler Szarlan).

The State Guard in Colorado used pigeon messengers as well. Governor Ralph L. Carr urged the Colorado State Legislature in 1942 to increase the Denver unit of the State Guard from 200 to 600 men. The guardsmen enlisted for only a year and would not be paid, but they would be available for rapid deployment to combat sabotage, quell rioting, and guard military and industrial complexes. The Denver Racing Pigeon Club donated 500 pigeons to the Guard to carry messages between headquarters in Denver and units in other towns, should communications be destroyed by the enemy.[67]

All over the country, pigeons trained with CAP, Civil Defense and State Guard units, and probably many other unrecorded groups, in some cases, forming large communications networks. As ever, the humble birds were ready to serve their country should the need arise.

CHAPTER 7

Staying Power

> ... *a single homing pigeon to let the handlers know they'd made it safely in.*—Col. Douglas C. Dillard, Korea, 1952

As communications continued to advance after World War II, pigeons and pigeoneers found less work. Both military and private companies developed increasingly sophisticated communications technology. By the late 1940s, navies of the world had highly advanced radio systems. After the war, the Navy's pigeoneer Specialist x rating changed to the Exclusive Emergency Service rating of ESX, later ESX-9792. When the new peacetime rating system structure was established, the separate identity of the pigeoneer was lost as a full-time active duty, and personnel were transferred to one of the peacetime general service ratings.[1]

The birds' value didn't fade quite so quickly with the U.S. Army. During the Korean War, the Army generally used equipment from World War II, with radio the mainstay of communications. As in many of World War II's theaters of operation, in Korea, the Army faced climate extremes, mountainous terrain and a lack of good roads. The distances between field headquarters were often too great for radios to connect. Batteries of the aging radio sets lasted only an hour or so. Wire communications proved difficult, with signalmen struggling to string wire through ridges, ravines and rice paddies. Telephone lines were hard to maintain, with enemy artillery and tanks constantly breaking them.[2]

The Signal Corps did introduce a few new devices: tactical radio teletype and improved ground radar to locate enemy mortar emplacements. In the air, the Signal Corps used planes to carry as much as 34,000 pounds of messages a month between the Eighth Army and its corps headquarters.[3] Aerial delivery worked especially well for maps and charts, and other bulky documents. Planes could do the job in a few hours while delivery by jeep might take days.

With so many advances in electronics and mobility, it seems

Chapter 7. Staying Power

Pigeoneer Frank Quatrochi with pigeon outside a Signal Corps breeding loft at Roppongi, Japan, early 1950s (courtesy Frank Quatrochi).

inconceivable that that Army would turn to pigeons, but they did. The birds had left an indelible mark on war communications—namely, their reliability. Overseen by Major Otto Meyer, chief of the Breeding and Training Center at Fort Monmouth, the first birds shipped to Korea from the center in 1951, with more following the next year. As they had in the world wars, these pigeon soldiers continued the tradition of reliable messenger service across the front lines. Corporals J. Thomas and F. Quatrochi of the 71st Signal Battalion were two pigeoneers who served in Korea. In a letter to Major Meyer in 1952, they described their arrival in Korea and initial setup, as well as their feelings about honoring their birds.

                                      Radio & Message Center Operations Co.
                                      51st Signal Battalion, Corps
                                      APO 358
                                      May 4, 1952

Otto Meyer
Pigeon Breeding & Training Center
Ft. Monmouth, N.J.

War Pigeons

Dear Major,

I have just arrived over in Japan, to pick up some birds that Cpl. Quatrochi has bred for us. While over here, he and I figured that we might as well give you a short account of some of our activities, so in this letter we will give you a picture of our operations.

A you know we arrived in Korea in March of '51 and were assigned to the 442 GHQ FEC. To put it plain, it was a fouled up mess. I won't go into detail about that deal because you already know about that, the condition we were in when Maj. Cole came over and got us out of there.

When we did get out of there, we were in Japan about a month, waiting on orders. We all thought that we would be shipped back to the ZI, but then Maj Cole heard of some outfit that was interested in using the birds, so he went over there and explained all the limitations, etc., to them and they agreed to the conditions that the birds would have to be be flown under. So we made preparations to go to Korea, one of which was to build a much needed breeding loft, which Cpl Quatrochi was put in charge of.

On 29 July we turned 18 pair of breeders over to Cpl. Quatrochi, on 30 July we flew to Korea, where we were assigned to our present units.

The conditions were much better, and although we did lose some birds while resettling, on the whole things went along pretty smoothly.

In Sept. they started using birds for frontline units having only radio as a sole means of communication. As soon as telephone and teletype communications were installed, the pigeon communication was discontinued.

This operation was only set up as a precautionary measure, and in that capacity was both efficient and successful.

To supplement the losses sustained during this operation, I received from Cpl Quatrochi twenty-two (22) Japanese birds. Although he did breed replacements, at the time there was a loft being set up in IX Corps, and they received the bulk of these. With the addition of these new birds I had then on hand (48) forty-eight birds. During the period from Oct. 51 to Feb. 52, I lost (20) twenty birds. These losses were incurred as a result of training flights only.

However, in Feb. and March there were a total of twenty-one (21) messages delivered by my loft, all of which were some importance, in one way or another. the milage on these flights is unknown but is assumed to be somewhere n the range of 100 miles.

All in all, the birds gave a very good performance of themselves, overcoming such obstacles as mountains, bad weather, predatory birds, and small arms fire. our birds out of this group that operated in Mar. and Feb., were wounded, one in two places, but nevertheless they delivered their messages.

Maybe we are getting sentimental, but we feel that some award be given to them, in recognition of their deeds, so we are going to ask Maj Cole what he thinks of the idea, that mabey they could get shipped back to Monmouth. If it does work out, I could accompany the birds, as I was informed that I would probly be rotated in June, so that would eliminate any need for another man to care for them while they are inroute.

Well Major, that is about all we have for now so I'll sign off, give my regards to everyone at the section.

Chapter 7. Staying Power

Sincerely,
(signed) Cpl. F. Quatrochi
(signed) Cpl. J. Thomas[4]

In the breeding and flying records that Corporal Thomas sent to Corporal Quatrochi, flight distances of his birds varied between 40 and 100 miles. The birds were often sent on classified flights, as this actual record shows. Neither the outfit the bird accompanied, nor the distance she flew was known to Corporal Thomas, though she was trained to fly to a number of locations near the North Korean border.

R&M Company, 51st Signal Battalion
APO 358
June 2, 1952

Subject: Pigeon Records (cont)
Sire: Band no. 034-AU-51-SBM
Color: Bl Ch Pd
Sex: Hen
Strain: Van Reel

Corporal Thomas with other pigeoneers next to a mobile loft, Korea (courtesy Frank Quatrochi).

War Pigeons

Bred by S. Singer of Jersey City, N.J.
From Belgium stock

Flight Record
Bird was settled at Taegu, Korea. In June '51 was sent to Japan. In July '51 was sent back to Korea (Uijongbu) and trained north to Kumhwa, Chorwon, Munsan-ni, and Yonchon Area.

   1st message flight: 1st Armd Amph Mar Bn   Distance—45 miles
   2nd message flight: Classified Flight   Distance—miles
   3rd message flight: " " "   Distance—miles
   4th message flight: " " "   Distance—Unknown
** Held for stock.

(signed)
Cpl. J.W. Thomas NCOIC
Pigeon Section

(** Not Mated)

Homing pigeons went on many secret missions in Korea. Starting in late 1950, with the Communist invasion of the Republic of South Korea in progress, the U.S. Eighth Army recognized that a number of anti–Communist partisan groups were fighting both the North Korea People's Army as well as North Korea Government's Interior Security Forces. It became apparent that these irregulars, if organized, armed and equipped for extensive ground combat missions, could aid in the defeat of the Communist forces.

Clandestine airborne operations, organized by the CIA and operated jointly with the Army, parachuted paramilitary units comprised of Army personnel, plus North and South Koreans and Chinese, behind lines, mostly in mountainous regions. These paramilitary agents collected intelligence about the status of North Korean troops and then made their way to boats waiting offshore, or through enemy and friendly lines. Some of these reports resulted in crucial changes in tactics, such as where to plan air strikes. However, many agents were inadvertently wounded or killed by friendly forces.

The U.S. Air Force supported the clandestine operations with a variety of aircraft, including C-47s, which could handle people and cargo drops on very small drop zones that required a low and slow flying mode. Careful training to execute a proper jump was needed along with close inspection of all equipment from parachutes to supply containers. A lack of careful inspection could result in a bad or tragic jump and loss of mission.

Colonel Douglas C. Dillard, a 26-year-old infantry officer from Georgia, was in charge of delivery and resupply of some of these joint

Chapter 7. Staying Power

CIA-Army airborne missions, code-named AVIARY.[5] A few took place early in the war, but the scale of operations grew dramatically starting in February of 1952. The missions were highly dangerous. The territory where paratroopers were dropped was remote and inhospitable. Radio communication did not exist in extreme mountainous and outlying regions, so agents were dropped with homing pigeons strapped to their legs.[6] These birds were often the only means of communication with their CIA and Army handlers waiting in the south. Just a single pair of pigeons to let the handlers know they had dropped safely in. In his book, *Tiger Hunters: Special Operations in Korea Behind the Lines of the Chinese and North Korean Forces*, Dillard recalls the use of pigeons in these difficult missions.

> On a short penetration mission in the summer of 1952, I conducted an intelligence agent team drop in the vicinity of Wonsan, North Korea. The team was given two sets of pigeons—each set on a different agent to ensure the survival of at least one set. The agents upon landing released the first set of pigeons before daybreak with a capsule message showing they had landed safely on the correct drop zone and had recovered their equipment. The morning of the second day, the second set of pigeons was released that carried a message indicating the agents had reached their operating base and would begin collecting operations. After the arrival of the pigeons, no further contact was made with the team.[7]

Retired Army bird GI Joe in front of Churchill Loft at Fort Monmouth, NJ, 1956. Only certified pigeon heroes lived in this special loft (courtesy Tommy DeRosa).

Despite some good results, the pigeon messenger system was short-lived in Korea. A high percentage fell prey to hawks. According to Pigeoneer Pratt, a total of 116 pigeons were sent to Korea, and 20 of them ended up in the talons of hawks. Birds and equipment returned to Fort Monmouth in the fall of 1954.[8]

War Pigeons

By the close of the Korean War, the pigeon's days as messengers in the Army were numbered. Electronic communications technology was making too much progress for them to compete. The Pigeon Breeding and Training Center at Fort Monmouth still had eight lofts with about 250 pigeons in each loft. Tommy DeRosa was in charge of one of the lofts, and he recalls the continual care of the birds, 24/7. This included extensive mobile loft training, and record and pedigree keeping. Even on holidays, someone was on duty. DeRosa was a handler for the retired hero, GI Joe, who lived in the select Churchill Loft with other famous war birds. DeRosa says, though, that GI Joe was only a hero because he happened to be the bird picked to carry that almighty important message in Italy that saved a village. "Lots of other birds could have done

Pigeoneer Tommy DeRosa holds World War II hero GI Joe at Fort Monmouth Breeding and Training Center, NJ, 1956 (courtesy Tommy DeRosa).

Chapter 7. Staying Power

the same thing," he said. "They were just doing their job, what they were trained to do, like human soldiers."[9] And, as with human soldiers, many more pigeons performed heroic flights than were recorded.

On November 30, 1956, the order was given to discontinue breeding and training pigeons and to dispose of them. The great pigeon sale took place on March 23, 1957. On that day, stated Major Ron Frain in an article for *Army Communicator*, "Fort Monmouth looked like a Rolling Stones concert. The pigeon lovers and breeders started to arrive at 2 a.m. to purchase the 1,018 birds that were to be sold. At five dollars a pair, a person was allowed to purchase one to five pairs of birds. All the birds were sold by 11:43 a.m. and hundreds of bird fanciers went home without so much as a feather."[10]

The birds designated heroes were not sold, and instead, presented to zoos. GI Joe went to the Detroit Zoological Gardens where he died on January 3, 1961. The Baltimore Zoo took Yank and Apex, the latter having flown more than 20 important combat missions in the India-Burma-China theater. Caesar and Flipper went to the Oak Park Zoo in Montgomery, Alabama. Caesar was credited with 44 combat flights in North Africa. Flipper was a 20-mission veteran of Europe. The National Zoo in DC got Anzio Boy and Global Girl. The former carried 388 messages in Italy, while Global Girl delivered 23 messages over far-flung areas in the Mediterranean theater. Lady Karen and 20-message Special Delivery went to the Dayton Museum of Natural History. Also in Ohio, the Cleveland Zoo got two birds, Pro Patria and Crossed Flags. The Woodland Park Zoo in Seattle, became the home of Geronimo and Eureka, both having made heroic flights in Europe. Scoop, a veteran of Algiers, ended up in the Scottsbluff, Nebraska, Zoo.[11]

In May 1957, the Pigeon Breeding and Training Branch of the U.S. Army School was discontinued. The lofts were closed. However, for years after, according to Major Frain, Otto Meyer gave a pigeon orientation to each Signal Officer Advanced Course. Perhaps he sought to instill the idea of reliability, of getting the message through.

In the Vietnam War (1955–1975), homing pigeons flew very briefly, again with irregular forces, although it's unclear where the birds came from. They may have been locally obtained, or a flock sent over before the lofts at Fort Monmouth closed.

As in Korea, partisan forces in rural communities combated Communist terrorism.

In a campaign to destroy Communist movement within the borders of South Vietnam, there was a need to complete a telecommunications

War Pigeons

network to enable military and government authorities to coordinate campaigns throughout the country. The CIA in 1957 had reported to the ambassador's office in South Vietnam about the importance of better and speedier communications for the Civil Guard posts for the counter-Communists campaigns. Without efficient communications, the Central Government was not able to react speedily to counter Communist campaigns. Nor were they able to reassure loyal villagers that they could count on quick support when needed. But, such a network was still years away, and the purchase of commercial or military radios for the militiamen in the thousands of hamlets and villages would create overwhelming problems in maintenance, battery supply, training and security. American signal planners could only propose that the rural security forces use simple communications, such as drums, smoke signals and homing pigeons.

A booklet about counterinsurgency tactics that included communications for long-range patrols and guerrilla forces was distributed to militiamen. It listed many of the primitive techniques already suggested: drums, flares, balloons, smoke, and pigeons.[12] But implementing even these simple signaling devices was difficult, involving coordination and lengthy education. Unusual items such as helium for balloons and pigeon feed, required special handling and storage. And villagers had other ideas for the birds. Said John D. Bergen in *A Test for Technology: The U.S. Army in Vietnam*, "Before carrier pigeons sent from Fort Monmouth could prove their worth, they succumbed to disease or landed in the cooking pots of hungry South Vietnamese militiamen."[13]

At least one pigeon did duty for the cause of freedom during the Cold War. In 1954, a pigeon named Lena was participating in a race from Munich to Katzenberg, Germany, some 270 miles. Lena got lost and landed in Pilsen, a town in communist Czechoslovakia where she was picked up by a Czech pigeon fancier. He recognized her German leg band and after she rested, he sent her home with a message addressed to Radio Free Europe:

> We plead with you not to slow down in the fight against Communist aggression, because Communism must be destroyed. We beg for a speedy liberation from the power of the Kremlin and the establishment of a United States of Europe.
> We always listen to your broadcasts. They present a completely true picture of life behind the Iron Curtain. We would like you to tell us how we can combat Bolshevism and the tyrannical dictatorship existing here.
> We are taking every opportunity to work against the regime and do everything in our power to sabotage it.
>
> (Signed), Unbowed Pilsen.[14]

Chapter 7. Staying Power

Lena arrived in Munich two days later, and the message was taken to Radio Free Europe. Lena was then given an all-expenses-paid airplane trip to the United States. She was greeted at New York like a celebrity, with 1000 pigeons released in her honor, including four "heroes" from World War II. A copy of her message was taken via pigeon courier to President Dwight D. Eisenhower. Lena spent the rest of her life at Fort Monmouth, no doubt in Churchill Loft.

Other than a brief duty in Vietnam, homing pigeons had not flown for the U.S. military since the Korean War, yet the power of the birds' abilities continued to impress. This time the U.S. Coast Guard called on their sharp eyesight. Homing pigeons have remarkable eyesight, able to see up to 50 miles at a decent height. They also recognize color, as well as part of the ultraviolet spectrum. On top of these characteristics, they are intelligent, quick learners, adaptable—wouldn't they make good spotters in Search and Rescue missions?

The Coast Guard tested the idea of using sharp-eyed pigeons for Search and Rescue missions from 1977 to 1983. The Project Sea Hunt pigeons were carried in a container attached to the underside of a helicopter to locate red, yellow or orange objects bobbing in the Pacific Ocean.

Their training began on land at the Navy's laboratory on Kailua, Hawaii. The birds first attended a ground school where they were taught to peck a lever every time they were shown red, yellow or orange, rewarded with food if they pecked at the right moment. After mastering the pecking, the birds were subjected to helicopter sounds, then strapped into a capsule and taken out to sea.

The Sea Hunt pigeons spotted a floating target 90 percent of the time on a helicopter's first pass, while the human air crew saw the object only 38 percent of the time.[15] The pigeons also spotted the object first during almost every trial.

Despite excellent results in all of the tests, the Coast Guard did not adopt Project Sea Hunt. The project was plagued by problems, including helicopter crashes. Project Sea Hunt never got out of the testing phase and ended in 1983 due to budget cuts.

Afterword

Where modernity stops, pigeons can still go through.—
Jean-Pierre Decool, 2012

Pigeons have flown for militaries for thousands of years, their role as couriers especially effective during sieges, where armies, or entire cities, were cut off from supplies and outside contacts. Although earlier mention is made of the use of homing pigeons in war, documented evidence began with the Romans more than 2000 years ago. Julius Caesar used pigeons as messengers in his conquest of Gaul. Hirtius and Brutus communicated by means of pigeon at the Siege of Modena in 43 BC. Genghis Kahn famously set up a massive pigeon post as he expanded the Mongol Empire in the 1100s. Homing pigeons were pressed into service during the Crusades. They served as couriers for the Saracens (Muslim soldiers) to convey information to their armies about the invading Crusaders. Pigeons were at the Siege of Acre in Syria in 1639. During the War of Independence in Holland, they flew messages into the besieged city of Leyden in 1575, bringing news of relief to its citizens and assurance that the Spaniards would be defeated. In 1849, pigeons were similarly employed by Venetians during the Siege of Venice.[1]

Modern military use of homing pigeons began in 1871with the Siege of Paris and continued through World Wars I and II where hundreds of thousands of homing pigeons were enlisted as messengers. They flew for the U.S. Army and intelligence agents in the Korean War and for the Iraqis in the 1990 conflict between Iraq and Kuwait.

Now, most countries have long since relegated their military flocks to a symbolic status or disbanded them altogether—with China a standout exception. In 1994, after 77 years of service, the Swiss military terminated use of their 30,000-bird-strong regiment. According to a *New York Times* article, this decision was questioned by some Swiss commanders. Modern communications can be intercepted by the enemy or jammed by electronic countermeasures, the officers said, in which case

Afterword

a few homing pigeons would prove highly useful.[2] In 2008, the Spanish Army followed suit and shut down their corps of pigeons, delivering the last few hundred to the Spanish Pigeon-Fancier Federation.[3] That leaves France as the last European country with a military pigeon loft. At Fort Mont-Valerien in Suresnes, just outside Paris, the Eighth Transmission Regiment keeps a small flock of homing pigeons for sake of tradition. The birds are raised and trained at the Mont-Valerien loft, and still race, but do no military service. At least at the moment. Lawmaker Jean-Pierre Decool believes homing pigeons are still a formidable communications tool and would like to boost the Mont-Valerien ranks. Without the defense minister's support, this isn't likely to happen, so Decool is pushing an alternative plan to use homing pigeons for homeland security. France operates some 58 nuclear powered reactors. If a major Fukushima-like accident occurred, for example, homing pigeons could help prevent a complete breakdown in communications. A mobile loft, explains Decool, would sit inside the security perimeter around the reactor, while a main loft would be situated outside, about 30 miles away. In case of an accident, the birds inside the perimeter would fly, undeterred, to their home loft with vital information.[4]

China harbors no skepticism about the value of homing pigeons in their military. While other countries are ridding their ranks of feathered fliers, China is building a veritable pigeon air force. According to several 2011 reports, the People's Liberation Army (PLA) is training up to 50,000 homing pigeons to deliver military information in the event their country's communications system breaks down. The PLA believes well-trained pigeons are the most effective short and medium distance communication tool if a collapse of signals occurs.

Some of the birds are being trained by a special unit of the PLA near Kunming, where in 1957 pigeon platoons were part of a contingency plan in case communications were cut off. On the base, hundreds of "jun ge" or military pigeons are trained to carry messages in case of an emergency or natural disaster[5] Another feathered force is being prepared to conduct missions between troops stationed at China's land borders, particularly in the remote, mountainous regions near the Himalayas. Trained to fly at speeds of nearly 75 miles per hour, the birds will carry loads of up to 3.5 ounces.[6]

The core of this new pigeon unit descends from an unusual source, according to Chen Wenguang, who founded the 1957 loft. In 1937, Lieutenant Claire Lee Chennault, a retired U.S. Army Air Corps pilot, was sent to help repel the Japanese invasion of mainland China. He trained

Afterword

Chinese pilots at Kunming and headed up a group of adventurous American aviators, who became known as Fei Hou, the Flying Tigers, the nickname bestowed on them after a December 20, 1941, raid on Japanese planes over Kunming.

The other "flying tigers" were the determined, unstoppable pigeons that Chennault is said to have brought with him to carry messages during his defense of China. Over difficult terrain and through unpredictable weather the birds flew intelligence and information as part of Chennault's communications network. The birds may have operated in 1941, during the Flying Tigers' efforts to defend the Burma Road, and again, when the Tigers flew cargo for the Chinese across the Hump, the dangerous eastern end of the Himalayan Mountains. After the war, Chennault allegedly left the birds behind. Some of the homing pigeons now being raised by the PLA are reputed to be descended from that intrepid flock.

Messaging via pigeons does have its vulnerabilities. The birds are limited, for the most part, to carrying messages one way. They rarely fly at night and are prey to hawks and sometimes veer off course in bad weather. The birds themselves, or the data they carry, are subject to loss by enemy action, or worse, to capture and exploitation of the data.

Despite some limitations, militia and resistance groups have taken advantage of the homing pigeon's simple and effective courier skills. In 2012, the Finnish fair-trade schooner, SV *Estelle*, sought to breach Israel's naval blockade on Gaza to bring essential goods to people living there. The Israel Defense Forces boarded the ship and found, among the crates, homing pigeons that carried digital memory cards of photos of Israeli soldiers using taser guns.[7] In the spring of 2016, a Jordanian border official said at a news conference that Islamic State militants used homing pigeons to deliver messages to operatives, including a Jordanian resident. The captured bird carried a letter with a phone number attached to its foot.[8]

In maintaining a corps of homing pigeons, the PLA may have precisely the right answer to global communications breakdowns, caused by everything from natural disasters to electronic warfare and cyber threats. From the very first use of homing pigeons in the military thousands of years ago, to the current Chinese regiments, homing pigeons provide an in-hackable and redundant flow of information. With climate change forcing extreme weather events, and electronic warfare and cyber attacks threatening to wreak havoc economically, politically and physically (an attack on the electric grid could shut down not only basic

Afterword

power, but also water supplies, cellphone towers, trains, airport landing lights, and much much more), what better reasons, and what better time, for militaries to once more have at hand a force of dependable and incorruptible homing pigeons.

Historian Frank Blazich agrees. In this era of electronic warfare, he argues that there are advantages to using an old technology, like pigeon couriers. In Syria, for example, Blazich explains that Russian electronic warfare systems have been sabotaging American electronics, knocking down communications and disabling aircraft and surveillance drones. Pigeons, says Blazich, are no substitute for drones, but they can offer:

> a low-visibility option to relay information. Pigeons can provide front line forces a covert means of transporting gigabytes of video, voice or still imagery and documentation over considerable distance with zero electromagnetic emissions or obvious detectability to radar. In an urban environment, pigeons can blend into the local avian population, further avoiding detection. The low cost of raising, maintaining and training them makes homing pigeons a quick and easy asset to distribute among a civilian population for wider military purposes, including electronic warfare.[9]

Dr. Blazich may be on to something.

Only traces of the U.S. military pigeon messenger services remain, artifacts and photographs found in museums or listed on eBay. However, Tommy DeRosa, the pigeon flier and former pigeoneer at Fort Monmouth, believes that descendants of former pigeoneers, or those enough influenced by them, maintain flocks of trained pigeons with the notion that their birds may be needed to carry messages for their country once more. Steadfast, determined, and reliable, homing pigeons brought out the best in our soldiers, seamen, airmen and Marines. They can do it again.

Appendix A: Instructions on Reception, Care and Training of Homing Pigeons in Newly Installed Lofts at U.S. Navy Air Bases

Navy Department
Office of Naval Operations
(Aviation)
Washington, D.C.
March 20, 1918.
Instructions on Reception, Care and Training of Homing Pigeons in Newly Installed Lofts at U.S. Navy Air Bases

(1) Men in charge of, or detailed to, homing pigeon lofts in process of construction and stocking with young birds, should see that the loft is scrupulously clean and prepared for the arrival of the birds. Close communication should be had with the Paymaster, to ascertain the arrival of the birds at the first practicable moment, and to arrange for their immediate transportation to the location of the loft. The birds arriving at the loft will all be young birds, varying from six to eight weeks of age, and ordinarily contained in two crates. These birds will have completed a lengthy trip by railroad, and will probably in a comparatively poor condition, because of delays in travel and possible lack of proper care and attention. Immediately upon the arrival of the birds at the loft, the pigeon attendant should carefully examine and handle each and every bird, separating the healthy birds from the sickly ones. Healthy birds should immediately be placed in a loft where they can obtain plenty of fresh drinking water, and fed sparingly. Sick birds should be isolated and kept by themselves until full recovery, as hereinafter described.

(2) As far as possible, dependent upon weather conditions, the front of the loft should be kept open, so that the birds will have plenty of sunlight and air, and at the same time familiarize themselves, to some extent, with the surrounding country.

Appendix A

(3) In stormy weather, where rain or snow is liable to beat into the loft, the outside upper half of the openings in front may be covered with swinging board flaps, hanging on hooks from the top of the openings, and held out at an angle of 45 degrees therefrom by means of a stick or support, and the lower half covered by a muslin covered frame fitting close in the dowelled front openings.

(4) While cold will not ordinarily injure the birds, it must be remembered that the new arrivals are young birds, not thoroughly inured to hardships, and that their worst enemies are drafts and currents of cold air. To obviate these, it is wise to construct four separate unbleached muslin covered frames, each fitting half of the outside dowelled front window frames, and on extremely cold nights to cover the entire front openings with these frames outside the dowels. Enough air and light will penetrate the muslin, but no drafts.

(5) The birds should be fed early every morning and about 4 or 5 o'clock every afternoon and given as much food as they will clean up in 10 minutes. Never allow food to remain indefinitely on the floor of the loft. It will quickly become soiled from the droppings, and prove a sure source of illness. Never feed birds before a flight, it makes them heavy, logy, inattentive and liable not to return promptly to the loft.

(6) Baths need not be given on extremely cold days; but should be given, if weather permits, every other day.

(7) If sand is available, spread a small quantity on the floor; it will serve to supplement the grit, (which is always kept before the birds to assist digestion,) and at the same time be an aid to cleanliness.

(8) The first morning after the arrival of the birds, dependent on the weather, plenty of fresh water should be available for baths, care being taken to remove such bath water whenever soiled, and replace with fresh water. Never allow water which has been used for bathing to remain in the loft, and birds must not be allowed to drink same.

(9) While the birds are confined, the pigeon attendant becomes familiar with them and gets them used to his presence and to the fact that feed is available at certain definite times. Each time the birds are to be fed, the attendant calls the birds by rattling a tin can in which buckshot or hard peas have been placed. The advantage of the rattling can over whistling is that the rattling can is a constant, never-varying sound, irrespective of who causes it, while the whistle varies with the individual and in case of change of attendants, is liable to upset the birds. Once the birds are used to the sound of the rattle and know that it means food, they will answer to the call quite readily. Never rattle the can without giving some feed to the birds.

(10) During this period the loft attendants make an exact inventory of the birds, giving band numbers, color, special markings and facts as to physical condition of each bird.

(11) An exact record of every occurrence in the loft must be carefully kept, showing all flights, and particulars of each bird's performance; any unusual occurrence must be specially noted, even though not understood, and all reports

Instructions on Reception, Care and Training of Homing Pigeons

must be recorded daily with the officer in charge of records.

(12) The following schedule gives approximate time to which it is necessary to confine the birds in the loft to acquaint them with their new surroundings:

6 weeks old—4 days
7 weeks old—5 days
8 weeks old—6 days

At the expiration of this period, and at about 3 or 4 o'clock in the afternoon, but not when it is raining or snowing or a fog or mist prevailing, and before the birds have their afternoon feed, the traps of the house should be opened and the birds allowed to go out of the traps on their own initiative. It is fatal to drive the birds out of the loft. If they are driven, they will fly wildly, and without knowledge of the country surrounding the loft, will lose themselves, and fail to return. The normal young bird on being permitted to go through the trap for the first time of its own free will, will perch on the landing board or roof of the pigeon loft and probably make a few short flights in the air, returning to the roof of the loft after each one, venturing further and further away from the loft at each succeeding flight. On the day selected, the birds should be fed rather lightly in the morning and kept rather sharp so as to have their appetites assist in bringing them back to the loft after their first flight in the open air.

(13) On the second day of liberation, the trap is to be opened at about 12 o'clock noon, and the birds allowed to go out of their own free will, remaining outside for perhaps one half an hour and then called in by the rattling can and given a very slight amount of food, just enough to let them know the reason for being called in; another flight of half an hour should be given just before feeding time.

(14) On the third day, the trap is opened before the birds are fed in the morning and they are allowed to go out of their own free will and fly around the loft for perhaps one half hour. On alighting on the roof of the loft they are called in by the feed rattle and again the regular amount of feed is given, as much as they will clean up in 10 minutes. In the afternoon, about 4 or 5 o'clock dependent upon weather conditions, they are allowed another flight, being fed as above, after they are called in to the loft.

(15) Never feed a bird anywhere except in the loft and never allow a bird to alight upon the ground, or on a tree house or building, in fact, anywhere, except on the roof of the loft. Never allow the birds to remain an indefinite time on the roof of the loft, always call them in by the can and give them a few grains of food.

(16) Never liberate a bird in a heavy fog, mist, rain, or snow, unless absolutely necessary. It serves no useful purpose, and may be the means of losing the bird.

(17) After the birds have taken to the wing well, and seem to enjoy their exercise around the loft, flying as it were in one compact body they are then ready for their initial tosses which must be single up at all times, giving each individual bird enough time to locate his own course or direction of flight. For further information see article on training.

Appendix A

(18) Never take a bird which is in poor condition for a flight. Every bird needs all of its strength and feathers to fly properly, and if it is not in such proper condition, it will be unable to return to its home. Unless weather conditions or accident prevent, never carry a bird back to the loft. Always liberate and allow a flight home, reducing the distance, if necessary.

(19) Scrupulous cleanliness is essential in every loft. The perches, nest boxes and floor must be cleaned every day. Water and bath cans should be sterilized. A trench should be dug perhaps 25 feet in the rear of the pigeon loft, into which should be dumped, every day, the cleanings and refuse from the loft. While one attendant is watching the birds outside another should be cleaning the loft and renewing drinking water and bathing water.

(20) All food to the birds should be sifted in a fine mosquito to wire sieve to remove all dust, etc. This sifting should also be dumped in the ditch, care being taken in summer time to keep the refuse covered with dirt, to avoid flies. Watch the food, and see that it is free from taint and mold. Defective grain is a certain forerunner of a full hospital.

(21) Except when the birds are allowed open trap, in the morning and evening, the trap leading outside the loft, should always remain closed permitting entry but not exit of birds.

(22) One of the attendants should always be on the lookout for return of birds after a practice liberation and give a few grains of food to each returning bird as a reward, making note of bird and time of return. In like manner, liberator should note birds released, with exact time and distance to be flown, and on the return to loft, compare record of return and prepare flight record.

(23) A few cardinal points: Each loft attendant should become intimately acquainted with each and every one of his birds, and overcome their fear and timidity. Emphasize the fact that he is their friend; that they will receive food, water and other comforts through him. Watch the birds carefully, both in and out of the loft. Isolate every sick bird, and if not sure of the ailment, consult freely with others. A thoroughly available hospital or sick bay can be easily constructed of an old packing box, 3 or 4 ft. square with the front covered with chicken wire. Raise it off of the ground to avoid rats, cats, etc., and face it where the birds will get all possible sunlight and be protected from drafts, wet and rain. A canvas or muslin flap over the front will protect the birds from cold and rain. Fresh water is the first essential for health and full recovery of the sick birds. Careful and regular feeding and plenty of fresh air and sunlight and the appropriate remedies obtainable from the hospital, will save most of the sick birds. A little tincture of Gentian is an excellent tonic for the birds, a small pinch of it being placed in their drinking water.

(24) The above rules are for the settling of the young pigeons in their new home, and are not intended to contemplate their immediate use by the Division or Military Unit to which they are attached. It will take from three to four weeks of training, as herein before set forth, to thoroughly acquaint the birds with their locality and to make them available for use by the Military Unit.

Instructions on Reception, Care and Training of Homing Pigeons

(25) Particular attention and care must be given to the method of catching, handling, liberating and trapping birds. If it is desired to catch a bird on a perch or board, walk slowly up to it, turning the head slightly in a different direction but watching the bird out of the corner of the eye. Slowly and smoothly raise both hands above the level of the bird and quickly swoop downward, bringing both hands together over the bird. By this downward motion it may be easily caught, even if it flies into the air.

(26) Attached photograph shows the proper method of holding a pigeon in the hand. It should be gently but firmly grasped with the hand, its keel in the palm, with the thumb and fingers encircling the body. The legs should be grasped between the index and second finger. In this way its wings and feet are permanently manacled. Extreme care must be taken not to bend, break, or pull out the flight or tail feathers or to frightened the birds by grasping them too tightly.

(27) Except when necessary, never make any quick movements when with the birds; move slowly and deliberately and never under any circumstances scare a bird in its home loft. Never trick a bird. Under no circumstances should a bird be caught when eating from the attendant's hand.

(28) Never handle a pigeon roughly in the trapping box. It is difficult enough to train a bird to trap quickly and fearlessly without adding to this difficulty by making it trap-shy. One of the most important phases of a bird's training is the trapping. A pigeon that will return and sit on the loft for 5, 10, or sometimes 30 minutes is a most imperfectly trained homer and not a reliable messenger. The utmost speed is desired, in the transmission of a message, and a slow trapping bird is a most unsatisfactory medium of communication. Begin with the first liberation and do all in your power to develop the youngsters into machine-like trappers.

(29) Avoid scaring birds violently from the roof of the loft. If they refuse to fly, gently force them from the roof, but never hurl pieces of board or other missiles at them.

(30) Upon receipt of any new addition to a loft the officer in charge of records shall forward the following information to the Supervisor Naval Reserve Flying Corps, Navy Annex, Washington, D.C.

>1st-Number of birds received
>2nd-Received from.
>3rd-Date Received.
>4th-Checked by.

A page in the record book shall then be assigned to each bird, which shall contain the following data: Ring no., Color and sex, Date of Hatch, Breeder, Brief Pedigree and record if flown previously.

(31) Cleanliness in the loft is no less essential than ventilation, particularly if many birds are kept. Therefore the loft should be cleaned out daily and a little fresh gravel or sand should be strewn on the floor after cleaning. Sitting pairs should not be disturbed during this process; neither should nests be disturbed

Appendix A

until youngsters are at least two weeks old when nests may be changed frequently to insure cleanliness. Grit pans should then be replenished with a supply of fresh grit, and drinking pans thoroughly cleansed and refilled with fresh water. It is desirable to perform the above duties while the birds are on the wing exercising.

(32) Youngsters should be banded about the seventh day on the right leg and the band should be placed so that the numbers will read upside down when the foot is on the floor. For example, put the top of the number nearest the ankle. An unrung youngster will indicate lack of attention and the attendant will be given a demerit.

(33) Mated pairs taking active part in delivering messages should only be allowed to raise one youngster in each nest, and great care should be taken so that one of the birds remain at home while the other is on a journey. Birds mated together that have produced young of meritorious value for carrying messages must be kept entirely for that purpose.

(34) As soon as the birds have taken to the wing well and seem to enjoy their exercise, flying in one compact body for miles around the loft, they may be put in the training baskets and liberated single toss,-one, two, four, six, eight, ten, twelve, fifteen, twenty, thirty, forty and fifty miles. The shorter distances, say up to and including fifteen miles can be indulged every day; beyond that distance and up to fifty miles every second day; and from fifty to one hundred miles every third day. Birds should by all means be liberated in the forenoon while undergoing this initial training and must not be fed until they return from their journey and enter the loft, when a small quantity of hemp or canary seed may be given.

(35) While the birds are not engaged in actual training flights, weather permitting, they must be exercised at least twice daily, allowing them to fly until they seem satisfied, and must not be disturbed after alighting on the loft or trap until every bird enters therein.

(36) The attendant in charge must at all times keep a sharp lookout for birds returning with a message while other birds are exercising. Otherwise the bird carrying some important message may mingle with the rest of the flock on returning and enter with the others unobserved. To avoid such an incident birds should be counted on leaving and entering the loft.

(37) Great care should be exercised on all birds returning from a journey and under no consideration should they be given liberty for exercise until they are again in the proper condition for same. This is absolutely necessary, as a bird in a tired condition will not submit to the work and will bring the other birds down with him, causing a great inconvenience to the trainer.

(38) If possible birds should always be trained in the direction they will be expected to carry their messages. Should it become necessary, have certain birds trained from the different directions, as a bird trained over the same course can be depended on to return with a greater amount of accuracy.

(39) Birds feeding young should not be detailed to long journeys until they disgorge the milky substance formed in their crops at that period, which takes from four to five days after the young are hatched.

Instructions on Reception, Care and Training of Homing Pigeons

(40) It is advisable that at least two birds should be entrusted to deliver the same message, and if important, three should be used. They should not be liberated together but at intervals of at least ten minutes. Great care should also be taken, should a strange bird enter the loft, to have the message forwarded to the proper authority.

(41) Provisions should be made if possible, with the officer in charge of air craft to instruct all men who may take pigeons on a journey to attach the following information in connection with the message: Time of liberation, approximate place and approximate distance. Blanks shall be provided for this purpose, together with a suitable message holder.

(42) The following feed formula has been adopted and shall be strictly adhered to:

50% Canada Peas
25% Argentine Corn
15% Kaffir Corn or Milo Maize
10% Whole Rice

Small quantities of hemp and canary seed must be fed the birds during the Moulting and Breeding season, at least once each day, also to birds returning from a journey. It is absolutely necessary that a good supply of grit must at all times be before the birds, as this enables them to digest their food and insures good health, which is necessary at all times.

(43) The following serial and register numbers have been adopted by the U.S.N.R.F. for pigeon bands to be used on all pigeons at the different Naval Air Stations in the U.S.A., and it is requested that all attendants become familiar with same in order to locate immediately the proper headquarters for stray messages.

Serial Number	Loft Designation Letter	Location of Loft
N.A.S.	18...................P.F.	Pensacola, Florida
N.A.S.	18...................H.R.	Hampton Roads, Va.
N.A.S.	18...................S.D.	San Diego, Cal.
N.A.S.	18...................M.F.	Miami, Florida
N.A.S.	18...................K.W.	Key West, Florida
N.A.S.	18...................C.M.	Cape May, N.J.
N.A.S.	18...................M.L.I.	Montauk, L.I., N.Y.
N.A.S.	18...................R.L.I.	Rockaway, L.I., N.Y.
N.A.S.	18...................C.H.	Chatham, Mass.
N.A.S.	18...................B.S.	Bay Shore, L.I., N.Y.

In addition to the identification band on each pigeon's right leg, every pigeon should be stamped on the fourth flight feather of the right wing, and the sixth

Appendix A

flight feather of the left wing. This marking to be done by means of the rubber stamps and ink pads provided for that purpose.

(44) The following cards will be furnished to enable attendants to keep complete daily record of every bird. Same must be turned in daily to the Officer in Charge of Records.

Date _____

Band No. _____

Time shipped from loft _____

In charge of _____

Time of liberation _____

Approximate place _____

Approximate distance _____

Time arrived at loft _____

Weather conditions _____

Weather conditions _____

Daily Breeding Report
Must be turned in daily to the Officer in Charge of Records.

Date _____

Band No. _____

Band No. of Sire _____

Band No. of Dam _____

General Remarks _____

---

(45) Forms like the following shall also be provided in order to take a general inventory on the first of every month.

Monthly Loft Inventory
To be turned in on the first day of every month to the Officer in Charge of Records.

PIGEONS

Number of breeders in loft _____

Number of trained birds in loft _____

Number of untrained birds in loft _____

Instructions on Reception, Care and Training of Homing Pigeons

Number of birds out for immediate duty which would otherwise be mentioned under trained birds_____

Number of sick birds in hospital_____

Total number of birds in loft_____

FEED

Canada Peas_____

Argentine Corn_____

Kaffir Corn or Milo Maize_____

Rice_____

Hemp Seed_____

Canary Seed_____

Grit_____

All other assortments not mentioned above_____

Total amount_____

(46) A monthly classification of birds shall be effected in the following order. This is absolutely essential as it will be necessary on special occasions to sent out the very best obtainable.

Class A-1

Will consist of birds that have delivered all the messages entrusted to them within a reasonable time, weather conditions considered.

Class A-2

Will consist of birds that have delivered 75% of their messages within a reasonable time, weather conditions considered.

Class A-3

Will consist of birds that have delivered 50% of their messages within a reasonable time, weather conditions considered.

Class A-4

Will consist of birds that have delivered 25% of their messages within a reasonable time, weather conditions considered.

Class A-5

Will consist of all untrained birds and mated pairs that have proven their worth in producing good reliable young.

No bird should be tolerated in the loft if, after the expiration of two years' training it has not acquired to Class A-3.

Appendix B.
Henri Marion's Patent for a Message Holder

(No Model.)

H. MARION.
MESSAGE HOLDER FOR USE WITH HOMING PIGEONS.

No. 569,111.   Patented Oct. 6, 1896.

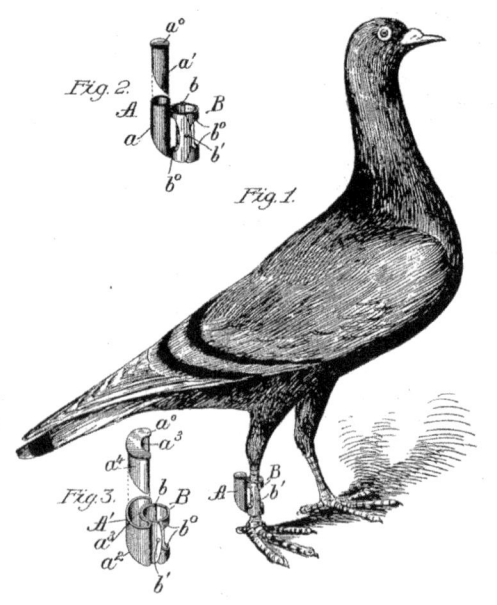

Henri Marion's Patent for a Message Holder

UNITED STATES PATENT OFFICE.

HENRI MARION, OF ANNAPOLIS, MARYLAND.

MESSAGE-HOLDER FOR USE WITH HOMING PIGEONS.

SPECIFICATION forming part of Letters Patent No. 569,111, dated October 6, 1896.

Application filed June 6, 1896. Serial No. 594,595. (No model.)

To all whom it may concern:

Be it known that I, HENRI MARION, a citizen of the United States, residing at Annapolis, in the county of Anne Arundel and State of Maryland, have invented certain new and useful Improvements in Message-Holders for Use with Homing Pigeons; and I do hereby declare the following to be a full, clear, and exact description of the invention, such as will enable others skilled in the art to which it appertains to make and use the same.

My invention relates to improvements in message-holders to be used in connection with homing or carrier pigeons.

It has hitherto been the custom to place the messages in quills and to tie these quills to one of the tail-feathers of the bird, but the quills containing the messages are often lost, thus rendering this method of transmitting messages at times unreliable.

According to my invention I attach the message-holder to the leg of the pigeon in such a way that the bird is unable to detach the same either by pecking at it or accidentally.

My invention will be understood by reference to the accompanying drawings, in which the same parts are indicated by the same letters through the several views.

Figure 1 represents the profile of a carrier-pigeon having one of my improved message-holders attached to one of the legs thereof. Fig. 2 represents in perspective the message-holder shown in Fig. 1 as detached from the leg of the pigeon and the box for holding the message being removed, and Fig. 3 represents a modified form of the message-holder in which the holder proper is curved to fit the leg of the bird.

The apparatus consists of a clasp or fastening and a box or case attached thereto, the clasp or fastening being of any suitable make that may be attached to the leg of the bird without causing injury thereto, while the box or case for holding the message may be of any preferred form of construction attached to the said clasp.

In Figs. 1 and 2 I have shown a box A, provided with a case a, and a box a', fitting in said case and having a beaded top a^0. This case a is secured to the clasp B, which is hinged, as at b, and is caught, as at b', by any suitable catch.

In order to obtain greater lightness, the two parts of the clasp B may be hollowed out, as shown at b^0.

The box a' should fit snugly in the case a, so as to be held firmly therein during the flight of the bird, and also should be approximately or wholly water-tight to protect the despatches from moisture.

In the form of device shown in Fig. 3 the clasp B is similar to that shown in Figs. 1 and 2; but the case a^2 and the box proper, a^4, are both curved, as at a^3, to fit the clasp B, which corresponds in general shape to the leg of the bird. Thus with the device shown in Fig. 3 a more compact structure is shown.

It will be obvious that one of the message-holders may be used on each leg of the bird, either to carry additional despatches or to better balance the bird in its flight.

I do not wish to limit myself to any particular form of clasp, spring, band, or anklet or to any particular form of despatch-holder. These may be arranged in a great variety of ways. Nor do I mean to limit myself to any particular material. The parts may be made of aluminium, zinc, brass, steel, silver, or celluloid, while the box may be of rubber, quill, or like material.

Having thus described my invention, what I claim, and desire to secure by Letters Patent of the United States, is—

1. A message-holder for use with homing pigeons, comprising a spring clasp or band adapted to be detachably connected to the leg of the pigeon, and a box or case for the message connected to said spring clasp or band, substantially as described.

2. In a message-holder for use with homing pigeons, the combination with the spring-clasp adapted to be detachably connected to the leg of the pigeon, and a box or case for the despatch rigidly attached to said clasp and removable therewith, substantially as described.

3. In a message-holder for use with homing pigeons, the combination with a hinged spring-

Opposite, above and next page: Homing pigeon with Henri Marion's patented message holder secured to a leg. The holder consisted of a capsule for the message and a clasp that safely attached it to a pigeon's leg. Marion's invention was the basis for future message holders used on thousands of war pigeons.

Appendix B

clasp adapted to be detachably connected to the leg of the bird, with a box or case attached to said clasp and adapted to hold the despatch, substantially as described.

4. In a message-holder for use with homing pigeons, the combination with a hinged clasp adapted to be detachably connected to the leg of the bird, of a case rigidly attached to said clasp, and a box for the message adapted to slide in said case and to be normally held therein, substantially as described.

In testimony whereof I affix my signature in presence of two witnesses.

HENRI MARION.

Witnesses:
FRANK B. MAYER,
J. R. WILMER.

Chapter Notes

Chapter 1

1. *Chambers Encyclopedia: A Dictionary of Universal Knowledge*, Vol. 2 (New York: Collier, 1888), 791.
2. Thomas J. Scharf, *History of Baltimore City and County* (Philadelphia: Louis H. Everts, 1993), 69–70.
3. Richard A. Schwarzlose, *The Nation's Newsbrokers*, Vol. 2 (Evanston, IL: Northwestern University Press, 1990), 54.
4. David Hochfelder, "The Telegraph," *Essential Civil War Curriculum*, www.essentialwarcurriculum.com/the-telegraph.html, accessed July 6, 2019.
5. "Those Who Served: The U.S. Army on the Frontier," *National Cowboy and Western Heritage Museum*, Oklahoma City, OK, www.nationalcowboymuseum.org/explore/served-u-s-army-frontier, accessed April 10, 2018.
6. James Schwoch, *Wired into Nature: The Telegraph and the North American Frontier* (Champaign: University of Illinois Press, 2018), 28.
7. Rebecca Robbins Raines, *Getting the Message Through: A Branch History of the U.S. Army Signal Corps*. (Washington, 1996), 45.
8. H.T.W. Allatt, "The Use of Pigeons as Messengers in War and the Military Pigeon System of Europe," *The Journal of the Royal United Services Institution*, Vol. XXX (1886–7): 113.
9. Michael Hill, *Elihu Washburne: The Diary and Letters of America's Minister to France During the Siege and Commune of Paris* (New York: Simon & Schuster, 2012), 62.
10. Robert Wooster, *Nelson A. Miles and The Twilight of the Frontier Army* (Lincoln: University of Nebraska Press, 1993), 69–70.
11. Nelson A. Miles, *Report of the Secretary of War at the 1st Session of the 44th Congress*, Vol. 1 (Washington, D.C.: GPO, 1875), 84.
12. Lt. William E. Birkimer, *Memoir on the Use of Homing Pigeons for Military Purposes*. Signal Service Notes (Washington, D.C.: Office of the Chief Signal Officer, 1882), 7.
13. *Ibid.*, 8.
14. *Ibid.*, 10.
15. *Ibid.*, 10.
16. *Ibid.*, 9.
17. Steven Trent Smith, "Light Conversation: after the Telegraph and Before the Radio, the Heliograph Provided Long-distance Wireless Communication," *Quarterly Journal of Military History*, 27 (2) (Winter 2015): 48.
18. Starr, E.S., "Homing Pigeons," *Century Magazine*, 32(3) (July 1886): 363.
19. *Ibid.*, 363.
20. Chris Marstall, "When the News Came on Wings," *Today's Globe*, August 20, 2011, https://www.bostonglobe.com/2011/08/23/when-news-came-wings.
21. Lt. William E. Birkimer, *Memoir on the Use of Homing Pigeons for Military Purposes*, 9.
22. *Report of the Chief Signal Officer of the Army to the Secretary of War, for the Year 1887*, Part 1 (Washington, D.C.: GPO, 1888), 6.
23. *Report of the Chief Signal Officer of the Army to the Secretary of War for the Year 1888* (Washington, D.C.: GPO, 1889), 47–49.

Notes—Chapters 2 and 3

Chapter 2

1. H.T.W. Allatt, "The Use of Homing Pigeons as Messengers in War and The Military Pigeon System of Europe," *The Journal of the Royal United Services Institutions*, Vol. 30 (1886–87):128.
2. Lt. Richard Wainwright, "Naval Coast Signals," *Proceedings of the U.S. Naval Institute* (XV, No. 1) (1889): 61.
3. *Ibid.*, 62.
4. *Ibid.*, 73.
5. Major General Donald Cameron, *An Aid to National Defense* (Toronto, Canada: Blackett Robinson, 1890), Preface.
6. *Ibid.*, 18.
7. *Ibid.*, 20.
8. *Ibid.*, 26.
9. Henri Marion, "Naval Messenger Pigeon Service," Professional Note, *Proceedings of the U.S. Naval Institute* (XVII, No. 58) (1891): 323.
10. Henri Marion, "Proposed Pigeon Naval Messenger Service," Professional Note. *Proceedings of the U.S. Naval Institute* (XVI) (1890): 439.
11. *Scientific American*, Vol. 23, December 6, 1890, 352–353.
12. Henri Marion, "Pigeons for Sea Service," *Proceedings of the U.S. Naval Institute* (XVIII, No. 4) (1892): 590.
13. *Ibid.*, 591.
14. *Ibid.*, 595.
15. Joseph C. Mosier, "The Naval Rendezvous of 1893," USS *San Francisco* Memorial Foundation, Inc., www.usssanfrancisco.org/story1.html, accessed August 20, 2019..
16. *Internal Revenue Record and Customs Journal*, Vol. 39, No. 18, May 1, 1893, 185.
17. *Internal Revenue Record and Customs Journal*, Vol. 39, No. 21, May 22, 1893, 161.
18. Henri Marion, "Pigeons for Sea Service," *Proceedings of the U.S. Naval Institute* (XIX, No. 4) (1893): 445.
19. A.M. Knight, "A Messenger Pigeon Service In Connection With Coast Defense," *Proceedings of the U.S. Naval Institute* (XX, No. 4) (1894): 790.
20. *Ibid.*, 792.
21. "Homing Pigeon Service," *The San Francisco Call*, Friday, June 7, 1895, 7.
22. "Homing Pigeons Ready to Fly," *The San Francisco Call*, Tuesday, July 14, 1896, 8.
23. Henri Marion, "Homing Pigeons for Sea Service," *Proceedings of the U.S. Naval Institute* (XXII, No. 3) (1896): 646.
24. *Ibid.*, 653.
25. *Ibid.*, 654.
26. Hiliary A. Herbert, Secretary of the Navy, to French E. Chadwick, Chief, Bureau of Equipment, January 11, 1896. Memorandum. ARC Identifier: 1742081, HMS/MLR Entry number PI-133 1216, Bureau of Equipment (BOE) Record Group (RG) 19, NARA, Washington, D.C.
27. Joseph N. Richards to Commander Bowman McCalla, May 18, 1896. Letter. ARC Identifier; 174081, HMS/MLR Entry number PI-133 1216, BOE RG 19, NARA Washington, D.C.
28. *The Advocate*, Topeka, KS, November 3, 1897, 7.
29. *Ibid.*
30. Henry G. Allen, *Allen's Living Topics Cyclopedia* (New York: Henry G. Allen & Co., 1897).
31. Jim Dolph, "The Shipyard Pigeon Cote," *Periscope*, Vol. 46, No. 2, August 11, 1989.
32. Lt. Charles Harlow to French E. Chadwick, BOE, Memo, April 15, 1892. ARC Identifier: 174081, HMS Entry number PI-133 1216, BOE, RG 19, NARA, Washington, D.C.
33. *Brooklyn Daily Eagle Almanac*, 1901, 425.
34. Professor Henri Marion to Hiliary A. Herbert, Letter, May 5, 1896. ARC Identifier: 174081, HMS Entry number PI-133 1216, RG 116, NARA, Washington, D.C.
35. Lt. Charles Harlow to French A. Chadwick, Letter, April 10, 1896. ARC Identifier: 174081, HMS Entry number: PI-133 1216, BOE, RG 19, NARA, Washington, D.C.
36. Jacob H. Gallinger, "Homing Pigeons for Sea Service," 55th Congress, 2nd Session, Document #328, July 7, 1898.

Chapter 3

1. Edgar Stauton Maclay, *History of the Navy, 1775–1901* (NY: D. Appleton & Co., 1901), 97–98.

Notes—Chapter 4

2. F.B. Anderson, "The Coast Signal System," *Proceedings of the U.S. Naval Institute* (XXV, No. 4), December 1899, 727–745.
3. Elinor DeWire, *The Light Keepers' Menagerie* (Sarasota, FL: Pineapple Press, 2007), 205–207.
4. *The United States Army and Navy Journal and Gazette*, Vol. 34, September 11, 1897, 27.
5. W.S. Schley, Chairman Light House Board to BOE, Memo, February 24, 1898, ARC Identifier: 1742081, HMS Entry number: PI-133 1216, NARA, Washington, D.C.
6. General A.C. Parkerson (editor) "Carrier Pigeon Service of the United States Navy," *How Uncle Sam Fights: Modern Warfare...How Conducted* (Baltimore: R.H. Woodward Co., 1898), 249–251.
7. A.T. Berry, Secretary Boston Homing Club, to John A. Long, Secretary of the Navy, Letter, March 18, 1898. ARC Identifier: 1742081, HMS Entry number: PI-133 1216, NARA, Washington, D.C.
8. E.F. Baker, President National Association of American Homing Pigeon Fanciers, to Secretary Long, Letter, April 9, 1898. ARC Identifier: 1732081, HMS Entry number: PI-133 1216, NARA, Washington, D.C.
9. "Coast Signal Service," *Report of the Secretary of the Navy* (Washington, D.C.: Navy Department, 1898).
10. *The U.S. Army and Navy Navy Journal and Gazette*, Vol. 35, February 5, 1898, 425.
11. Eugene Hale, *Homing Pigeons*, 55th Congress, 2nd Session, April 18, 1898.
12. *Ibid.*, 7.
13. *Ibid.*, 4.
14. Letter from E.F. Baker to Royal B. Bradford, Chief, BOE, Letter, 23 April 1898, ARC Identifier: 1742081, HMS Entry number: Pi-133 1216, NARA, Washington, D.C.
15. Baker to Bradford, Letter, June 16, 1898. ARC Identifier: 1742081, HMS Entry number: Pi-133 1216, NARA, Washington, D.C.
16. "Pigeons to the Front," *The New Zealand Press*, Vol. 55, issue 1046, May 26, 1898, 2.
17. "Homing Pigeons in War," *The Hawaiian Gazette*, July 12, 1898, 7.
18. Lt. Col. Max L. Marshall (ret.) (editor), *The Story of the U.S. Army Signal Corps* (New York: Franklin Watts, 1965), 137.
19. *Report of the Commission Appointed by the President to Investigate the Conduct of the War Department in the War with Spain*, 55th Congress, Vol. 2, Washington, D.C.: GPO, 1900.
20. L.S. Howeth, *History of Communications-Electronics in the United States Navy* (Washington, D.C.: GPO, 1963), 13.
21. Nina Morgan, "Guglielmo Marconi," In: *Pioneers of Science* (New York: Bookwright Press, 1991), 22.
22. Rebecca Robbins Raines, *Getting the Message Through: A Branch History of the U.S. Army Signal Corps* (Washington, D.C.: Center of Military History, U.S. Army, 1996), 105.
23. Howeth, *History of Communications-Electronics in the United States Navy*, 27.
24. *Ibid.*, 28.
25. R.B. Bradford, "The Marconi System of Wireless Telegraphy," *Annual Report of the Navy Department for the Year 1900*, October 1, 1900, 319–320.
26. Bradford, "Wireless Telegraphy," *Annual Report of the Navy Department for the Year 1901*, October 1, 1901, 380–381.
27. *Turf, Field & Farm Journal*, Vol. 70, December 20, 1901, 1240.
28. "Miscellaneous Reports," *Report of the Secretary of the Navy*, Annual Report of the Navy Department, 1902.

Chapter 4

1. Capt. D.C. Buscall, "Progress of the American Racing Pigeon Union," *American Pigeon Journal* 10 (January 1921), 114.
2. Wendell Mitchell Levi, *The Pigeon* (Sumter, SC: Levi Publishing, Inc., 1969), 7.
3. Clarence C. Clendenen, *Blood on the Border: The United States Army and the Mexican Irregulars* (New York: Macmillan, 1969), 334.
4. Clyde F. Wicker, "Carrier Pigeons, an Aid to Preparedness," *New York Times*, July 16, 1916.
5. Sue Morris, "Transitions: Pittsburgh

Notes—Chapter 4

After WWI," *The Historical Dilettante* (blog), historicaldilettante.blogspot.com/2019/01/transitions-pittsburgh-after-wwi.html, accessed June 13, 2019.

6. *Report of the Chief Signal Officer to the Secretary of War, for the Year Ending June 2, 1919.* Washington, D.C.: GPO, 1919, 338–339.

7. "Protection of Homing Pigeons U.S. Problem," *San Francisco Chronicle,* May 31, 1918.

8. Frank A. Blazich, Jr. "Feathers of Honor: U.S. Army Signal Corps Pigeon Service in World War I, 1917–1918," Society for Military History Annual Meeting, Columbus, OH, May 10, 2019, 5.

9. *Ibid.*, 11.

10. *Ibid.*, 11.

11. Capt. Terry M. Mays, "A Signal Company for the Birds," *Army Communicator,* Summer 1987, 28.

12. Levi, *The Pigeon,* 10.

13. *Ibid.*

14. Mays, "A Signal Company for the Birds," 24.

15. *Ibid.*, 29.

16. *The American Legion Weekly,* "They Winged Their Way Through Skies of Steel," August 29, 1919, 8.

17. Christoph Bergs, "The History of the U.S. Air Service in World War I," April 10, 2017. http://centenaire.org/en/autour-de-la-grande-guerre/aviation/history-us-air-service-world-war-i.

18. Duane Colt Denfield, "Second Lieutenant Ray Delhauser Takes Command of Camp Lewis Pigeoneer Training on May 13, 1918," HistoryLink.org, Essay 20328, posted April 10, 2017.

19. War Department, "The Homing Pigeon: Care and Training for Military Purposes" (Washington, D.C.: GPO, 1920), 49–50.

20. *The Pigeoneer: Students Manual for all Arms,* Prepared Under the Direction of the Chief Signal Officer, Manual No. 33, Unit Operation No.13 (Washington, D.C.: GPO, 1924),91–93.

21. Maj. Gen. George Owen Squire, Correspondence 1917–1919, RG 120, Box 128, NARA, Washington, D.C.

22. Frank Blazich, Jr., "America's Kaiser: How a Pigeon Served in Two World Wars," *O Say Can You See* (blog), National Museum of American History, February 11, 2019. http://americanhistory.si.edu/blog/kaiser.

23. Christopher H. Sterling (editor). *Military Communications, From Ancient Times to the 21st Century* (Santa Barbara, CA: ABC-CLIO, 2008), 485.

24. Lt. James J. McAttee, "The Homing Pigeon: A Fearless Messenger in Time of War," *Flying Officers of the USN* (Washington, D.C.: Naval Aviation War Book Committee), August, 1919.

25. Marion B. Cothren, *Pigeon Heroes: Birds of War and Messengers of Peace* (New York: Coward-McCann, Inc., 1944), 85.

26. *The Lusitania Resource: History, Passenger and Crew Biographies, and Lusitania Facts,* www.rmslusitania.info, accessed November 4, 2017.

27. TomTulloch-Marshall (compiler), "Tom, I'm Done, Throw Me Overboard," *Roll of Honour Regiments Q Ships,* www.roll-of-honour.com/Regiments-Q-ships-1.html, 2001.

28. Robert H. Moulton, "Feathered Fliers Aid Our Airmen," *The Ohio Farmer,* May 3, 1919, 18.

29. Sterling, *Military Communications: From Ancient Times to the 21st Century,* 10.

30. A.B. Feuer, *The U.S. Navy in World War I: Combat at Sea and in the Air* (Westport, CT: Praeger, 1999), 121.

31. *Ibid.*, 129.

32. Lt. James J. McAttee, "Winged Messengers," *The Country Gentleman,* September 20, 1919, 50.

33. Adrian O. Van Wyen, *Naval Aviation in WWI* (Honolulu: University Press of the Pacific, 2005), 30.

34. E.T. Wooldridge (editor), *The Golden Age Remembered* (Annapolis, MD: Naval Institute Press, 1998), 16.

35. James J. McAttee, "A Fearless Messenger in Time of War," *Flying Officers of the USN,* Washington, D.C.: Naval Aviation War Book Committee, August 1919.

36. A.B. Feuer, *The U.S. Navy in World War I: Combat at Sea and in the Air,* 130–131.

37. *Ibid.* 132–133.

38. McAttee, *Winged Messengers,* 52.

39. Kelly Duffy, "Pigeons: Not Just Air Rats," *National Museum of the American*

Notes—Chapter 5

Sailor, https://sailorsattic.wordpress.com/2018/04/26/pigeons-not-just-air-rats/.

40. *Instructions on Reception, Care and Training of Homing Pigeons in Newly Installed Lofts at U.S. Navy Air Bases.* Office of Naval Operations, Aviation. Navy Department (Washington, D.C.: GPO), 1918.

41. Wooldridge, *The Golden Age Remembered*, 32–33.

42. Roy A. Grossnick (editor), *Kite Balloons to Airships ... the Navy's Lighter-Than-Air Experience* (Stockton, CA: University of the Pacific, 2004), 10.

43. *Ibid.*, 12.

Chapter 5

1. Rebecca Robbins Raines, *Getting the Message Through: A Branch History of the U.S. Army Signal Corps* (Washington, D.C.: Center of Military History, U.S. Army, 1996), 222.

2. Chrissie Reilly, and Floyd Hertweck, "Peacetime Pigeons," *CECOM History Is for the Birds* (blog), March 2, 2012, www.army.mil/cecom_history.

3. Alfred R. Lee, "Homing Pigeons: Their Care and Training," *Farmer's Bulletin No. 1371* (Washington, D.C.: U.S. Department of Agriculture, 1924), 1.

4. *Report of the Chief Signal Officer to the War Department for the Year Ending June 1920*, Washington, D.C.: GPO, 1920, 63.

5. Robert W. Cermak, "Pioneering Aerial Forest Fire Control: The Army Air Patrol in California, 1919–1921," *California History*, Vol. 70, No. 3, Fall, 1991, 290–305.

6. S.W. (Bill) Smith, "90th Aero Squadron on Patrol," *Museum News*, Terrell County Memorial Museum, March 3, 2016, www.terrellmuseum.info.

7. U.S. Marine Corps, *Marine Barracks, Quantico, 1930* (Quantico, VA: U.S. Marine Corps, 1930), 26.

8. Joint Base Andrews, "NAF Washington History," *Fact Sheet*, February 2, 2017. www.jba.af.mil.

9. Robert H. Moulton, "Feathered Fliers Aid Our Airmen," *The Ohio Farmer*. May 3, 1919, 18.

10. "Training Pigeons to Be Mile-An-Hour Fliers," *Courier-Journal*, Louisville, KY, January 24, 1916, 87.

11. Henry Kubec, "Flights Made by Pigeons at the Naval Air Station, Anacostia, D.C.," Personal Note, ca. mid–1920s.

12. "Training Pigeons to Be Mile-An-Hour Fliers," *Courier-Journal*, 87.

13. "Homing Pigeons in the Navy," *St. Landry Clarion*, Opelousas, LA, July 17, 1920, 3.

14. "Sundry Legislation Affecting the Naval Establishment," Hearing Before the Committee on Naval Affairs of the House of Representatives, 66th Congress, 3rd Session (Washington, D.C.: GPO, 1921), 108.

15. Bruce Linder, "Coronado for the Birds" (blog), January 20, 2014 https://coronadohistory.org/static/media/uploads/historical%20coronado/Field%20Guide/coronado_for_the_birds.pdf.

16. John Fry, *U.S.S. Saratoga (CV3) An Illustrated History of the Legendary Aircraft Carrier 1927–1946* (Atglen, PA: Schiffer Publishing, Ltd., 1996), 12.

17. Gary Craven Gray, *Radio for the Fireline: A History of Electronic Communication in the Forest Service, 1905–1975* (Washington, D.C.: Department of Agriculture, U.S. Forest Service, 1982), 11–12.

18. Lt. Cdr. Richard E. Byrd, "Flying Over the Arctic," *National Geographic*, November 1925, 524.

19. Cmdre. Ben H. Wyatt, USN (Ret.), *Alaskan Aerial Survey Detachment*, Condensed from *World's Work Magazine*, February 1927. http://historian.iwarp.com/research.htm.

20. Colleen Mondor, "1926 Aerial Survey of Southeast Alaska Improbable, but Successful," *Anchorage Daily News*, August 1, 2014, updated September 28, 2016. http://adn.com/bush-pilot/article/aviations-long-relationship-fishing-industry-dates-1926/2014/08/01/.

21. Olen Cole, Jr., "African-American Youth in the Program of the Civilian Conservation Corps in California, 1933–42, An Ambivalent Legacy," *Forest and Conservation History* (35), July 1991, 124.

22. Suzy Goodsell, "Pigeons Delivered Flour Orders" (blog), July 5, 2012, www.generalmills.com.

23. Paula Allen, "Homing Pigeons

Notes—Chapter 6

Helping Military, Express with Fast Communications, Football Game Film Delivery," *San Antonio Express-News*, November 23, 2017. http://www.expressnews.com/sa300/article/Homing-pigeons-help-military-Express-with-fast-12380312.php.
24. *Ibid.*
25. Joelle Parker, Personal Communication, January 2010.

Chapter 6

1. Wendell Mitchell Levi, *The Pigeon* (Sumter, SC: Levi Publishing, 1969), 12.
2. *Ibid.*, 13.
3. *Ibid.*, 13.
4. United States War Department, Technical Manual, No. 11–410, *The Homing Pigeon* (Washington, D.C.: The War Department, 1940), 3.
5. Levi, *The Pigeon*, 14.
6. Karen Jensen, "Birds of War," *World War II Magazine*, March 9, 2018, https://www.historynet.com/birds-of-war.htm.
7. United States War Department, Signal Pigeon Company Handbook, *War Department Field Manual FM11–80* (Washington, D.C.: War Department, 1944), 1.
8. *Ibid.*, 4–7.
9. Lt. Col. Joseph F. Spears, "The Flying Telegraph," *National Geographic Magazine*, April 1947, 553.
10. United States War Department, Signal Pigeon Company Handbook, *War Department Field Manual FM11–80*, 4.
11. *Ibid.*, 4.
12. U.S. Army Medical Department, Office of Medical History, *Army Signal Pigeons*, Chapter XVIII, 646. https://history.amedd.army.mil/booksdocs/wwii/vetservicewwii/chapter18.htm.
13. United States War Department, Signal Pigeon Company Handbook, *War Department Field Manual FM11–80* (Washington, D.C.: War Department, 1944), 13.
14. *Ibid.*, 20.
15. Lt. Col. Jerome Pratt (Ret.), *Courageous Couriers* (Warrenton, MO: American Pigeon Journal Company, 1977), 30.
16. United States Army, *The Pigeoneer,*

Student Manual for All Arms, United States Army Training Manual No. 32. Washington, D.C.: GPO, 1924, 56.
17. Pratt, *Courageous Couriers*, 34.
18. *Ibid.*, 68.
19. *Ibid.*, 69–70.
20. *Ibid.*, 81.
21. *Ibid.*, 92.
22. David Price Cannon, "Frank Hauck of the Signal Pigeon Company," World War II Operation Log. https://frankhauck.blogspot.com, December 13, 2009.
23. Gordon H. Hayes, *The Pigeons That Went to War* (self-published, 1981), 21–22.
24. *Ibid.*, 23.
25. *Ibid.*, 24.
26. *Ibid.*, 24.
27. *Ibid.*, 29–30.
28. *Ibid.*, 66.
29. *Ibid.*, 72.
30. *Ibid.*, 77–78.
31. Lindsay Keating, "Pigeons in Bras Go to War," Stories from the Museum Blog, National Museum of American History, September 4, 2013, https://americanhistory.si.edu/blog/2013/09/pigeons-in-bras-go-to-war.html.
32. Edwin T. Woodhall, *Spies of the Great War*, Kindle Edition, Endeavor Compass, 2015. Chapter 17.
33. Gordon Corera, *Secret Pigeon Service: Operation Columba, Resistance and the Struggle to Liberate Europe* (London: William Collins, 2018), 21.
34. Ben Fenton, "Documents Reveal Role of Winged Spies," *The Telegraph*, 20 March 2007. https://www.telegraph.co.uk/news/1546107/Documents_reveal_role_of_winged_spies.html.
35. Jennifer Spangler, *The World War II Pigeons and the Secret Columba Messages* (Denver, CO: Outskirts Press, 2018), 3.
36. *Ibid.*, 3.
37. *Ibid.*, 12.
38. *Ibid.*, 11.
39. Corera, *Secret Pigeon Service*, 44.
40. Spangler, *The World War II Pigeons and the Secret Columba Messages*, 6–7.
41. *Ibid.*, 1–2.
42. Stephen Shapiro, "Subversive Pigeons," *The Devil of History* (blog), January 16, 2016. devilofhistory.wordpress.com.
43. Spangler, *The World War II Pigeons and the Secret Columba Messages*, 34.

Notes—Chapter 7

44. Hayes, *Pigeons That Went to War*, 25.
45. Pratt, *Courageous Couriers*, 92.
46. *Ibid.*, 120.
47. Office of Strategic Services, "Detachment 101," http://www.soc.mil/OSS/det-101.html.
48. Levi, *The Pigeon*, 21.
49. C. Kay Larsen, "Bravo Zero: The Coast Guard Auxiliary in World War II," U.S. Coast Guard Auxiliary, 2012. wow.uscgaux.info/uploads_wowll/l-DEPT/pdf_files/AuxHx.pdf.
50. James R. Powell, and Alan B. Flanders. *Wolf at the Door: the World War II Antisubmarine Battle for Hampton Roads, Virginia* (Richmond, VA: Brandywine Publishers, Inc., 2003), 8..
51. C. Kay Larson, "Bravo Zero: The Coast Guard Auxiliary in World War II," U.S. Coast Guard Auxiliary, 2012.
52. Powell and Flanders, *Wolf at the Door: the World War II Antisubmarine Battle for Hampton Roads, Virginia*, 35.
53. *Ibid.*, 41.
54. C. Kay Larson, "Bravo Zero: The Coast Guard Auxiliary in World War II," U.S. Coast Guard Auxiliary, 2012.
55. Stephen Shapiro, "Trawling for Spies," *The Devil of History* (blog), June 1, 2017, devilofhistory.wordpress.com.
56. Bureau of Aeronautics, U.S. Navy, Newsletter No. 187, 1 February 1943, 16–17.
57. Juanita Lovret, "Homing Pigeons Used as Secret Weapons in World War II," *Orange County Register*, March 29, 2011.
58. California State Racing Pigeon Organization Newsletter (Spring 2015), 29.
59. Joy Bright Hancock, *Lady in the Navy* (Annapolis: Naval Institute Press, 1972), 137.
60. Grace and Knickerbacker Davis, "Everybody's Weekly," *Philadelphia Inquirer*, March 12, 1944, 2.
61. Civil Air Patrol Bulletin (No. 10) 3 April 1942..
62. Civil Air Patrol, *Illinois Wingover* (No. 5): May, 1942
63. Robert E. Neprud, *Flying Minutemen: The Story of the Civil Air Patrol* (New York: Duell, Sloan & Pearce, 1948), 88.
64. California State Racing Pigeon Organization Newsletter (Spring 2015) 28–31.

65. *Ibid.*
66. "Pigeons Earn Wings in State Guard Service," *Los Angeles Times*, January 26, 1942.
67. Douglas R. Hurt, *The Great Plains During World War II* (Lincoln, NE: University of Nebraska Press, 2008), 87.

Chapter 7

1. Charles A. Malin, "Ratings and the Evolution of Jobs in the Navy," (Washington, D.C.: Naval History and Heritage Command, 1971). www.history.navy.mil.
2. Rebecca Robbins Raines, *Getting the Message Through: A Branch History of the U.S. Army Signal Corps* (Washington, D.C.: Center of Military History, U.S. Army, 1996), 324.
3. *Ibid.*, 325.
4. Jennifer Spangler, "Frank Quatrochi, 71st Signal Battalion Korean War Pigeoneer," *Racing Pigeon Digest*, February 1, 2019, pp. 39–41.
5. Annie Jacobsen, *Surprise, Kill, Vanish: The Secret History of CIA Paramilitary Armies* (Boston: Little, Brown & Co., 2019), 48.
6. *Ibid.*,49.
7. Col. Douglas C. Dillard, *Tiger Hunters: Special Operations in Korea Behind the Lines of the Chinese and North Korean Forces, 1950–1953* (Bloomington, IN: Xlibris, 2010), 17.
8. Lt. Col. Jerome Pratt (Ret.), *Courageous Couriers* (Warrenton, MO: American Pigeon Journal Company, 1977), 128.
9. Tom DeRosa, Personal Communication, June14, 2019.
10. Major Ron Frain, "The Signal Corps Was for the Birds," *The Army Communicator*, Winter, 1976.
11. Jerome Pratt, *Courageous Couriers*, 123.
12. John D. Bergen, *A Test for Technology: the U.S. Army in Vietnam* (Washington, D.C.: Center of Military History, U.S. Army, 1986), 25.
13. *Ibid.*, 60.
14. Alex Mayer, "The Pigeon Who Crashed the Iron Curtain," RadioFree Europe/RadioLiberty, October 23, 2009. http://pressroom.rferl.org/a/off_mic_

pigeon_who_crashed_iron_curtain/1859287.html.

15. George C. Wilson, "In Search and Rescue, the Eagle Eyes are Pigeons," *The Washington Post*, July 31, 1979, https://www.washingtonpost.com/archive/politics/1979/07/31/in-sea-rescues-the-eagle-eyes-are-pigeons/3

Afterword

1. Wendell Mitchell Levi, *The Pigeon* (Sumter, SC: Levi Publishing, 1969), 5.

2. Robert L. Kroon, "Swiss Budget Cutters Clip Army's Platoon of Carrier Pigeons," *New York Times*, December 23, 1994.

3. "Army Retires Carrier Pigeons," The Town-Crier.com, English Language Newspaper, Costa del Sol, Spain, April 7, 2008.

4. Gabriele Parussini, "In France, a Mission to Return the Military's Carrier Pigeons to Active Duty," November 11, 2012. www.WSJ.com.

5. Chengeheng Jiang, "China's Most Secret Weapon: The Messenger Pigeon," March 2, 2011. www.time.com.

6. Adrienne Mong, "China Raises Tiny Reserve Army," September 10, 2011. http://behindthewall.msnbc.msn.com.

7. Jason Ditz, "Israel Bashes Provocation of Carrier Pigeons on Gaza Flotilla," October 29, 2012. Antiwar.com.

8. "ISIS Uses Homing Pigeons to Carry Messages, Jordanian Official Says," *Fox News*, May 6, 2016. foxnews.com/world/2016/05/06.

9. Frank Blazich, Jr. "In the Era of Electronic Warfare, Bring Back Pigeons," January 16, 2019, https://warontherocks.com/2019/01/in-the-era-of-electronic-warfare-bring-back-pigeons/.

Bibliography

Primary Sources

Annual Report of the Navy Department for the Year 1902. "Miscellaneous Reports." GPO: Washington, D.C.

Baker, E.F., President, National Association of American Homing Pigeon Fanciers. Letter to John A. Long, Secretary of Navy, April 9, 1898. ARC Identifier: 1742081, HMS Entry number: PI-133 1216, NARA, Washington, D.C.

_____. Letter to Royal B. Bradford, Chief, Bureau of Equipment (BOE), April 23, 1898. ARC Identifier: 1742081, HMS Entry number: PI-133 1216, NARA, Washington, D.C.

_____. Letter to Royal B. Bradford, June 16, 1898. ARC Identifier: 1742081, HMS Entry number: PI-133 1216, NARA, Washington, D.C.

Berry, A.T., Secretary Boston Homing Club. Letter to John A. Long, Secretary of the Navy, March 18, 1898. ARC Identifier: 1742081, HMS Entry number: PI-133 1216, NARA, Washington, D.C.

Birkimer, Lt. William E. *Memoir on the Use of Homing Pigeons for Military Purposes.* Signal Service Notes. (Washington, D.C.: Office of the Chief Signal Officer, 1882).

Blazich, Frank A., Jr. "Feathers of Honor: U.S. Army Signal Corps Pigeon Service in World War I, 1917–1918." Society for Military History Annual Meeting, Columbus, OH, May 10, 2019.

Bradford, R.B. "The Marconi System of Wireless Telegraphy." *Annual Report of the Navy Department for the Year 1900.* October 1, 1900.

_____. "Wireless Telegraphy." *Annual Report of the Navy Department for the Year 1901.* October 1, 1901.

Chadwick, BOE, Memo, 15 April 1892. ARC Identifier: 174081, HMS Entry number PI-133 1216, BOE, RG 19, NARA, Washington, D.C.

Coast Signal Service. *Report of the Secretary of the Navy.* Washington, D.C.: Navy Department, 1898.

DeRosa, Tom. Personal Communication, June 14, 2019.

Gallinger, Jacob H. "Homing Pigeons for Sea Service." Presented at the 55th Congress, 2nd Session, Document #328, July 7, 1898.

Harlow, Lt. Charles. Letter to French A. Chadwick, April 10, 1896. ARC Identifier: 174081, HMS Entry number: PI-133 1216, BOE, RG 19, NARA, Washington, D.C.

Hazen, Maj. Gen. W.B. *The School and the Army in Germany and France, With a Diary of Siege Life at Versailles,* New York: Harper & Bros., 1872.

Hill, Michael. *Elihu Washburne: The Diary and Letters of America's Minister to France During the Siege and Commune of Paris.* New York: Simon & Schuster, 2012. 62.

Kubec, Henry. "Flights Made by Pigeons at the Naval Air Station, Anacostia, D.C." Personal Note, ca. mid–1920s.

Bibliography

Marion, Professor Henri. Letter to Hiliary A. Herbert, May 5, 1896. ARC Identifier: 174081, HMS Entry number PI-133 1216, NARA, Washington, D.C.

Miles, Nelson A. *Report of the Secretary of War at the 1st Session of the 44th Congress*, Vol. 1. Washington, D.C.: GPO, 1875.

Office of Naval Operations, Aviation. *Instructions on Reception, Care and Training of Homing Pigeons in Newly Installed Lofts at U.S. Navy Air Bases*. Navy Department. Washington, D.C.: GPO, 1918.

Parker, Joelle. Personal Communication, January 2010.

Report of the Chief Signal Officer of the Army to the Secretary of War, for the Year 1887, Part 1. Washington, D.C.: GPO, 1888.

Report of the Chief Signal Officer of the Army to the Secretary of War for the Year 1888. Washington, D.C.: GPO, 1889.

Report of the Chief Signal Officer to the Secretary of War, for the Year Ending June 2, 1919. Washington, D.C.: GPO, 1919.

Report of the Chief Signal Officer to the War Department for the Year Ending June 1920, Washington, D.C.: GPO, 1920.

Report of the Commission Appointed by the President to Investigate the Conduct of the War Department in the War With Spain. 55th Congress, Vol 2., Washington, D.C.: GPO, 1900.

Schley, W.S. Memo, Chairman Light House Board to BOE, February 24, 1898. ARC Identifier: 1742081, HMS Entry number: PI-133 1216, NARA, Washington, D.C.

Squire, Maj. Gen. George O., Chief Signal Officer, AEF. Correspondence 1917–1919, RG 120, Box 128, NARA, Washington, D.C.

Sundry Legislation Affecting the Naval Establishment. Hearing Before the Committee on Naval Affairs of the House of Representatives, 66th Congress, 3rd Session. Washington, D.C.: GPO, 1921.

United States Army, *The Pigeoneer: Students Manual for all Arms*. Prepared Under the Direction of the Chief Signal Officer, Manual No. 33, Unit Operation No.13. Washington, D.C.: GPO, 1924.

United States War Department. *The Homing Pigeon: Care and Training for Military Purposes*. Washington, D.C.: GPO, 1920.

United States War Department. Signal Pigeon Company Handbook. *War Department Field Manual FM11–80*. Washington, D.C.: War Department, 1944.

United States War Department. Technical Manual, No. 11-410, *The Homing Pigeon*. Washington, D.C.: The War Department, 1940.

Secondary Sources

The Advocate, Topeka, KS, November 3, 1897.

Allatt, H.T.W. "The Use of Pigeons as Messengers in War and the Military Pigeon System of Europe." *The Journal of the Royal United Services Institution*, Vol. 30 (1886–7).

Allen, Henry G. *Allen's Living Topics Cyclopedia*. New York: Henry G. Allen & Co., 1897.

Allen, Paula, "Homing Pigeons Helping Military, Express with Fast Communications, Football Game Film Delivery." *San Antonio Express-News*, November 23, 2017. http://www.expressnews.com/sa300/article/Homing-pigeons-help-military-Express-with-fast-12380312.php.

Anderson, F.B. "The Coast Signal System." *Proceedings of the U.S. Naval Institute* (XXV, No. 4), December 1899.

Bibliography

Bergen, John D., *A Test for Technology: The U.S. Army in Vietnam*. Washington, D.C.: Center of Military History, U.S. Army, 1986.

Bergs, Christoph. "The History of the U.S. Air Service in World War I," April 10, 2017. http://centenaire.org/en/autour-de-la-grande-guerre/aviation/history-us-air-service-world-war-i.

Birkimer, Lt. William E. *Memoir on the Use of Homing Pigeons for Military Purposes*. Signal Service Notes. Washington, D.C.: Office of the Chief Signal Officer, 1882.

Blazich, Frank A., Jr. "America's Kaiser: How a Pigeon Served in Two World Wars." *Oh Say Can You See* (blog). National Museum of American History, February 11, 2019. http://americanhistory.si.edu/blog/kaiser.

Bradford R.B. "The Marconi System of Wireless Telegraphy." *Annual Report of the Navy Department for the Year 1900*. October 1, 1900.

Brooklyn Daily Eagle Almanac, 1901.

Bureau of Aeronautics, US Navy. Newsletter No. 187, February 1, 1943.

Buscall, Capt. D.C. "Progress of the American Racing Pigeon Union." *American Pigeon Journal* 10 (January 1921).

Byrd, Lt. Cdr. Richard E. "Flying Over the Arctic." *National Geographic*, November 1925.

California State Racing Pigeon Organization. Newsletter (Spring 2015).

Cameron, Maj. Gen. Donald. *An Aid to National Defense*. Toronto, Canada: Blackett Robinson, 1890.

Cannon, David Price. "Frank Hauck of the Signal Pigeon Company." World War II Operation Log. https://frankhauck.blogspot.com, December 13, 2009.

Cermak, Robert W. "Pioneering Aerial Forest Fire Control: The Army Air Patrol in California, 1919–1921." *California History*, Vol. 70, No. 3, Fall, 1991.

Chambers Encyclopedia: A Dictionary of Universal Knowledge, Vol. 2. New York: Collier, 1888.

Civil Air Patrol Bulletin (No. 10), 3 April 1942.

Civil Air Patrol. *Illinois Wingover* (No. 5): May, 1942.

Clendenen, Clarence C. *Blood on the Border: The United States Army and the Mexican Irregulars*. New York: Macmillan, 1969.

Cole, Olen, Jr. "African-American Youth in the Program of the Civilian Conservation Corps in California, 1933–42, An Ambivalent Legacy." *Forest and Conservation History* (35), July 1991.

Corera, Gordon. *Secret Pigeon Service: Operation Columba: Resistance and the Struggle to Liberate Europe*. London: William Collins, 2018.

Cothren, Marion B. *Pigeon Heroes, Birds of War and Messengers of Peace*. New York: Coward-McCann, Inc., 1944.

Courier-Journal. Louisville, KY. January 24, 1916.

Davis, Grace and Knickerbacker. "Everybody's Weekly." *Philadelphia Inquirer*, March 12, 1944, 2.

Denfield, Duane Colt. "Second Lieutenant Ray Delhauser Takes Command of Camp Lewis Pigeoneer Training on May 13, 1918." HistoryLink.org, *Essay 20328*, posted April 10, 2017.

DeWire, Elinor. *The Light Keepers' Menagerie*. Sarasota, FL: Pineapple Press, 2007.

Dillard, Col. Douglas C. *Tiger Hunters: Special Operations in Korea Behind the Lines of the Chinese and North Korean Forces, 1950–1953*. Bloomington, IN: Xlibris, 2010.

Ditz, Jason. "Israel Bashes Provocation of Carrier Pigeons on Gaza Flotilla." October 29, 2012, Antiwar.com.

Bibliography

Dolph, Jim. "The Shipyard Pigeon Cote." *Periscope*, Vol. 46, No. 2, August 11, 1989.
Duffy, Kelly. "Pigeons: Not Just Air Rats." *National Museum of the American Sailor*. https://sailorsattic.wordpress.com/2018/04/26/pigeons-not-just-air-rats/.
Fenton, Ben. "Documents Reveal Role of Winged Spies," *The Telegraph*, 20 March 2007. https://www.telegraph.co.uk/news/1546107/Documents_reveal_role_of_winged_spies.html.
Feuer, A.B. *The US Navy in World War I: Combat at Sea and in the Air*. Westport, CT: Praeger, 1999.
Frain, Maj. Ron. "The Signal Corps Was for the Birds." *The Army Communicator*, Winter, 1976.
Fry, John. *U.S.S. Saratoga (CV3) An Illustrated History of the Legendary Aircraft Carrier 1927–1946*. Atglen, PA: Schiffer Publishing, Ltd., 1996.
Gallinger, Jacob H. "Homing Pigeons for Sea Service." Presented at the 55th Congress, 2nd Session. Document #328, July 7, 1898.
Goodsell, Suzy. "Pigeons Delivered Flour Orders" (blog). July 5, 2012, www.generalmills.com.
Gray, Gary Craven. *Radio for the Fireline: A History of Electronic Communication in the Forest Service, 1905–1975*. Washington, D.C.: Department of Agriculture, US Forest Service, 1982.
Grossnick, Roy A. (Editor). *Kite Balloons to Airships...the Navy's Lighter-Than-Air Experience*. Stockton, CA: University of the Pacific, 2004.
Hale, Eugene. *Homing Pigeons*. 55th Congress, 2nd Session, April 18, 1898.
Hancock, Joy Bright. *Lady in the Navy*. Annapolis: Naval Institute Press, 1972.
Hawaiian Gazette, July 12, 1898.
Hayes, Gordon H. *The Pigeons That Went to War*. Self-published, 1981.
Hochfelder, David. "The Telegraph," *Essential Civil War Curriculum*. Accessed July 6, 2019. www.essentialwarcurriculum.com/the-telegraph.html.
Howeth, Capt. L.S. *History of Communications-Electronics in the United States Navy*. Washington, D.C.: GPO, 1963.
Hurt, Douglas R. *The Great Plains During World War II*. Lincoln: University of Nebraska Press, 2008.
"Instructions on Reception, Care and Training of Homing Pigeons in Newly Installed Lofts at US Navy Air Bases." *Office of Naval Operations, Aviation*. Navy Department. Washington, D.C.: GPO, 1918.
Internal Revenue Record and Customs Journal, Vol. 39, No. 18, May 1, 1893; Vol. 39, No. 21, May 22, 1893.
"ISIS Uses Homing Pigeons to Carry Messages, Jordanian Official Says," *Fox News*, May 6, 2016. foxnews.com/world/2016/05/06.
Jacobsen, Annie. *Surprise, Kill, Vanish: The Secret History of CIA Paramilitary Armies*. Boston: Little, Brown, 2019.
Jensen, Karen. "Birds of War." *World War II Magazine*, March 9, 2018. https://www.historynet.com/birds-of-war.htm.
Jiang, Chengeheng. "China's Most Secret Weapon: The Messenger Pigeon," March 2, 2011. www.time.com.
Joint Base Andrews. "NAF Washington History." *Fact Sheet*, February 2, 2017. www.jba.af.mil
Keating, Lindsay. "Pigeons in Bras Go to War." Stories from the Museum Blog, National Museum of American History, September 4, 2013.
Knight, A.M. "A Messenger Pigeon Service in Connection with Coast Defense." *Proceedings of the US Naval Institute* (XX, No. 4) 1894.

Bibliography

Kroon, Robert L. "Swiss Budget Cutters Clip Army's Platoon of Carrier Pigeons." *New York Times*, December 23, 1994.
Kubec, Henry. "Flights Made by Pigeons at the Naval Air Station, Anacostia, D.C." Personal Note, ca. mid–1920s.
Larsen, C. Kay. "Bravo Zero: The Coast Guard Auxiliary in World War II." U.S. Coast Guard Auxiliary, 2012. wow.uscgaux.info/uploads_wowll/l-DEPT/pdf_files/AuxHx.pdf.
Lee, Alfred R. "Homing Pigeons: Their Care and Training." Farmer's Bulletin No. 1371. Washington, D.C.: U.S. Department of Agriculture, 1924.
Levi, Wendell Mitchell. *The Pigeon*. Sumter, SC: Levi Publishing, 1969.
Linder, Bruce. "Coronado for the Birds" (blog). January 20, 2014. https://coronadohistory.org/static/media/uploads/historical%20coronado/Field%20Guide/coronado_for_the_birds.pdf.
Lovret, Juanita. "Homing Pigeons Used as Secret Weapons in World War II." *Orange County Register*, March 29, 2011.
The Lusitania Resource: History, Passenger and Crew Biographies, and Lusitania Facts. Accessed November 4, 2017. www.rmslusitania.info.
Maclay, Edgar Stauton. *History of the Navy, 1775–1901*. New York: D. Appleton & Co., 1901.
Malin, Charles A. "Ratings and the Evolution of Jobs in the Navy." Washington, D.C.: Naval History and Heritage Command, 1971. www.history.navy.mil.
Marion, Henri. "Naval Messenger Pigeon Service." Professional Note, *Proceedings of the U.S. Naval Institute* (XVII, No. 58) 1891.
_____. "Homing Pigeons for Sea Service." *Proceedings of the U.S. Naval Institute* (XXII, No. 3) 1896.
_____. "Homing Pigeons for Sea Service." *Proceedings of the U.S. Naval Institute* (XIX, No. 4) 1893.
_____. "Homing Pigeons for Sea Service." *Proceedings of the U.S. Naval Institute* (XVIII, No. 4) 1892.
_____. "Proposed Pigeon Naval Messenger Service." Professional Note. *Proceedings of the U.S. Naval Institute* (XVI) 1890.
Marshall, Lt. Col. Max L. (Ret.) (Editor). *The Story of the U.S. Army Signal Corps*. New York: Franklin Watts, 1965.
Marstall, Chris. "When the News Came on Wings." *Today's Globe*, August 20, 2011. https://www.bostonglobe.com/2011/08/23/when-news-came-wings.
Mayer, Alex. "The Pigeon Who Crashed the Iron Curtain." *RadioFreeEurope/Radio Liberty*, October 23, 2009. http://pressroom.rferl.org/a/off_mic_pigeon_who_crashed_iron_curtain/1859287.html.
Mays, Capt. Terry M. "A Signal Company for the Birds." *Army Communicator*, Summer 1987.
McAttee, Lt. James J. "The Homing Pigeon: A Fearless Messenger in Time of War." *Flying Officers of the USN*. Washington, D.C.: Naval Aviation War Book Committee, August 1919.
Mondor, Colleen. "1926 Aerial Survey of Southeast Alaska Improbable, but Successful." *Anchorage Daily News*, August 1, 2014, updated September 28, 2016. http://adn.com/bush-pilot/article/aviations-long-relationship-fishing-industry-dates-1926/2014/08/01/.
Mong, Adrienne. "China Raises Tiny Reserve Army." September 10, 2011, http://behindthewall.msnbc.msn.com.
Morgan, Nina. "Guglielmo Marconi." *Pioneers of Science*. New York: Bookwright Press, 1991.

Bibliography

Morris, Sue. "Transitions: Pittsburgh After WWI." *The Historical Dilettante* (blog). Accessed June 13, 2019. historicaldilettante.blogspot.com/2019/01/transitions-pittsburgh-after-wwi.html.

Mosier, Joseph C. "The Naval Rendezvous of 1893." USS *San Francisco* Memorial Foundation, Inc. Accessed August 20, 2019, www.usssanfrancisco.org/story1.html.

Moulton, Robert H. "Feathered Fliers Aid Our Airmen." *The Ohio Farmer.* May 3, 1919.

Naval History and Heritage Command. *Dictionary of American Naval Aviation Squadrons*, Vol. 2. Accessed July 21, 2019. http://www.history.navy.mil/content/dam/nhhc/research/hhistories/naval-aviat Naval ion/dictionary-of-american-naval-aviation-squadrons-volume-2/pdfs/Chap_1.pdf.

Neprud, Robert E. *Flying Minutemen: The Story of the Civil Air Patrol.* New York: Duell, Sloan & Pearce, 1948.

Office of Strategic Services, "Detachment 101," http://www.soc.mil/OSS/det-101.html.

"Pigeons to the Front." *The New Zealand Press*, Vol. 55, issue 1046, May 26, 1898.

Parker, Joelle. Personal communication, January 2010.

Parkerson, General A.C. (editor). "Carrier Pigeon Service of the United States Navy" *How Uncle Sam Fights: Modern Warfare...How Conducted.* (Baltimore: R.H. Woodward Co., 1898).

Parussini, Gabriele. "In France, a Mission to Return the Military's Carrier Pigeons to Active Duty." November 11, 2012. www.WSJ.com.

"Pigeons Earn Wings in State Guard Service." *Los Angeles Times*, January 26, 1942.

Powell, James R., and Alan B. Flanders. *Wolf at the Door: The World War II Antisubmarine Battle for Hampton Roads, Virginia.* Richmond, VA: Brandywine Publishers, Inc., 2003.

Pratt, Lt. Col. Jerome (Ret.). *Courageous Couriers.* Warrenton, MO: American Pigeon Journal Co., 1977)

Raines, Rebecca Robbins. *Getting the Message Through: A Branch History of the U.S. Army Signal Corps.* Washington, D.C.: Center of Military History, U.S. Army, 1996.

Reilly, Chrissie, and Floyd Hertweck. "Peacetime Pigeons." *CECOM History is for the Birds* (blog), March 2, 2012. www.army.mil/cecom_history.

St. Landry Clarion, Opelousas, LA, July 17, 1920.

The San Francisco Call, June 7, 1895 and July 14, 1896.

Scharf, Thomas J. *History of Baltimore City and County.* Philadelphia: Louis H. Everts, 1993.

Schwarzlose, Richard A. *The Nation's Newsbrokers*, Vol. 2. Evanston, IL: Northwestern University Press, 1990.

Schwoch, James. *Wired Into Nature: The Telegraph and the North American Frontier.* Champaign: University of Illinois Press, 2018.

Scientific American, Vol. 23, December 6, 1890, 352–353.

Shapiro, Stephen. "Subversive Pigeons." *The Devil of History* (blog). January 16, 2016. devilofhistory.wordpress.com.

Smith, Steven Trent. "Light Conversation: After the Telegraph and Before the Radio, the Heliograph Provided Long-distance Wireless Communication." *Quarterly Journal of Military History*, 27 (2) (Winter 2015).

Smith, S.W. (Bill). "90th Aero Squadron on Patrol." *Museum News*, Terrell County Memorial Museum, March 3, 2016. www.terrellmuseum.info.

Spangler, Jennifer. *The World War II Pigeons and the Secret Columba Messages.* Denver, CO: Outskirts Press, 2018.

Bibliography

Spears, Lt. Col. Joseph F. "The Flying Telegraph." *National Geographic Magazine*, April 1947.

Starr, E.S. "Homing Pigeons." *Century Magazine*, 32(3) July 1886.

Sterling, Christopher H. (editor). *Military Communications: From Ancient Times to the 21st Century.* Santa Barbara, CA: ABC-CLIO, 2008.

"Sundry Legislation Affecting the Naval Establishment." Hearing Before the Committee on Naval Affairs of the House of Representatives, 66th Congress, 3rd Session. Washington, D.C.: GPO, 1921.

"They Winged Their Way Through Skies of Steel." *The American Legion Weekly*, August 29, 1919.

"Those Who Served: The U.S. Army on the Frontier." *National Cowboy and Western Heritage Museum*, Oklahoma City. Accessed April 10, 2018. www.nationalcowboymuseum.org/explore/served-u-s-army-frontier.

The Town-Crier.com, English Language Newspaper, "Army Retires Carrier Pigeons." Costa del Sol, Spain. April 7, 2008.

Tulloch-Marshall, Tom (compiler). "Tom, I'm Done, Throw Me Overboard," Roll of Honour Regiments Q Ships, www.roll-of-honour.com/Regiments/Q-ships-1.html, 2001.

Turf, Field & Farm Journal, Vol. 70, December 20, 1901, 1240.

The United States Army and Navy Journal and Gazette, Vol. 34, September 11, 1897, 27.

US Army Medical Department, Office of Medical History. *Army Signal Pigeons*, Chapter XVIII. https://history.amedd.army.mil/booksdocs/wwii/vetservicewwii/chapter18.htm.

US Marine Corps. *Marine Barracks, Quantico, 1930.* Quantico, VA: US Marine Corps, 1930.

Van Wyen, Adrian O. *Naval Aviation in WWI.* Honolulu: University Press of the Pacific, 2005.

Wainwright, Lt. Richard. "Naval Coast Signals." *Proceedings of the U.S. Naval Institute*, XV, No. 1 (1889).

Wicker, Clyde F. "Carrier Pigeons an Aid to Preparedness." *New York Times*, July 16, 1916.

"Wireless Telegraphy." *Annual Report of the Navy Department for the Year 1901.* October 1, 1901.

Woodhall, Edwin T. *Spies of the Great War.* Kindle Edition, Endeavor Compass, 2015.

Wooldridge, E.T. (editor). *The Golden Age Remembered.* Annapolis, MD: Naval Institute Press, 1998.

Wooster, Robert. *Nelson A. Miles and the Twilight of the Frontier Army.* Lincoln: University of Nebraska Press, 1993.

Wyatt, Cdre. Ben H., (Ret.). *Alaskan Aerial Survey Detachment.* Condensed from *World's Work Magazine*, February 1927. http://historian.iwarp.com/research.htm.

Index

Numbers in **_bold italics_** indicate pages with illustrations

Abell, Arunah S. 7
Academy *see* U.S. Naval Academy
Advocate newspaper 42
AEF *see* American Expeditionary Force
Aeromarine Company 108
Afghan War 55
Africa 61
African American Company 2923-C 107
Afrika Corps 123
HMS *Agamemnon* 71
agents 124, 127, 129, 136, 141, 156, 157, 162
An Aid to National Defense 25–26
air raid drills 147
Air Service *see* U.S. Army Air Service
airships 93, 94, 141, 142
Aisne-Marne Offensive 73–74
Akron, Ohio 93
Alaska 106, 107, 116
Albany County Homing Club 13
Alcatraz 62
Allatt, Capt. H.T.W. 23, 24
Allied forces 3, 128, 136
American Civil War 8, 9, 11, 12, 17, 27, 32, 44, 55
American Expeditionary Force (AEF) 68, 71, 76, 80, 85
American Legion 83
The American Pigeon Journal 65
The American Pigeon Keeper 65
American Pigeon Service *see* U.S. Army Signal Corps Pigeon Service
The American Racing Pigeon News 65
American Racing Pigeon Union 65, 69
America's Cup 17
Anacostia, Washington, D.C. 100, **_100_**, 101, **_101_**, 102, **_102_**, 103, 104
Angeles National Forest 98
Annapolis, Maryland 21, 23, 27, 30, 31, 32, 35, 36, 39, 41, 45, 46, 51, 54, 83, 84
Annual Report of the Signal Officer 17
anti-submarine warfare 84, 138, **_139_**
Antwerp, Belgium 47

Anzio, Italy 125
Anzio Boy (pigeon) 159
Apache 15
Apennine Mountains **_125_**
Apex (pigeon) 159
Arctic 106
Ardennes Campaign 119
Arizona 15, 66
Army *see* U.S. Army
Army Balloon and Airship School 96
Army Communicator 159
Arnold, Col. H. H. 97
Arnoux, C.T. 16, 17
Ashantee War 55
Asia 11, 116
Atlantic City, New Jersey 32
Atlantic Coast 30, 33, 47, 56, 64
Aurora, Illinois 71
Austin, Texas 108
Austria 24
Auxiliary Coast Guard patrols 140
AVIARY operation 157
aviation camps 69
aviators 76, 80, 86, 87, 91, **_99_**, 101, 104, 164
Axis powers 3, 128, 145

B-25 bomber 136
Bailey, Roderick 128
Baker, E.F. 53, 56
balloons 10, 11, 85, 93, 96, 128, 143, 160; *see also* lighter-than-aircraft
Baltimore, Maryland 7, 8, 53, 56, 57, 159
Baltimore Sun 7, 58
Baltimore Zoo 159
Barham, Capt. Harold 150
Bartoldi, Frédéric Auguste 10
Battle of the Bulge 121
Bejá, Tunisia 123, 134
Belgium 3, 11, 24, 39, 47, 86, 117, 119, 120, 121, 128
Belknap, Rear Adm. George E. 36
Bennett, James Gordon 62

195

Index

Benson, Lt. W.S. 32, 33
Berry, A.T. 53
Bhamo, Burma 136
Birkhimer, 1st Lt. William E. 13, 14
USS *Birmingham* 83
Bishop, California 150
Bizerte, Tunisia 134
Black Magic (pigeon) 133
Black 92nd Infantry Division 74
Black Shirts 123
Blackie Halligan (pigeon) 137
Blanchette (pigeon) 81
blockade 58, 164
bloom 113
Board of Aeronautics, U.S. Navy 84
BOE *see* Bureau of Equipment
bombers 86, 132, 133, 134, *141*
Boon Island, Maine 51
Boston 7, 17, 30, 36, 40, 43, 53, 56
Boston Daily Mail 7
Boston Globe 17
Boston Homing Club 53
Boucq, France 71
Boulogne, France 7
Bournemouth, England 61
Bradford, Cmdre. Royal B. 56, 63
Brazil 34
Brewer, Charles 119
Britain *see* Great Britain
British Isles 84
British Military Intelligence 128
British Naval Service 84
British 10th Corps, British Army 134
Brittany, France 130
USS *Brooklyn* 51
Brooklyn, New York 29, 35, 44, 64
Brooklyn Daily Eagle Almanac 44
Brooklyn Navy Yard 44, 46, 54
Brooks Airfield, Texas 96
Brown, David 133
Brown, Rear Adm. George 44, 45
Brutus 162
Buffalo, New York 54
Bureau of Aeronautics 142, 143
Bureau of Equipment (BOE) 40, 45, 46, 47, 50, 52, 56, 62, 63
Burma Queen (pigeon) 136
Burma Road 164
Burns, SSgt. W.M. 146
Buscall, Lt. David C. 68, 71

C-47 airplane 156
California 41, 77, 97, 98, 101, 107, 141, 142, 150
California Club 150
California Sperry Flour Company 107
California State Guard 150
Calvados, France 129

Cameron, Maj. Gen. Donald R. 4, 25, 26
camouflage 122
Camp, John F. 108
Camp Claiborne, Louisiana 113
Camp Crowder, Missouri 112, 135
Camp Furlong, New Mexico 66, 67
Camp La Cienega, California 107
Camp Vail, New Jersey 95
Canada 3, 18, 19, 26, 27, 173, 175
CAP *see* Civil Air Patrol
Cape Charles, Virginia 43, 51
Cape Hatteras, North Carolina 138
Cape Henry, Virginia 39
Cape May, New Jersey 35
capstan 32, 44
Captain Fulton (pigeon) *122*
Captain Lederman (pigeon) 136
Caribbean 57
Carney, Lt. John L. 68, 69, 71, 72
Carr, Gov. Ralph L. 151
Carranza, Venustiano 66
Cassino, Italy 125, 126, *126*, 127
CCC *see* Civilian Conservation Corps
Central Intelligence Agency (CIA) 5, 135, 156, 157, 160
Central Pacific 116, 135
Central Pacific Railroad 8
Central Powers 65
Century Magazine 16
Cervera, Adm. Pascual 57
Charleston, South Carolina 23, 141
Charrot, John Douglas 128
Chatham, Massachusetts 91, 101, 173
Chen Wenguang 163
Chennault, Lt. Claire Lee 163
Cher Ami (pigeon) 80, 95
Cherbourg, France 120
Chesapeake Bay 31, 56, 57
Chester, Cdr. Colby M. 32, 34, 36
Chief Joseph 12
Childs, George 35, 36
China 116, 117, 162, 163, 164
USS *China* 60
China-Burma-India Theater 116, 135
Churchill Loft 95, 135, *157*, 158, 161
CIA *see* Central Intelligence Agency
Cincinnati, Ohio 56
SS *Circassia* 16
Civil Air Patrol (CAP) 5, 138, 145, 146, 151;
    Alabama Wing 145; Chicago Heights Airport Wing 145; Nevada Wing 146
Civil Defense Corps 145
Civil War *see* American Civil War
Civilian Conservation Corps (CCC) 107
Civilian Defense Council 5, 147, *147*, *149*
clandestine operations 156
Cleveland, Pres. Grover 24, 35, 49
Cleveland National Forest 98, 107

196

Index

Cleveland Zoo 159
Cline, Joe 86
Coast Guard *see* U.S. Coast Guard
Coast Guard Auxiliary and Reserves 138
Coast Signal Service 50, 54
Coastal Convoy System 138
Coastal Picket Force 140
Cob Dock 44
Coco Solo, Panama 91
Cold War 160
Colonia Dublán, Mexico 66
Colorado 9, 59, 151
Colorado State Guard 151
Colorado State Legislature 151
COLUMBA 128; *see also* Operation Columba
Columba livia 3
Columbia 62
Columbus, Christopher 34
Columbus, New Mexico 66
Colvi Vecchia, Italy 134
Comanche 12
combat 71, *74*, 112, 113, 115, 116, 122, 124, *125*, *126*, 134, 156, 159
communications 5, 6, 8, 9, 12, *12*, 15, 18, 21, 22, 23, 25, 26, 30, 34, 37, 42, 50, 55, 56, 59, 60, 61, 65, 67, 72, 74, 81, 82, 96, *97*, 108, 110, 118, 119, 135, 139, 145, 150, 151, 152, 153, 154, 158, 160, 162, 163, 164, 165
Communist forces 156
Congress *see* U.S. Congress
USS *Constellation* 32, 33, 44
Convoy (naval) 57, 84, 85, 93, 137, 138, 139, 142
Cornieville, France 71
Coronado Historical Society 104
Corpus Christi, Texas 96
Corsica 134
cote 18, 21, 26, 29, *31*, 32, 33, 35, 37, 40, 41, *41*, 42, 43, *43*, 44, 45, 46, 47, 48, 52, 54, 58
counterinsurgency tactics 160
Country Gentleman (magazine) 90–91
couriers 1, 5, 7, 10, 20, 22, 33, 46, 53, 55, 58, 67, 72, 77, 78, 84, 86, 98, 102, 104, 112, 115, *122*, 124, 127, 145, 146, 161, 162, 164, 165
Craig, Daniel H. 7, 8, 17
Cramp, Edgar S. 36
Crisp, Skipper Tom 85
Crossed Flags (pigeon) 159
Crusades 162
Cuba 17, 18, 20, 45, 49, 52, 56, 57, 58, 59, 60, 61, 108
Cuisy Bill (pigeon) 82
Culligan, Stan 149
Curtiss float planes 83
Curtiss HS-2L flying boats 92

Curtiss JN-4D airplane 98
Curtiss JN-4H airplane 98
cyber threats 164

Dagron, M. René 10
Dahlgren guns 32
Daily Express newspaper 61
Daly, Master-at-Arms 1st Class 44
Davis, Cdr. John 57
Davis, Grace and Knickerbacker 144
Dayton, Ohio 2
Dayton Museum of Natural History 159
D-Day 117
Decool, Jean-Pierre 162, 163
Delhauer, 2nd Lt. Ray 77
Denfield, LCdr. G.W. 62
Denmark 11, 24
Denver, Colorado 151
Denver Racing Pigeon Club 151
Department of Agriculture *see* U.S. Department of Agriculture
DeRosa, Tom 135, *157*, 158, *158*, 165
Desatoya Mountains, Nevada 146
Detroit Zoological Garden 159
Dewey, Cmdre. George 56, 57, 59, 60, 62
Dickin Medal 134
Dillard, Col. Douglas C. 152, 156, 157
dirigibles 93, *141*, 143; *see also* lighter-than-aircraft
USS *Dolphin* 34, 35, 51
Donovan, Col. William 135; *see also* Office of Strategic Services (OSS)
Doolittle, Jimmy 99, 100
double-tossed 115
drones 165
DuBois, Coert 97

Eagle Pass Airfield, Texas 98
Eighth Transmission Regiment 163
Eisenhower, Pres. Dwight D. 161
El Caney, Cuba 57
El Paso, Texas 99
electronic warfare 164, 165
elephants, Castor and Pollux 23
Ely, Eugene 83
Endicott Board 50
England 7, 8, 23, 24, 39, 47, 55, 61, 63, 76, 85, 86, 88, 117, 119, 120, 129, 130, 131, 135
Englewood, California 150
English Channel 7, 61
Entente Powers 65, 86
espionage 127, 128
SV *Estelle* 164
Etah (Greenland) 106
Eureka (pigeon) 159
Europe 7, 8, 11, 24, 26, 27, 39, 47, 61, 64, 65, 66, 68, 76, 91, 93, 116, 119, 135, 137, 147, 159

197

Index

Exeter blitz 118
Exposition Park Armory, California 150
Express Newspaper Company 108

F-5-L seaplane 102
Fall River, Massachusetts 29, 33, 53, 56
Farallon Islands 38
Fifth Army Corps 57
Fifth Infantry *see* U.S. Army 5th Infantry
Fifth Naval District 138
Figaro newspaper 38
Fire Island Light-ship 62
First Aero Squadron 66, 76
First Aeronautic Detachment 85
First Colorado Infantry 59
Flanders 2, 87, 130
Flanders, Alan B. 138
Flipper (pigeon) 159
Florence, Italy 125
Flying Huntress 61
Flying Tigers 164
FM radio 110
Forgotten Voices Of The Secret War 128
Forsyth, Brig. Gen. James W. 11
Fort Benning, Georgia 112
Fort Custer, Montana 15
Fort Hamilton, New York 62
Fort Huachuca, Arizona 15
Fort Jackson, South Carolina 113
Fort Keogh, Montana 14, 15
Fort Lewis, Oregon 77
Fort Mason, California 62
Fort Meade, Maryland 113
Fort Meyer, Virginia 82, 76
Fort Monmouth, New Jersey 69, 82, 83, 95, 110, 114, 135, 149, 153, 157, *157*, *158*, 159, 160, 165
Fort Monroe, Virginia 35
Fort Mont-Valerien, Suresnes, France 163
Fort Sam Houston, Texas 96
Fort Taylor, Florida 17
Frain, Maj. Ron 159
France 2, 3, 7, 10, 11, 23, 24, 38, 39, 47, 61, 71, 73, 75, 76, *77*, *78*, 85, 86, 89, 91, *91*, *92*, 117, 119, 128, 130, 131, 132, 134, 163
Franco-Prussian War 23
Franklin, Benjamin 9
free balloons 93, 96, 143; *see also* lighter-than-aircraft
frontier 8, 9, 14, 24, 56
Fukushima 163
Futa Pass, Italy 125, *125*

Gafsa, Tunisia 133
Gambetta, Léon 11
USS *Gannet* 106
Gaul 162
Gaza 164

Genghis Kahn 162
Germans 1, 2, 65, 67, 75, 82, 119, 121, 125, 126, 127, 129, 130, 132, 133
Germany 11, 13, 24, 34, 47, 68, 76, 82, 119, 129, 130, 137, 160
Geronimo 16
Geronimo (pigeon) 159
GI Joe (pigeon) 133, 134, 135, *157*, 158, *158*, 159
Gilkie, Thomas 36
Glendale, California 150
Global Girl (pigeon) 159
Glynco, Georgia 142
Golden Gate Bridge 150
Goodrich, Capt. Casper 53
Governor's Island, New York 62
Grant, Arizona 15
Great Britain 3, 7, 24, 34, 61, 65, 84, 86, 91, 93, 128, 133, 134, 137
Great Plains 8, 9, 12, 13, 14
Great War 67, 95; *see also* World War I
Greely, Adolphus W. 17, 18, 20, 39
Greene, Gen. Francis 59, 60
Ground Observer Corps 145
Guadalcanal 137
Guantanamo, Cuba 57
Gulf of Mexico 45, 52, 138, 139, 140, 192
Gulfport, Mississippi 120
Gunpowder (pigeon) 71
Gurkhas 127

Hael, Marie 23
Hahn, Glen 149
Hale, Sen. Eugene 55
Halifax, Nova Scotia 27
Hangman's Hill 127
Harley-Davidson motorcycle *75*
Harlow, Lt. Charles H. 45, 46, 48, 51, 58
Hauck, Cpl. Frank 6, 119, 120
Havana, Cuba 17, 20, 39, 56, 58
Hawaii 52, 69, 95, 161
Hawaiian Gazette 57, 58, 60
Hayes, Charles L. 107
Hayes, Sgt. Gordon H. 121, 122, 124, 125, 126
Hazen, Col. William B. 11, 12, 17
Hearing Before the Committee on Naval Affairs of the House of Representative, 1921 95
Hearst, William Randolph 49
heliograph 10, 15, 16, 29, 66, 72, 84
Henry, Joseph 9
Herbert, Hilary A. 40, 45
Herbert, Lila 35
Herford, Germany 121
Higginson, Cdr. Frances J. 29, 30, *31*, 44
Highlands, New Jersey 62
Hill, Ens. F.K. 36

198

Index

Himalayan Mountains 163, 164
Hindenburg Line 2
Hirtius 162
Hitchcock, Texas 142
Hitler, Adolf 137
Holland 3, 34, 39, 117, 119, 120, 128, 129, 162
Hong Kong 56
Hoorn, Holland 129
Houma, Louisiana 142
Howell, Wing Cdr. Eugene 146
Hudson River 34
Hump 164; *see also* Himalayan Mountains
Hunt, Geoffery 60

Idaho 105
Imperial Army 82
Inaugural Animals Medal of Bravery Award Ceremony 134; *see also* Dickin Medal
USS *Indiana* 51
Indians 8, 9, 12, 14, 56
intelligence (information) 25, 46, 77, 127, 128, 130, 132, 133, 134, 135, 136, 137, 139, 156, 157, 164
Internal Revenue Record and Customs Journal 36
International Code of Signals 22
International Naval Rendezvous 34
USS *Iowa* 51
Iraq 162
Ireland 61, 85
Iron Curtain 160
Islamic State militants 164
Isle of Wright 61
Israel Defense Forces 164
Italy 11, 24, 34, 47, 85, *122*, 125, *125*, 126, *126*, 133, 134, 158, 159

Japan *153*, 154, 156
Japanese 110, 135, 136, 137, 142, 163
Jefferson, Thomas 9
Jerry 118, 121, 123
SS *John Ericsson* 120
John Silver 2, 3
The Journal (newspaper) 49
Journal of the Royal United Services Institution 23
Julius Caesar 162
Julius Caesar (pigeon) 133, 159
Jungle Joe (pigeon) 136
USS *Juniata* 29
Just Jerry (pigeon) 127

Kachin Rangers 135
Kailua, Hawaii 161
Kaiser (pigeon) 82, 83
Kaja-Boy (pigeon) 81
Kansas 9, 42

Kasserine Pass, Tunisia 133
Katzenberg, Germany 160
Kelly, Joseph 140
Key West, Florida 17, 18, 20, 21, 26, 28, 30, 39, 40, 45, 46, 51, 56, 58, 60, 64, 66, 91, 101, 108
Key West Pigeon Loft 40, 45
Killingholme, England 88
King Bloomfield (pigeon) 81
Kiowa 12
kite balloon 93; *see also* lighter-than-aircraft
Knight, Lt. Austin 36, 37
Koening, Edward 38
Koestar, Lt. Charles 110
Korean War 5, 152, 158, 161, 162
Kotlin Island 61
Kremlin, Soviet Union 160
Kubec, Chief Quartermaster Henry 101, 102, *102*
Kunming, China 163
Kuwait 162

Lady Astor (pigeon) 124
Lady Karen (pigeon) 159
Lakewood, Ohio 71
USS *Langley* 104, *105*, 106
Lansing, Michigan Civilian Defense Council 147, *147*, *148*, *149*; *see also* Civilian Defense Council
Las Guasimas, Cuba 57
Le Croisic, France 87, 89
Lederman, Capt. Morris Y. 117, 135, 136
Lee, Consul General Fitzhugh 56
Lena (pigeon) 160, 161
Lewes, Delaware 36
Lewis, Jim 150
Lewis gun 93, 88
USS *Lexington* 104
Leyden, Holland 162
life-savings stations 25, 47, 50
light-ship 37, 47
lighter-than-aircraft (LTA) 93, 104, 141, 142, 143
lighthouses 25, 27, 37, 43, 47, 50, 51, 52
Linder, Bruce 104
Loening amphibious airplane 106
Loire Valley, France 23
London 7, 134
London Telegraph 128
Long, John D. 50, 52, 53, 64
Long Beach, California 150
long-range patrols 160
Los Angeles Times 150
LTA *see* lighter-than-aircraft
Lunga River, Solomon Islands 137
RMS *Lusitania* 67, 84
Luxembourg 119, 120

199

Index

Maastrick, Holland [Maastricht] 120
Macmillan, Donald E. 106
Maidenform Brassiere 127
USS *Maine* 24, 52
Manasquan, New Jersey 108
Mandalay, Burma 136
Manhattan Homing Pigeon Club 58
Manila 58, 59, 60
Manila Bay 56, 59, 62
Manning, Margaret 35
Manoubia 22, 38, 39, 40, 47
Marconi, Guglielmo 61, 62, 63
Marconi System of Wireless Telegraphy 63
Mare Island Navy Yard 40, 41, *41*, 42, 64
Marine Club 150
Marine Corps *see* U.S. Marine Corps
Marion, Henri 22, 23, 27, 28, 29, 30, 31, 32, 33, 34, 36, 37, 39, 41, 45, 46, 47, 48, 52, 57, 58, 64, 87, 91, 103
Mary of Exeter (pigeon) 118
Massachusetts 4, 29, 56, 91, 101, *139*
USS *Massachusetts* 51
Master Brian (pigeon) 127
Maymyo, Burma 136
Mayport, Florida 141
McAtee, Lt. J.J. 65, 87
McCalla, Cdr. Bowman 41
McIntee, William 83
McKinley, Pres. William 49, 52, 54, 56
Mediterranean 116, 159
merchant ships 44, 56, 84, 91, 137, 138, 139
Merritt, Maj. Gen. Wesley 58, 59, 60
message capsule 2, 46, 79, 115, 124, *147*
Meuse-Argonne Offensive 1, 2, 74, 76, 98
Mexican-American War 27
Mexican Punitive Expedition 66, 68, 76, 77
Mexico 66, 68, 77, 99
Meyer, Maj. Otto 153, 159
MI 14 128
Miami, Florida 51, 101, 173
microphotography 10
Miles, Gen. Nelson A. 7, 12, 14, 15, 16
military communications 5, 23
Military Division of the Pacific 14
military pigeons 6, 36, 70, 110, 112, 114, 163
Miss Peggy (pigeon) 127
Mission Boy's Club 150
mobile lofts 71, 72, 112, 122, 124
The Mocker (pigeon) 81
Mongol Empire 162
Monkey Face (pigeon) 133
USS *Monongahela* 36
Montana 8, 12, 14, 15
Morrison, F.H.S. 49, 55, 56
Morse code 22, 63, 66
Moser, Herman 71
mosquito fleet 44, 45

motorcycle 71
Mt. Wilson, California 97
Munich, Germany 160
Mussolini 123
Myer, Albert J. 8, 14, 22
Myitkyina, Burma 136

Nancy (pigeon) 86, 87
Naples, Italy 125
NAS *see* U.S. Naval Air Stations
Natashima, Sashi 150
National Army 68
National Defense Act of 1916 67
National Federation of American Pigeon Fanciers 16, 49, 55
National Guard 5, 67, 68, 69, 76, *97*; 28th Infantry Division 82
National Museum of the U.S. Air Force 2
National Zoo, Washington D.C. 159
Native American 8
Naval Academy *see* U.S. Naval Academy
Naval Act of 1916 67
Naval Appropriations Act, 1911–1912 83
naval aviators 86, 91, 95, 104
naval militia 47, 54, 78
Naval Operations Post 138
naval vessels 85, 30, 41, 48
Naval War College 39
Navesink Lighthouse, New Jersey 62
Navy *see* U.S. Navy
Navy Department *see* United States Navy Department
Nebraska 8
Nelson 85
New Caledonia 116
New England 52, 53, 56
USS *New Hampshire* 29, 44
New Jersey 16, 35, 56, 62, 69, 95, 108, 110, 112, 141, 143
New London, Connecticut 30, 34
New Mexico 9, 15, 66
New York 4, 7, 13, 16, 17, 29, 30, 35, 40, 49, 54, 58, 62, 63, 67, 78, 120, 124, 127, 161
USS *New York* 35, 40, 43, 46, 51, 53, 58, 63
New York City 34, 54, 124
New York Harbor 35, 62
New York Herald 62
New York Homing Pigeon Club 13
New York Sun 7
The New York Times 68, 162
Newark, New Jersey 35
Newport, Rhode Island 26, 29, 30, *31*, 32, 39, 40, 44, 64
Nez Perce 12
Niblack, Lt. A.P. 40
night flying 76, 116
Ninetieth Aero Squadron 98
Ninth Army Ground Forces 119

Index

Norfolk, Virginia 30, 40, 43, 44, 45, 46, 64, 138
Norfolk Naval Shipyard 138
Norfolk Navy Yard 44, 51, 104
Normandy 117, 120, 129, 130
North America 8, 26, 93
North Atlantic Squadron 51
North Carolina 138
North Dakota 8
North Hollywood, California 150
North Island, California 92, 104
North Korea Interior Security Forces 156
North Korea People's Army 156
North Sea 86
Northampton, Massachusetts
Northern Cheyenne 12
Norwood Institute for Girls and Young Ladies 23
nuclear power reactors 163

Oak Park Zoo, Alabama 159
Ocean Gem 17
Office of Civilian Defense (OCD) 145
Office of Naval Intelligence (ONI) 140
Office of Strategic Services (OSS) 4, 117, 135
Oflerman, Louis 13
The Ohio Farmer (magazine) 85
Oklahoma 9
Old Dominion Homing Pigeon Club 13
Old 17 (pigeon) 126
USS *Olympia* 62
one-way communication 115
Operation Columba 129
Operation Log of 278th SPC Overseas 1st Platoon 120; *see also* U.S. Army Signal Corps Pigeon Service
Orange County Register 142
Oregon 105
Osterburg, Germany 121
Ottawa, Canada 26
Outer Banks 138

Pacific (Ocean) 60, 92, 161
Pacific Theater 135, 136, 148
Panama 69, 91, 95, 116
Panama Canal Zone 91, 95, 116
Panzer division 121
parachute 100, 115, 124, 127, 128, 131, 136, 156
paramilitary units 156
paratroopers 117, 121, 127, 157
Paris 7, 10, 11, 23, 38, 53, 71, 85, 120, 162, 163
Parker, Joel 108
Pasadena, California 150
Patch, Gen. Alexander M. "Sandy" 137
Patton, Lt. Gen. George C. 133

Pauillac, France 91
Pearl Harbor, Hawaii 110
Pearson, Lt. Alexander 99
Peerless Pilot (pigeon) 91, **92**
Pensacola, Florida 30, 84, 85, 93, 101, 173
People's Liberation Army (PLA) 163, 164
Periscope (magazine) 43
Perry, Mathew C. 45
Pershing, Gen. John J. 2, 66, 67, 68, 77, 85
Le Petit Journal 38
Petite Rosette (pigeon) 81
Philadelphia 7, 8, 13, 14, 30, 32, 35, 36, 53, 56
Philadelphia Inquirer 143–144
Philadelphia Public Ledger 35
Philippines 56, 57, 59, 60, 95
photograph 54, 107, 108, 146, 147, 165, 171
Phythian, Capt. R.L. 37
Pigeon Breeding and Training Headquarters 69
pigeon messenger service 18, 24, 27, 28, 34, 36, 37, 38, 46, 49, 51, 55, 57, 59, 83, 91, 98, 101, 103
Pigeon Roost barge 106
pigeon stations 11, 25, 29, 33, 46
pigeon whistles 116
pigeoneer 6, 66, 67, 69, **69**, 72, 74, 78, 79, 81, 95, 96, 101, 110, 112, 114, 115, 116, 117, 119, 120, 121, 123, 124, 127, 133, 135, 143, 144, 148, **150**, 152, 153, **153**, **155**, **158**, 165
The Pigeoneer Student Manual for All Arms 79, 92, 116
Pigeons That Went To War 121
Pilsen, Czechoslovakia 160
Pittsburgh, Pennsylvania 69
PLA *see* People's Liberation Army
Plains *see* Great Plains
Plains Indians 8
Plymouth, England 117, 118
The Poilu (pigeon) 81
Point Judith, Rhode Island 29–30
Pointe du Croisic, France 39
USS *Ponce* 62
Poncho Villa 66, 67
Popov, Alexander 61
Porte des Ternes, Paris 10
Portland, Maine 34
Portsmouth, New Hampshire 30, 34, 42, 64
Portsmouth Navy Yard 42, 43, **43**
Portugal 24
Potomac River 98, 100, **102**
Poutré, Sgt. Maj. Clifford 110, 112, 114
Powell, James R. 138
Pratt, Lt. Col. Jerome 117, 119, 157
USS *Preble* 32
Premier (pigeon) 82
Preparedness Movement 67
President Wilson (pigeon) 81

201

Index

The Press Weekly (New Zealand) 58
Pretty Baby (pigeon) 71
Pro Patria (pigeon) 159
Proceedings of the U.S. Naval Institute 22, 24, 28, 29, 30, 32, 39, 40
Project Sea Hunt 161
Prudholm, England 63
Prussian Army 11; see also Franco-Prussian War
Prussians 10
Puerto Rico 52
Pulitzer, Joseph 49
USS Puritan 51

Q ships 84, 85, 139
Quantico, Virginia 100
Quatrochi, Cpl. F. 153, *153*, 154, 155, *155*

radar 110, 152, 165
radio *41*, 61, 62, 65, 72, 83, 84, 85, 93, 98, 99, 100, 101, 104, 106, 108, 110, 113, 119, 123, 131, 136, 139, 140, 142, 143, 145, 146, 150, 152, 154, 157, 160
Radio Free Europe 160, 161
radio teletype 152
Rampont, France 2, 80
Red Cross 119
Red River, Texas 12
Red Star Pigeon Club 13
Redcock (pigeon) 85
Redlands, California 150
Reliable (pigeon) 82
USS Relief
Reno, Nevada 146
Republic of South Korea 156
Resistance 129
Rhineland Campaign 119
Richards, Joseph N. 41
Richmond, Florida 142
Richmond, Virginia 35
Rimburg, Holland 121
Rio Grande River 99
Rockaway, New York 93
Romans 162
Rommel, Gen. Erwin 123
Roosevelt, Franklin D. 107
Roosevelt, Theodore 51, 52, 57, 67
Rosenthal, Ida 127
Ross Airfield, California 77, 97
Rough Riders 57
Royal Air Force 117, 130
Russell, Col. Edgar 71
Russia 11, 24, 34, 129, 131, 165

sabotage 120, 121, 141, 151
Saco, Maine 43
Safi, French Morocco 121
Saint John's, Newfoundland 63

Saint Louis 29, 30
St. Mihiel Drive 74
St. Nazaire, France 39, 86
Saint Petersburg, Russia 61
St. Simon, Georgia 141
Salerno, Italy 125
Sampson, Sgt. Adam 124
Sampson, Cmdre. P. 57, 58, 59
San Antonio, Texas 108
San Antonio Express 107
San Bernardino National Forest 98
San Francisco Call 38
San Francisco Civil Defense Council 150
San Francisco Racing Pigeon Club 150
San Juan, Cuba 57
San Pedro, California 150
Sandy Hook, New Jersey 56
Santa Ana, California 142
Santa Barbara, California 150
Santiago, Cuba 57, 59
Saracens 162
USS *Saratoga* 104
Schley, Capt. W.S. 50
Schouler, Cdr. John 50
Scientific American 30
Scoop (pigeon) 159
Scottsbluff, Nebraska Zoo 159
Sea Frontier defense system 140
seaplanes 85, 86, 87, 93, 100, 102, 106
Search and Rescue (SAR) 146
Secretary of the Navy 35, 36, 40, 52, 62, 64, 84
Seigfried Line [Siegfried] 120
Selected Masters and Informants (SMI) 141
Sessa, Italy *122*
Seventy-First Signal Battalion 153
Severn River 31
Shafter, Gen. William 57, 59
Shamokin, Pennsylvania 56
Shamrock 62
USS *Shark* 45
Sheridan, Maj. Gen. Philip H. 11
shrimpers 139, 140
Shwebo, Burma 136
Sicard, Adm. Montgomery 43
Siege of Acre 162
Siege of Modena 162
Siege of Paris 10, 11, 23, 53, 162
Siege of Venice 162
Signal Corps *see* U.S. Army Signal Corps
Signal School, Fort Leavenworth, Kansas 95
signal stations 9, 25, 50, 52, 54, 56
Sioux 12
Sixth Naval District 141
Smith, Ens. Kenneth R. 89
Smithsonian Institution 9
Solomon Islands 137
Sorbonne, Paris 23

202

Index

South Dakota 8
South Vietnam 159, 160
South Weymouth, Massachusetts 141
Southern Cheyenne 12
Southwest Pacific 135, 116
Spain 11, 24, 34, 49, 52, 54, 56, 58, 59
Spangler, Jennifer 128
Spanish-American War 24, 49, 57, 59, 60, 78, 83
Spanish Army 163
Spanish Pigeon-Fancier Federation 163
Special Delivery (pigeon) 159
Specialist x rating 144
spies 3, 121, 127, 141
squeakers 69, 82, 123
Squire, 1st Lt. George O. 61, 62, 80
USS *Standish* 36
Starr, E.S. 16, 32
State Naval Militia 50, 54
stationary lofts 69, 71
Statue of Liberty 10
Staub, John 88, 89
Steinway Pigeon Club of New York City 124
Steubenville, Ohio 13
Stevenson, Robert Louis 2
submarine 67, 68, 84, 85, 87, 89, 90, 91, 93, 134, 137, 138, 139, 140; warfare 68
summer cruises 28, 30, 31, 36
Sutton, Capt. Charles Z. 77
Swanker, Sgt. Lewis 71
Sweet, Lt. George C. 83
Swiss military 162
sympathizers 128
Syria 165

Tampa, Florida 57
Tangier Island, Virginia 104
taser guns 164
Taylor, Charles 17
Tebessa, Algeria 133
telegraph 4, 8, 9, 10, 17, 22, 24, 25, 26, 33, 35, 37, 42, 43, 50, 55, 59, 60, 61, 63, 65, 66, 84, 99, 113, 146
telephone 1, 4, 25, 42, 50, 55, 59, 60, 65, 66, 72, 75, 84, 96, 97, 108, 113, 115, 145, 146, 150, 152, 154
Ten Years War 49
Texas 9, 12, 51, 54, 66, 76, 96, 98, 108, 112, 113, 142
USS *Texas* 51
Thailand 136
Thiaumont, France 75
Thomas, Cpl. J.W. 153, 154, 155, 156
Tiger Hunters: Special Operations in Korea Behind the Lines of the Chinese and North Korean Forces 157
Tillamook, Oregon 142
Times-Picayune newspaper 108

Tokyo, Japan 99
Tongeren, Belgium 121
torpedo boats 46, 58, 87
torpedoes 84, 138
Toulon, France 29
Tours, France 10, 22
Tower of London 134
trenches 1, 2, 71, 72, 73
Trenton, New Jersey 56
Truman, Pres. Harry 83, 150
Tunisia *122*, 133
Turkey 11
Twelfth Army Group 117, 119

U-boats *see Unterseebooten*
Union Pacific Railroad 8
United States 3, 7, 14, 17, 23, 27, 29, 30, 39, 48, 49, 51, 52, 53, 55, 58, 61, 64, 65, 67, 83, 85, 91, 93, 119, 137, 161
U.S. Air Force 156
U.S. Army 8, 9, 11, 13, 14, 15, 16, 17, 18, 21, 27, 39, 45, 56, 59, 60, 61, 65, 66, 67, 68, *70*, 76, *77*, *78*, 81, 82, 83, 92, 95, 96, 97, 100, 102, 104, 107, 110, 111, 114, 120, 122, 126, 134, 138, 141, 152, 153, 156, 157, 158, 162, 163
U.S. Army Air Service 76, 77, 79, 97, 110, 116, 135, 146
United States Army and Navy Journal and Gazette 51
U.S. Army 5th Infantry 12
U.S. Army Signal Corps 1, 2, 8, 9, 10, 15, 17, 22, 59, 60, 62, 66–69, *70*, 71, 72, 76, *77*, 77, *78*, 82, 83, 95, *97*, 108, 112, 113, 114, 117, 124, 134, 135, 140, 149, *151*, 152, *153*
U.S. Army Signal Corps Pigeon Service 71, 112, 113, 115, 119
U.S. Army Signal Pigeon Companies: provisional 6681st Signal Pigeon Company 116; 209th Signal Pigeon Company 116; 277th Signal Pigeon Company 115; 278th Signal Pigeon Company 115; 279th Signal Pigeon Company 116; 280th Signal Pigeon Company 113, 116; 280th Signal Pigeon Company, 2nd Platoon 116; 281st Signal Pigeon Company 113; 281st Signal Pigeon Company, 1st Platoon 116; 282nd Signal Pigeon Company 115; 283rd Signal Pigeon Company 113; 284th Signal Pigeon Company 116; 285th Signal Pigeon Company 116; 828th Pigeon Replacement Company 113; 828th Signal Pigeon Company, non-combative 117, 135
U.S. Army Signal Service 8, 10, 17, 18, 20
U.S. Army Vest 127
U.S. Army Veterinary Service 114
U.S. Board of Fortification 24

Index

U.S. Coast Guard 5, 138, 139, 140, 143, 161
U.S. Congress 9, 34, 40, 49, 55, 67, 70, 141
U.S. Department of Agriculture 21, 97–98
U.S. Department of War 10, 52, 60, 112
U.S. 8th Army 156
U.S. First Army 2
U.S. Forest Service 5, 104, 107
U.S. Geological Survey 106
U.S. Lighthouse Service 43
U.S. Marine Corps 74, 95, 100, 137
U.S. Marine Corps Signal School 100
U.S. military 5, 31, 64, 134, 161, 165
U.S. National Archives and Records Administration (NARA) 6
U.S. National Park Service 107
U.S. Naval Academy 21, 22, 23, 28, 29, 30, 31, 32, 33, 35, 36, 37, 38, 39, 40, 41, 58
U.S. naval air stations 84, 85, 93, 96, 100, 101, 101, 104, 141, 143, 144, 173
U.S. Naval Air Stations (NAS): Bay Shore 101; Chatham 101; Key West 101; Lakehurst 141, 142, 143, 144; Miami 101; Moffett Field 141; Montauk 101; North Island 104; Pensacola 101; Rockaway 101; San Diego 101, 104
U.S. Naval Aviation 83
U.S. Naval Institute 28, 111, 116, 141
U.S. Naval Pigeon Messenger Service 47, 48, 63, 64, 83, 103
U.S. Navy 5, 6, 18, 21, 22, 23, 27, 28, 30, 33, 34, 35, 40, 42, 43, 44, 45, 52, 53, 55, 56, 57, 58, 59, 61, 63, 64, 65, 83, 85, 86, 93, 95, 100, 102, 104, 105, 106, 110, 137, 138, 139, 141, 141, 142, 143, 151, 152, 161
United States Navy Department 38, 39, 40, 43, 47, 51, 52, 54, 58, 59, 61, 62
United States Training Center, Newport, Rhode Island 29
U.S. Weather Bureau 21, 38
Unterseebooten (U-boats) 84, 85, 91, 93, 94, 137, 138, 139, 140
Utah 8
Utica, New York 4

vaccinations 114
Valkenborg, Holland [Valkenburg] 120
Vallejo Homing Pigeons Lofts 41
Verdun 2, 80, 81, 82
USS *Vermont* 44
Veterinary Service *see* U.S. Army Veterinary Service
Vietnam War 159
Vimy Ridge, France 71
Virginia Beach, Virginia 138

SS *Waesland* 16
Wainwright, Lt. Richard 24, 25, 28, 40, 42, 50, 52
walkie-talkies 110
Wallabout Channel 44
War Department *see* U.S. Department of War
War of 1812 27
Warren, Lt. Alfred K. 92
Washburne, Elihu 11
Washington D.C. 7, 8, 10, 22, 23, 26, 30, 35, 37, 38, 42, 45, 51, 53, 55, 56, 58, 59, 60, 61, 62, 83, 134
Watsonville, California 58, 59
WAVES 142, 143, 144
Webb, Lt. John A. 117
Weeksville, North Carolina 141
West Enders 150
West Virginia 138
Western Front 68
Wetzel, William 42
Weyler, Gen. Valeriano 49
Wheeling, West Virginia 56
White Plains, New York 4
Wicker, Cyrus F. 68
wicker baskets 71, 74
wig-wag signaling system 22
Williams, Herman 122
Williams, William C. 51
Wilson, Pres. Woodrow 66, 67
Wimereaux, France 61
Windsor, Ontario 27
wireless telegraphy 61, 63
Wolf at the Door 138
Wonsan, North Korea 157
Wood, Col. Leonard 57
Woodbury, New Jersey 32
Woodland Park Zoo, Washington 159
Woodman, H.C. 117
The World (newspaper) 49
World War I 1, 3, 21, 65, 70, 71, 73, 74, 79, 82, 84, 92, 93, 97, 101, 104, 110, 112, 127, 144
World War II 3, 5, 6, 10, 82, 99, 108, 110, 112, 114, 115, 122, 125, 126, 127, 128, 134, 137, 141, 145, 152, 158
The World War II Pigeons and the Secret Columba Messages 128
Wright brothers 83
Wright Flyer 76
Wyoming 8

Yachts 16, 17, 56, 61, 62, 138, 140
Yank (pigeon) 133, 159

Zulu War 55

www.ingramcontent.com/pod-product-compliance
Ingram Content Group UK Ltd.
Pitfield, Milton Keynes, MK11 3LW, UK
UKHW042005140426
5217IPUK00015B/987